Expo 2

Resource and Assessment File
Nouvelle Edition

Rouge

Clive Bell

Nancy Brannon

Michael Wardle

heinemann.co.uk

✓ Free online support
✓ Useful weblinks
✓ 24 hour online ordering

01865 888080

Heinemann is an imprint of Pearson Education Limited, a company incorporated in England and Wales, having its registered office at Edinburgh Gate, Harlow, Essex, CM20 2JE. Registered company number: 872828

www.heinemann.co.uk

Heinemann is the registered trademark of Pearson Education Ltd

First published 2008

12 11 10 09 08
10 9 8 7 6 5 4 3 2 1

British Library Cataloguing in Publication Data is available from the British Library on request.

ISBN 978 0 435 39284 0

Designed by Ken Vail Graphic Design
Produced by Ken Vail Graphic Design and TechType
Original Illustrations © Pearson Education Ltd 2004
Illustrated by Beehive Illustration (Theresa Tibbetts) and Mark Ruffle
Cover photo © Digital Vision/Robert Harding
Printed in the UK by Ashford Colour Press Ltd

Acknowledgements
Every effort has been made to contact copyright holders of material reproduced in this book. Any omissions will be rectified in subsequent printings if notice is given to the publishers.

Contents

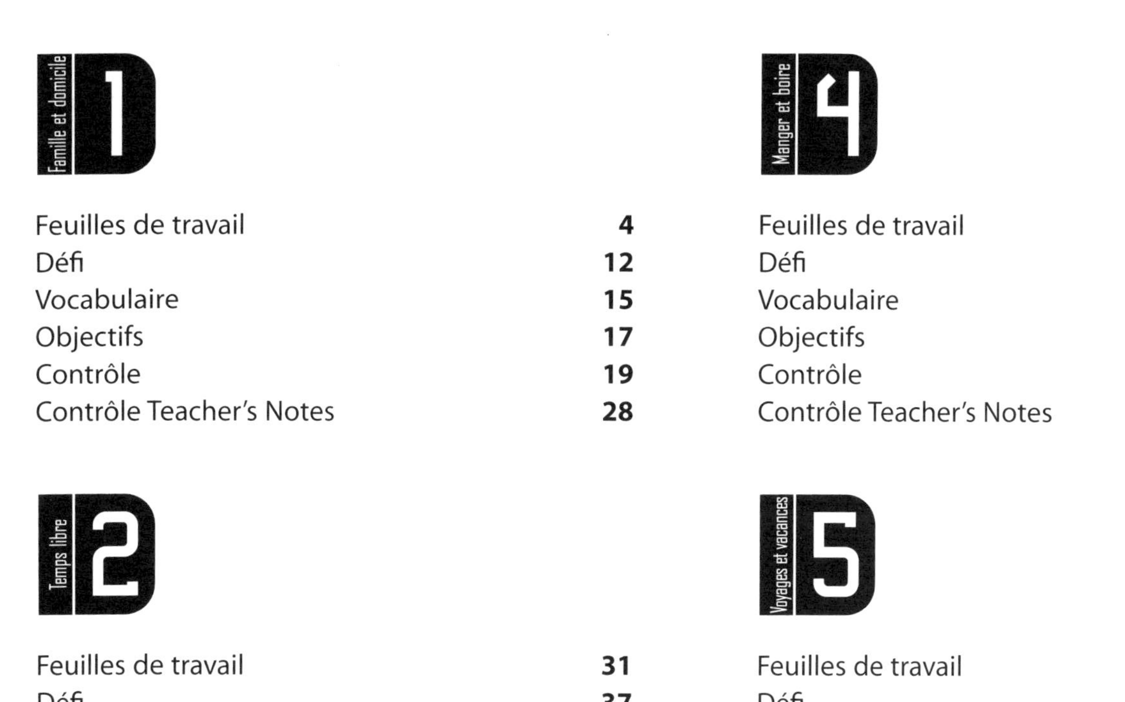

Famille et domicile
1
Manger et boire
4

Les sorties
3

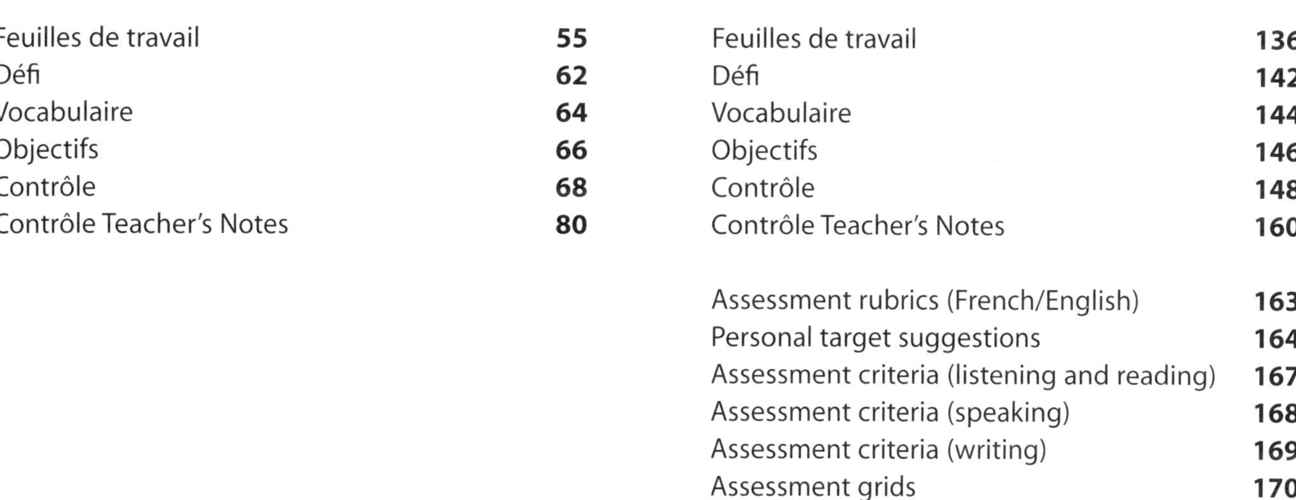

Les copains et Fin d'année
6

Thinking skills

Odd-one-out

A Work in a group. Look at the verbs below and circle the one which you think is the odd-one-out in each row. You might have different ideas from other people. Get ready to explain and justify your answers.

1 adores adore adorez adorent

2 travaillons déteste collectionnez habitons

3 joue aime regarde déteste

4 j'adore je travaille je voyage je collectionne

5 il aime les animaux il aime le sport il aime faire du ski il aime la musique

6 on écoute de la musique on fait du skate on adore la lecture on travaille dans le jardin

B Work with a partner. Read the sentences below and copy out the text, putting the lines in the correct order.

Mon père s'appelle Christophe et ma belle-mère s'appelle …

pas le sport, mais elle collectionne
frère, Laurent, adore faire du
Françoise. Ma mère s'appelle Anne-Marie et elle habite
joue souvent au tennis et elle écoute de la
à Paris. Comme passe-temps, papa aime
des photos de Tom Cruise! Mon demi-
musique dans sa chambre.
la lecture et le football. Françoise n'aime
ski et il voyage beaucoup pour le travail. Ma sœur, Sophie,

Grammaire

Les verbes en *-er*

A **Write down eight verbs with an infinitive ending in *-er*.**

____

____

When you look up a verb in the dictionary or a glossary, it will be written in the **infinitive.**
Here are the present tense endings of **-er** verbs – the biggest group of infinitives.
Don't forget to take off the **-er** first!

je regard**e**	nous regard**ons**
tu regard**es**	vous regard**ez**
il/elle/on regard**e**	ils/elles regard**ent**

je changes to **j'** before a vowel or silent **h** → **j'a**ime, **j'h**abite.
Verbs that end in **-ger** have a special form for **nous**: nous mang**e**ons, nous voyag**e**ons.

B **Write the infinitives, given in brackets below, in the correct form. There are some verbs you know and some that are new. If you can't work out what they mean, look them up.**

1 Je ______________________ au foot. (jouer)
2 Mon frère ______________________ de la musique. (écouter)
3 Nous ______________________ la lecture. (aimer)
4 Elle ______________________ dans un magasin. (travailler)
5 Ils ______________________ des croissants. (manger)
6 Vous ______________________ des livres d'Astérix. (collectionner)
7 Tu ______________________ bien le français. (parler)
8 J' ______________________ mes professeurs. (admirer)

C **You have not met the infinitives below. Write them in the correct form. Look up what the words mean, if you can't work them out.**

1 Je ______________ la souris. (chasser)
2 Chérie, tu ______________. (ronronner)
3 Blanche ______________ tout le temps. (tomber)
4 Ils ______________ sur la table. (sauter)
5 Nous ______________ les enfants. (chercher)
6 Vous ______________ au lit. (rester)

Lesson starter

Masculine and feminine nouns for jobs

Work with a partner. Complete the grid with the masculine and feminine forms of the nouns for jobs and the English meanings.

	masculin	féminin	anglais
	vendeur	vendeuse	*shop assistant*
1	serveur	serveuse	
2	coiffeur		*hairdresser*
3	mécanicien	mécanicienne	
4	électricien		*electrician*
5		pharmacienne	*chemist*
6	infirmier	infirmière	
7	ouvrier		*labourer, factory worker*
8		fermière	*farmer*

Learning skills

The many meanings of *faire*

A The following sentences all use the verb *faire*. Find the form of *faire* used in each sentence and write down what it means in each case.

1 Qu'est-ce que tu fais quand il pleut? __________
Tu fais de la natation à la piscine? __________

2 S'il neige, je fais du ski, mais le __________
soir, je fais mes devoirs. __________

3 Ce soir, mon frère fait la cuisine. __________
Il fait une pizza. __________

4 Le week-end, on fait du sport, __________
on fait les magasins ou __________
on fait du skate dans le parc. __________

5 Ici, en été, il fait très chaud, __________
mais en hiver, il fait assez froid. __________

B How many different verbs in English can be used to translate *faire*? What does this tell us about the differences between languages?

____

C Here are some new expressions with *faire*. Work them out or look them up in a dictionary. Then categorise them by copying them into the correct box and give the English meaning.
Will you look them up in the dictionary under *faire*? Why (not)?!

____

faire un gâteau
faire beau (il fait beau)
faire le ménage
faire de la musculation
~~faire le lit~~
faire mauvais (il fait mauvais)
faire des crêpes

Keep-fit activities	Weather	Household chores	Cookery	English meaning
		faire le lit		*to make the bed*

Grammaire

Les verbes en *-ir* et *-re*

A Complete the verbs.

Subject pronouns	-ir verbs	-re verbs
je/j'	fin	attend
tu	fin	attend
il/elle/on	fin	attend
nous	fin	attend
vous	fin	attend
ils/elles	fin	attend

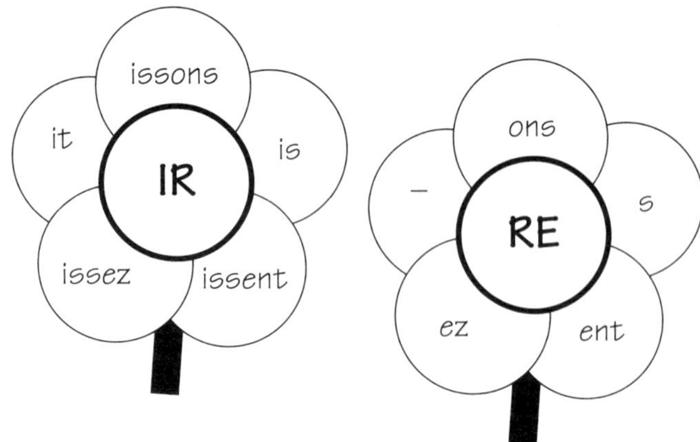

B Complete the sentences with the verbs given in brackets.

Some of the verbs below you know, and some are new. If you come across a new verb and haven't got a dictionary to hand, what do you do? Try to make an 'educated guess'. Then check to see if you were right.

	Guess	Check
1 Il ______________ le bus. (attendre)	☐	☐
2 Nous ______________ nos devoirs. (finir)	☐	☐
3 Le boulanger ______________ du pain. (vendre)	☐	☐
4 Ils ______________ du train. (descendre)	☐	☐
5 Vous ______________ le jeu. (choisir)	☐	☐

Some **-ir** and **-re** verbs, such as **partir**, **voir**, **boire**, **faire** and **lire** are irregular. These verbs don't follow the same pattern as regular **-ir** and **-re** verbs. You just have to learn them!

C Complete the sentences with the verbs given in brackets.

1 Elle ______________ à 8h. (partir)

2 Nous ______________ du café au petit déjeuner. (boire)

3 Vous ______________ du judo. (faire)

4 Ils ______________ des magazines de sport. (lire)

5 Je ______________ toujours de l'eau. (boire)

Famille et domicile

1 Grammaire

Les verbes irréguliers

In this module, you have met a lot of **irregular verbs** in the present tense. **Irregular** means they don't follow the patterns you have learnt for regular **-er**, **-ir** and **-re** verbs.

A **Complete the paradigms of *avoir* and *être*. Check your answers before you go on to task B.**

avoir *to have*		**être** *to be*	
j'______	nous ______	je ______	nous ______
tu ______	vous ______	tu ______	vous ______
il/elle/on ______	ils/elles ______	il/elle/on ______	ils/elles ______

B **Complete the sentences with the correct part of *avoir* or *être*.**

1 Tu ________ vendeuse.
2 Ils ________ un chat.
3 Je ________ grande.
4 Vous ________ au chômage.
5 Il ________ une demi-sœur.
6 Nous ________ un appartement à Paris.
7 Elle ________ sportive.
8 Tu ________ des frères et des sœurs?

C **Complete the paradigms of the irregular verbs *faire*, *aller* and *venir*.**

faire *to do/make*	**aller** *to go*	**venir** *to come*
je fais	je ________	je viens
tu ________	tu vas	tu ________
il/elle/on fait	il/elle/on ________	il/elle/on ________
nous ________	nous ________	nous venons
vous faites	vous ________	vous ________
ils/elles ________	ils/elles vont	ils/elles ________

allons **font** **vais** **vient** **viennent** **allez** **fais** **faisons** **viens** **va** **venez**

D **Unjumble the verbs in brackets to complete the sentences.**

1 Je (siva) __________ au collège à 8h.
2 Il (vntie) __________ chez moi.
3 Nous (oainfss) __________ du ski.
4 Ils (nitveenn) __________ ce soir.
5 Vous (lalze) __________ au café.
6 Ils (onft) __________ du judo.

E **Fill in the missing verbs in these sentences.**

1 Elles ______________ à Paris.
2 Vous ______________ du sport?
3 Vous ______________ d'Angleterre.
4 Tu ______________ en France.

Learning skills

A Work with a partner. Look at the bold words in these groups of sentences. Say the sentences and tick the correct columns.

- In some of the groups below, you **always** hear or pronounce the final consonant of the words in bold.
- In some groups, the final consonant is **either** silent **or** heard/pronounced.

		Silent	Heard/Pronounced
1	Il s'appelle **Michel**.		
	Michel Chassagne est moniteur de ski.		
	Michel adore son métier.		
2	Le réveille-matin sonne. Il est **six** heures.		
	Ma maison, c'est le numéro **six**.		
	Il y a **six** personnes dans la maison.		
3	Je saisis **mon** anorak …		
	… et **mon** snowboard.		
	Mes skis sont dans le **salon**.		
4	J'attends **mes** élèves.		
	J'aime beaucoup le **cours**.		
	Mes cours finissent à 13h.		

B Answer the questions in English.

1 Which final consonant in the sentences above is always heard? ____________

2 **x** as a final consonant is silent in front of another consonant (e.g. **six personnes**), but heard/pronounced in front of a vowel or a silent **h** (e.g. **six heures**). Is it silent or heard/pronounced at the end of a sentence?

____

3 **n** and **s** as final consonants are silent at the end of a sentence and in front of another consonant. When are they heard/pronounced? ____________

4 Look at these examples. What is unusual about the word **fils**? ____________

Je suis fils unique. | **Voici mon fils.** | **Mon fils s'appelle Michel.**

C Read this text aloud. Take care with the final consonants on the bold words – should you pronounce them or are they silent?

Je m'appelle **Michel** Chassagne et je suis moniteur de ski. J'habite avec **deux** collègues, Jean-Pierre et **Alex**. À **dix** heures, je commence **mes cours** de ski. **Mes** élèves sont sympas. Il y a **dix** personnes dans la classe. À midi, je prends le déjeuner avec **mon** copain, **Pascal**. Je me couche à vingt-**deux** heures.

Grammaire

Les petits mots très utiles

High-frequency words are useful little words that can appear at any time in any topic. You need to use them a lot.
depuis means 'since' and you use it with the present tense to say how long you have been doing something (literally 'since when you have been doing it').
Look at these examples:

J'**habite** en France **depuis** six ans.	I **have been living** in France for six years.
J'**apprends** le français **depuis** deux ans.	I **have been learning** French for two years.

Look at the verbs in both sentences. In French, the verbs are in the **present tense**, and in English, the verbs are in the **past tense**.

A **Answer the questions with the information given. Translate your answers into English.**

1 Il habite à Paris depuis quand? ______________________

____

10 ans

2 Il travaille dans le magasin depuis quand? ______________

____

juillet

3 Elle est journaliste depuis quand? __________________

____

3 ans

4 Il fait du skate depuis quand? ____________________

____

2 ans

5 Elle fait ses devoirs depuis quand? ________________

____

B **Use the connectives from the box to join as many of these sentences as possible to make the text more interesting.**

You have also met some other useful little words called **connectives.** They are used to join sentences and here are some you have met so far:
et = and **mais** = but **quand** = when
parce que (**parce qu'** in front of vowels) = because

Salut! Je m'appelle Serge. J'ai 25 ans. Je suis serveur dans un restaurant à Paris. J'aime bien mon travail. C'est intéressant. Quelquefois, c'est difficile. Je ne travaille pas le jeudi. J'aime faire du sport.

Défi

La vie d'un(e) scientifique – Préparation

A Which sentences (A–H) contain the information for 1–8? Unscramble the poster. (Levels 3–5)

1 Name and nationality of the scientist ☐
2 Character ☐
3 Where he works ☐
4 What he is interested in ☐
5 What he really loves in his work ☐
6 What he will research in the future ☐
7 When he usually starts and ends his working day ☐
8 What he does when he has the time ☐

F Quand j'ai le temps, j'écoute de la musique classique.

B Ce qui m'intéresse, c'est la gravité.

G Je suis scientifique et je travaille dans un laboratoire à Zürich en Suisse.

D Je suis très intelligent et modeste.

C Dans l'avenir, je vais faire des recherches en mécanique quantique.

E Je m'appelle Albert Einstein et je suis allemand.

H **Moi, j'adore la relativité générale.**

B Choose a card and use the details to write sentences along the lines of those in activity A.

Charles Darwin – anglais
intelligent et gentil
Édimbourg en Écosse
l'histoire naturelle
l'évolution humaine
la sélection naturelle
9h00 – 17h00
Je vais à l'église.

Marie Curie – polonaise / française
intelligente et sérieuse
Paris en France
le polonium
la radioactivité
le radium
6h00 – 18h00
Je lis les romans.

Défi
La vie d'un(e) scientifique

Assignment 1 Challenge

Use the sentences from activity A as a model to write about the daily life of a famous scientist. Choose a scientist and research information on him/her. At points, you may also need to use your imagination.

Assignment 1 Support grid

Level 3	Give four pieces of information, joining them together where appropriate.	*Je m'appelle Albert Einstein et je suis allemand.*
Level 4	Write a short paragraph on the scientist; include the full range of information covered in the cards in activity B. Include opinions, intensifiers and adjectives.	*Je suis très intelligent et modeste. Ce qui m'intéresse, c'est la gravité.*
Level 5	Write a short paragraph as in Level 4. Justify the opinions given and say what the scientist is going to do in the future. Use a dictionary to add something original.	*Ce qui m'intéresse, c'est la gravité parce que c'est fascinant. Dans l'avenir, je vais faire des recherches en mécanique quantique.*

Assignment 1 Judging grid

Points for language level as shown plus 1 point for each of the other criteria.

L3 = **1**, L4 = **2**, L5 = **3**		Paragraph well presented		
Image of scientist's work included		Clear and striking title		
Photo or picture of scientist included		Full picture of scientist's life given		Total
Interesting information included		Imaginative details included		/10

La vie d'un(e) scientifique: guidelines for teachers

For general guidelines on how to get the most out of the *Défi* sections, see page 14.

Use this alongside or instead of exercise 8 on page 15 of the Pupil's Book.

1 Hand out the activity sheet and work through activity A with the pupils. Pupils more confident in their research skills should then complete activity B for extra language practice.

2 Pupils then research the life and work of a scientist (living or from the past) and write a paragraph on him/her. Pupils with less developed research skills can use the information given for Charles Darwin or Marie Curie in activity B. Pupils will need to use their imagination too, to fill in the more mundane details of being a famous scientist.

Science Programme of Study	1.3 Key concepts; cultural understanding
Levels accessed	NC Levels 3–5
Key vocabulary	*Expo 2 Rouge* Pupil's Book, Module 1, pages 22–23

Défi sections

Guidelines for teachers

Cross-curricular focus

The challenges are cross-curricular in approach, allowing teachers to develop links with other curriculum areas and also cover non-linguistic skills. Each challenge focuses on a different curriculum area. The Programme of Study for that area is listed in the teacher's notes. Teachers can build upon the links to other subject areas to help pupils develop a broader range of skills. Thus, the challenges are contextualised and the outcomes have relevance beyond the MFL classroom.

Assessment for learning

Assessment for learning strategies form the basis of the teaching process in the challenges. Pupils are given both a support grid and a judging grid. The support grid gives guidelines on the type and level of French required. The judging grid assesses the linguistic and non-linguistic skills that the pupils have developed while completing the tasks. This grid can be used either as a self-assessment tool or as a way of peer-assessing in class.

Skills based

In addition to the curriculum link, the challenges further develop a range of skills, relating in particular to presentations, both oral and written.

For speaking tasks, group work and organisation are practised, as are pronunciation, clarity and whole group presentation skills.

For writing tasks, the focus on presentation covers the effective use of colour and font, layout, titles, labelling, etc.

Throughout there is the possibility of using ICT or other media, although this is not required to complete the task itself. There are also Top Tips to help guide pupils in their planning.

Structure of teaching

There are two sheets to support teaching: the activity sheet and the challenge sheet. These can be used in presenting the challenge as follows:

The big picture: start by looking at the challenge generally. What is the challenge? What do students think is involved? What might they need to do in preparation?

Preparation: pupils use the activity sheet. The tasks there consist of modelled or structured activities: these support pupils by guiding them through the process they need to follow in order to complete the challenge. Pupils do these in the same pairs/groups in which they will do the challenge.

Progression: pupils use the challenge sheet (with the support grid and judging grid as a guide on what to include) to complete the task.

Performance: pupils either perform the task or show their results to the group. They self-assess and/or peer-assess the presentations.

Review: discuss with pupils what went well and what went less well. How would they complete the same task differently if they were to do it again?

Vocabulaire

Les verbes en -er	*-er verbs*
adorer	*to love*
aimer	*to like*
collectionner	*to collect*
détester	*to hate*
écouter	*to listen to*
habiter	*to live*
jouer	*to play*
manger	*to eat*
parler	*to speak, talk*
regarder	*to look at, watch*
travailler	*to work*
voyager	*to travel*

La famille	*The family*
mon demi-frère	*my stepbrother*
mon beau-père	*my stepfather*
ma belle-mère	*my stepmother*
ma demi-sœur	*my stepsister*
mon frère	*my brother*
ma mère	*my mother*
mon père	*my father*
ma sœur	*my sister*
chez nous	*at our house*
divorcé	*divorced*
Il/Elle s'appelle ...	*He/She is called ...*
donc	*therefore*
surtout	*especially*

Les pronoms	*Pronouns*
je	*I*
tu	*you*
il	*he, it*
elle	*she, it*
on	*we, one*
nous	*we*
vous	*you*
ils	*they*
elles	*they (f)*

Les métiers	*Jobs*
Je suis ...	*I am ...*
Il/Elle est ...	*He/She is ...*
au chômage	*unemployed*
coiffeur (coiffeuse)	*a hairdresser*
infirmier (infirmière)	*a nurse*
mécanicien(ne)	*a mechanic*
médecin	*a doctor*
musicien(ne)	*a musician*
professeur	*a teacher*
programmeur (programmeuse)	*a computer programmer*
secrétaire	*a secretary*
serveur (serveuse)	*a waiter/waitress*
vendeur (vendeuse)	*a shop assistant*
Il/Elle travaille dans ...	*He/She works in ...*
un bureau	*an office*
un collège	*a school*
un garage	*a garage*
un hôpital	*a hospital*
un magasin	*a shop*
un restaurant	*a restaurant*
une usine	*a factory*
chez (+ name of firm)	*at (+ name of firm)*

Où?	*Where?*
J'habite dans ...	*I live in ...*
le nord	*the north*
le sud	*the south*
l'est	*the east*
l'ouest	*the west*
le centre	*the centre*
de	*of, from*
l'Angleterre	*England*
l'Écosse	*Scotland*
l'Irlande du Nord	*N. Ireland*
le Pays de Galles	*Wales*
ici	*here*
J'habite ici depuis ...	*I have lived here for ...*
un an	*a year*
un mois	*a month*
Je viens d'Écosse.	*I come from Scotland.*
maintenant	*now*

Vocabulaire

Quel temps fait-il?	*What's the weather like?*
il fait chaud	*it's hot*
il fait froid	*it's cold*
il y a du vent	*it's windy*
il y a du brouillard	*it's foggy*
il y a du soleil	*it's sunny*
il y a des orages	*it's stormy*
il neige	*it's snowing*
il pleut	*it's raining*

Les conjonctions	*Connectives*
car	*because*
donc	*therefore*
mais	*but*
ou	*or*
où	*where*
parce que	*because*
puis	*then*
quand	*when*
si	*if*

Les verbes en *-ir*	*-ir verbs*
finir	*to finish*
saisir	*to grab*

Les verbes en *-re*	*-re verbs*
attendre	*to wait for*
descendre	*to go down*

Les verbes irréguliers	*Irregular verbs*
boire (je bois)	*to drink*
lire (je lis)	*to read*
partir (je pars)	*to leave*
prendre (je prends)	*to take*
voir (je vois)	*to see*

Les expressions de temps	*Time expressions*
comme d'habitude	*as usual*
d'habitude	*usually*
quelquefois	*sometimes*
l'après-midi	*in the afternoon*
tous les jours	*every day*
tout de suite	*immediately*

Objectifs

Nom: ....

Year 7 Attainment			This module (M1) targets	
Listening			Listening	
Speaking			Speaking	
Reading			Reading	
Writing			Writing	

Before	Level 3 (Short sentences linked together, short conversations)	Mid	End
	Ask a partner his/her name and age, and to describe his/her personality. Respond to these questions.		
	Give three sentences saying what a member of my family likes and dislikes.		
	Give three sentences saying what a member of my family does in his/her spare time.		
	Give three sentences explaining what a member of my family does as a job and where he/she works. **G** Use the masculine or feminine form of the job as appropriate.		
	Give three sentences about where I live, where it is in the country and how long I have lived there.		
	Ask a partner what the weather is like, and respond to this question. Ask a partner what he/she does with his/her family if it is cold. **G** Respond to this question using the *nous* form.		

Before	Level 4 (short texts and longer conversations, short presentations)	Mid	End
	In a short paragraph describe where the various members of my (imaginary) family live and say who I live with. Include opinions and connectives. **G** Include at least one negative.		
	Give a short presentation describing two members of my family. Include details on their hobbies and how often they do these hobbies. Mention one thing they don't like (using *il/elle n'aime pas*). Include connectives.		
	In a short paragraph describe the job of a member of my family, giving details of what job he/she does, where he/she works and an example of what he/she does at work. Include opinions, adjectives, connectives and intensifiers. **G** Include at least one negative.		
	Working with a partner, interview each other on where we live, where it is in the country, how long we have lived there and whether or not we like it there. Use adjectives and connectives. **G** Include at least one negative.		
	In a short paragraph describe what I do in different types of weather. Use both *si* and *quand*.		
	In a short paragraph, describe a typical day in the life of a person who does an interesting job. **G** Use *il/elle* forms of verbs. Give details of daily routine, what he/she does at work and his/her hobbies.		

Objectifs

Nom: ....

Before	Level 5 (Longer texts and more detailed conversations, longer presentations)	Mid	End
	Give a presentation introducing myself and my family, and the likes, dislikes and hobbies of family members (talking about at least four people). Include reasons for opinions. Say what these people are going to do this evening. **G** Use the near future tense and include at least two negatives.		
	Write a text about where I live, what the weather is like there and what activities I do in different types of weather. Say what I am going to do at the weekend, giving plans for different types of weather. Include opinions, using appropriate time expressions. Use the near future tense and include two negatives.		
	Write a text about a day in the life of a famous person, giving details of his/her morning routine, his/her work day and his/her hobbies. Say what he/she has done recently or is going to do in the near future, using appropriate time expressions. Include reasons for opinions. **G** Use the perfect or near future tense and include at least two negatives.		

Personal Targets	Mid	End

Target Setting

Fill in the levels you reached in Year 7, then decide which level you are aiming for in Module 1 in each skill.

Go to the objective grid for your target level and decide which objectives you are going to focus on. You may want to include an objective from the level below or the level above, to help you make the transition from a lower to a higher level. Put a mark in the **Before** column for your chosen objectives.

To help you fill in your personal targets, you may like to refer to pages 164–166 for ideas.

1 Contrôle

Famille et domicile

Nom: ....

Expo 2R Listening

Écouter 1

A Listen and tick the correct box. (Level 3)

1 He works ...

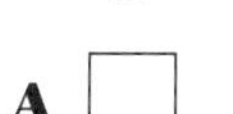

A ☐ **B** ☐ **C** ☐

2 He has worked there for ... years

A 2 ☐ **B** 10 ☐ **C** 12 ☐

3 He is a ...

A ☐ **B** ☐ **C** ☐

4 He likes ...

A ☐ **B** ☐ **C** ☐

5 He hates ...

A ☐ **B** ☐ **C** ☐

6 At weekends, he ...

A ☐ **B** ☐ **C** ☐

Points	
Niveau	

B Listen and choose one correct statement for each member of Nabila's family. Write the appropriate letter. (Level 4)

Example: Nabila G

1 Her dad ☐

2 Her mum ☐

3 Her half-brother ☐

4 Her big sister ☐

5 Her little sister ☐

6 Her uncle ☐

A likes spiders

B works in a hospital

C likes tennis

D likes pizza

E works in an office

F likes cats

G likes doing sport

H collects cards

I likes skateboarding

J likes football

K works in a shop

Points	
Niveau	

Contrôle

Nom: ....

Écouter 2

A **Écoute. Note les détails en français. (Level 4)**

Exemple: Hôtel: Expotel

Travail: **A** ____________________

Région: **B** ____________________

Heures?

commence: **C** ____________________

finit: **D** ____________________

Âge minimum: **E** ____________________

Qualité nécessaire: **F** ____________________

Points	
Niveau	

B **Écoute. Écris les bonnes lettres dans la grille. (Level 5)**

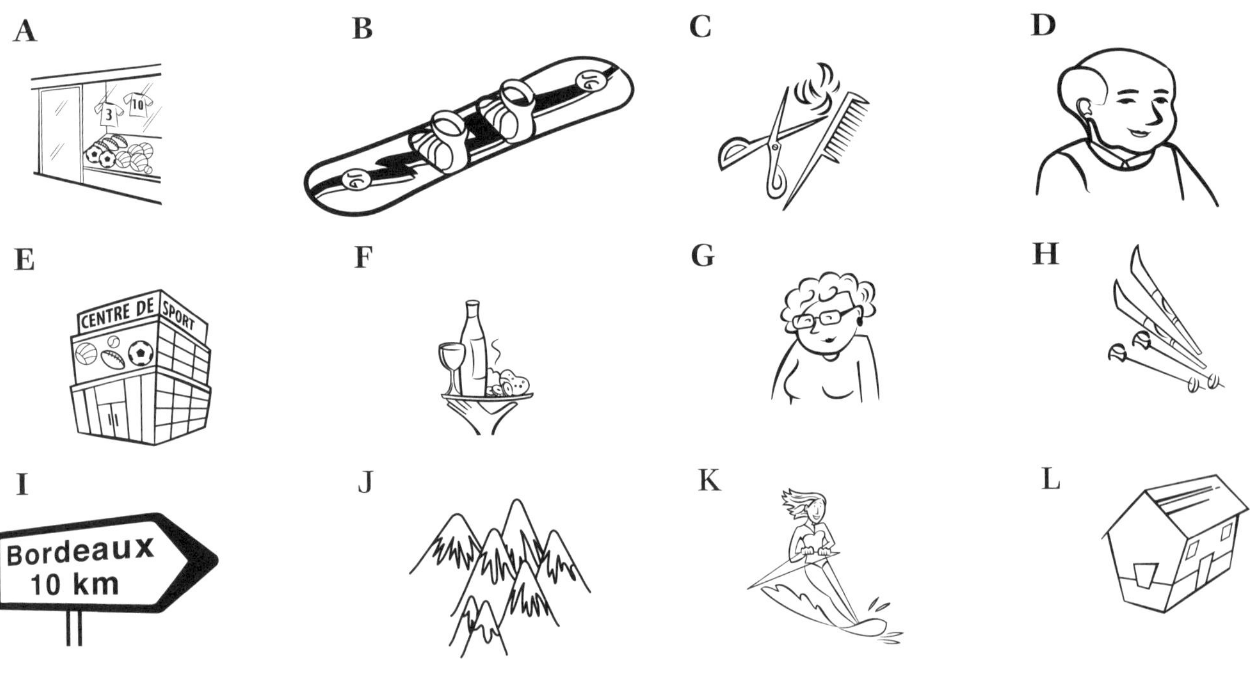

Maintenant Roselyne ...	Dans le futur, Roselyne
Exemple: L	

Points	
Niveau	

Nom: ....

Parler 1

Réponds aux questions de ton professeur ou de ton ami/amie. (Tu peux inventer les détails.) Pose des questions à ton/ta partenaire aussi. (Levels 3–4)

- Comment s'appelle ta mère/ton frère?
- Qu'est-ce qu'il/elle aime?
- Qu'est-ce qu'il/elle n'aime pas?
- Il/Elle fait quel métier?

Level information	Pupil support	Example
You can show achievement at Level 3 or 4 depending on how you carry out the task.		
Level 3: Ask and answer the questions.	• Choose a person in your partner's family and ask: his/her name, what she/he likes, what he/she dislikes, what his/her job is. Respond.	■ *Comment s'appelle-t-il/elle?* ● *Elle s'appelle Valérie.*
Level 4: As Level 3, but include adjectives, intensifiers, connectives and negatives.	• Choose a person in your partner's family, and ask: his/her name, what he/she likes, what he/she dislikes, what his/her job is, where he/she works. • Extend your answers by giving more than one thing he/she likes and dislikes and include his/her opinion of his/her job.	■ *Qu'est-ce qu'elle aime?* ● *Elle aime les chats et les CD. Elle adore Elton John, mais elle n'aime pas Maroon 5.*

Contrôle

Nom: ....

Parler 2

Réponds aux questions de ton professeur ou de ton ami/amie. Pose des questions à ton/ta partenaire aussi. (Levels 3–5)

- Où habites-tu? C'est où?

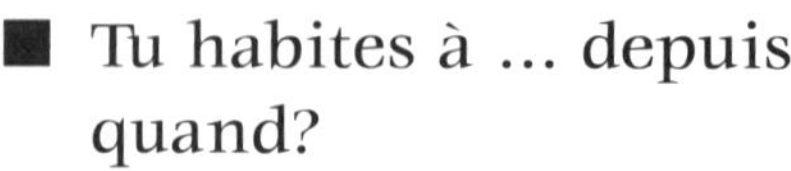

- Tu habites à ... depuis quand?

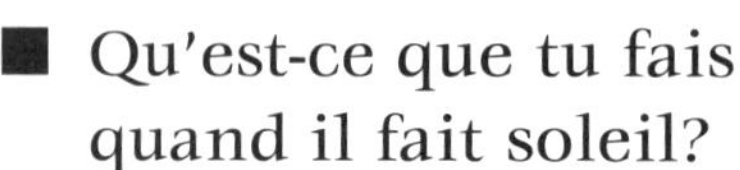

- Qu'est-ce que tu fais quand il fait soleil?

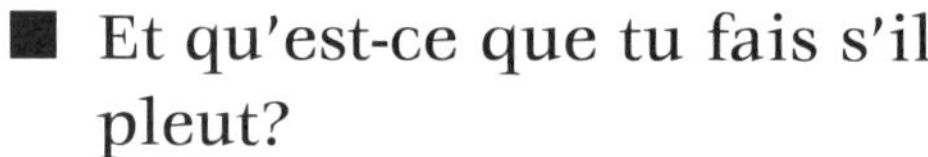

- Et qu'est-ce que tu fais s'il pleut?

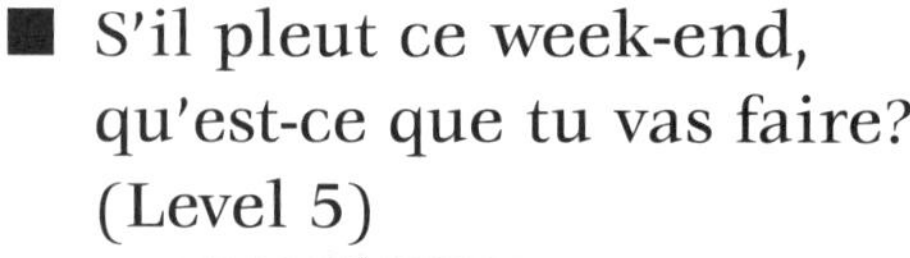

- S'il pleut ce week-end, qu'est-ce que tu vas faire? (Level 5)

5 ANS

10 ans

12 ans

Level information	Pupil support	Example
You can show achievement at Levels 3, 4 or 5 depending on how you carry out the task.		
Level 3: Ask and answer three questions.	• Ask your partner where he/she lives and where that is located. Respond. • Ask how long he/she has lived there. • Ask each other what you do when it is sunny and when it is raining. Respond.	■ *Où habites-tu? C'est où?* ● *J'habite à Leeds, dans le nord de l'Angleterre.*
Level 4: As Level 3, but include adjectives, intensifiers, connectives and negatives.	• When talking about where you live, give an opinion. • Give two activities that you do when it is sunny and when it is raining; mention one activity that you do not do.	*Quand il pleut, je joue au tennis parce que j'adore faire du sport. Je ne regarde pas la télé quand il fait chaud!*
Level 5: As Level 4, but your conversation needs to make reference to the future as well as the present and use appropriate time expressions. Include reasons for your opinion.	• When discussing what you do when it is sunny and when it is raining, give reasons. Add information on what you like doing. • Ask what he/she is going to do this weekend if it is raining. Respond, giving information about when you are going to do activities.	*Ce week-end, s'il y a du soleil, je vais faire du vélo parce que j'aime mon vélo. Samedi soir, je vais aller au cinéma.*

Lire 1

A Lis. Choisis un titre pour chaque paragraphe. (Level 3)

Exemple: Je m'appelle Luc, et j'ai quatorze ans. Je suis français. [F]

1 Mon beau-père est électricien et ma mère travaille dans un grand magasin. Elle est vendeuse. ☐

2 Je suis assez grand. J'ai les cheveux blonds et assez longs. Je suis très actif et sympa. ☐

3 J'aime le sport: je joue au foot et je fais du skate. Le week-end, je fais du vélo et je regarde la télé. ☐

4 J'habite à Perpignan dans le sud-ouest de la France. J'habite dans un appartement au centre. ☐

5 À Perpignan il fait très chaud en été. En automne, il fait beau mais quelquefois il y a des orages. ☐

6 Mes parents sont divorcés. J'habite avec ma mère. J'ai une demi-sœur. Elle s'appelle Charlotte. ☐

A Mes passe-temps
B Mon ami
C Les métiers de mes parents
D Le climat chez moi
E Mes grands-parents
F Mes détails personnels
G Où j'habite
H Une description de moi
I Ma famille

Points	
Niveau	

B 'a' Read and tick the correct answer. (Level 4)

Example: How old is Luc?
A fifteen ☑ **B** sixteen ☐ **C** seventeen ☐

1 Where in France does he live?
A north ☐ **B** south ☐ **C** east ☐

2 What job does he do?
A nurse ☐ **B** waiter ☐
C mechanic ☐

3 What is his hair like?
A long and black ☐ **B** short and black ☐
C long and blond ☐

4 What are his hobbies?
A football ☐ **B** video games ☐ **C** music ☐

5 What does he like doing when it's sunny?
A playing cards ☐ **B** swimming ☐
C cycling ☐

6 Where does he go when it's raining?
A swimming pool ☐ **B** café ☐ **C** shops ☐

Points	
Niveau	

Forum des Jeunes

Comment t'appelles-tu?
Je m'appelle Luc.
Quel âge as-tu?
J'ai quinze ans. Mon anniversaire est le 5 novembre.
Où habites-tu?
J'habite à Pontivy dans l'est de la France. J'habite dans une grande maison avec ma famille. J'aime bien habiter ici – c'est super.
Tu travailles?
Oui, je travaille dans un café le week-end.
Comment es-tu?
J'ai les cheveux noirs et longs – Je suis assez intelligent et un peu timide.
Quels sont tes intérêts?
J'adore écouter de la musique, je collectionne des CD. Je déteste les jeux vidéo et je ne suis pas sportif.
Que fais-tu avec tes amis le week-end?
S'il fait beau, je retrouve mes amis et on fait du vélo au parc. S'il pleut, on va au café et on joue aux cartes.

Contrôle

Nom: ....

Lire 2

A **Lis Passage A sur page 25. Écris les lettres dans le bon ordre. (Level 4)**

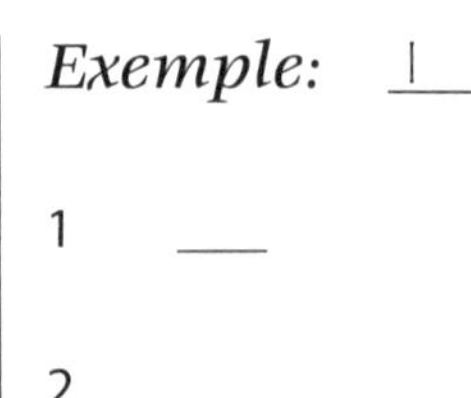

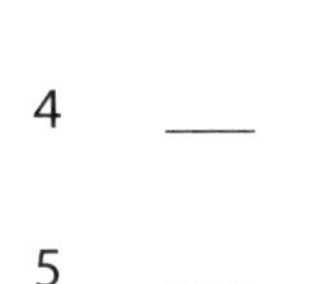

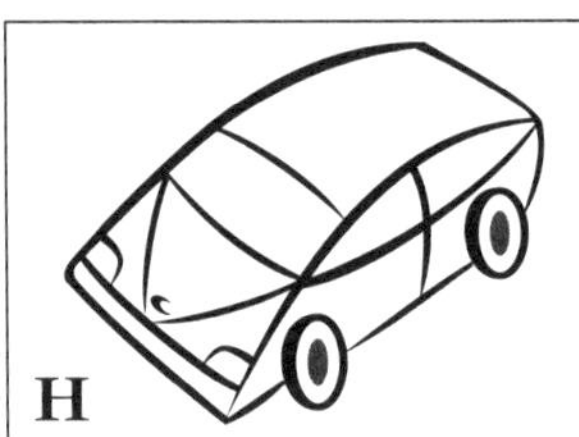

Exemple: I

1 ___

2 ___

3 ___

4 ___

5 ___

6 ___

Points	
Niveau	

B **Lis Passage A et Passage B à la page 25. Complète les phrases. (Level 5)**

se douche · la guitare · le samedi · ses collègues · le volley · son métier · le tennis · va aller au cinéma · va lire · à 12h · chez lui · tard · le mardi · à 9h · va faire du shopping

Exemple: Karim est vendeur.

1 Le soir, il n'aime pas rentrer ______________________.

2 Avant de manger le soir, il ______________________.

3 Il pratique ______________________.

4 Demain, il va se lever ______________________.

5 S'il pleut demain, il ______________________.

6 Il va retrouver ses amis ______________________.

Points	
Niveau	

Nom: ....

Lire 2

Passage A

Je m'appelle Karim et je suis vendeur dans un grand magasin à Paris. D'habitude, je me lève à 9h. Je regarde un peu la télé, puis je m'habille. Normalement, je pars au travail à 10h. Quand j'arrive, je mange un croissant et je bois du café. Je finis à 19h et je vais au supermarché pour faire du shopping. Puis je rentre chez moi en autobus. J'arrive vers 20h30. Je suis fatigué et c'est trop tard pour sortir. Le soir, c'est vraiment difficile de retrouver mes amis et je n'aime pas ça. Je me douche et puis je dîne. Je joue de la guitare tous les soirs. Je me couche vers 23h et je lis un livre ou quelquefois un magazine.

Passage B

Travailler dans un grand magasin, c'est un métier difficile et quelquefois ennuyeux. De temps en temps il y a des clients impatients, mais mes collègues au magasin sont sympas et marrants. On s'amuse bien! Quand je ne travaille pas, j'aime faire du sport. Je suis membre d'un club de volley et je joue trois fois par semaine. Le mardi et le samedi, je ne travaille pas, donc je me lève à midi. Demain, c'est mardi! Normalement, je vais au cinéma, mais demain s'il fait beau je vais regarder un match de tennis. S'il pleut, je vais faire les magasins. Je viens de Nice où il y a du soleil tous les jours et ici, à Paris, il pleut souvent et il fait froid. C'est affreux ça, mais j'aime bien Paris. Demain soir, je vais aller au café avec mes amis. On va au café tous les mardis, on bavarde et on joue aux cartes.

Contrôle

Nom: ....

Écrire 1

A **Lis le site internet. Copie et adapte les phrases pour toi et ta région. (Level 3)**

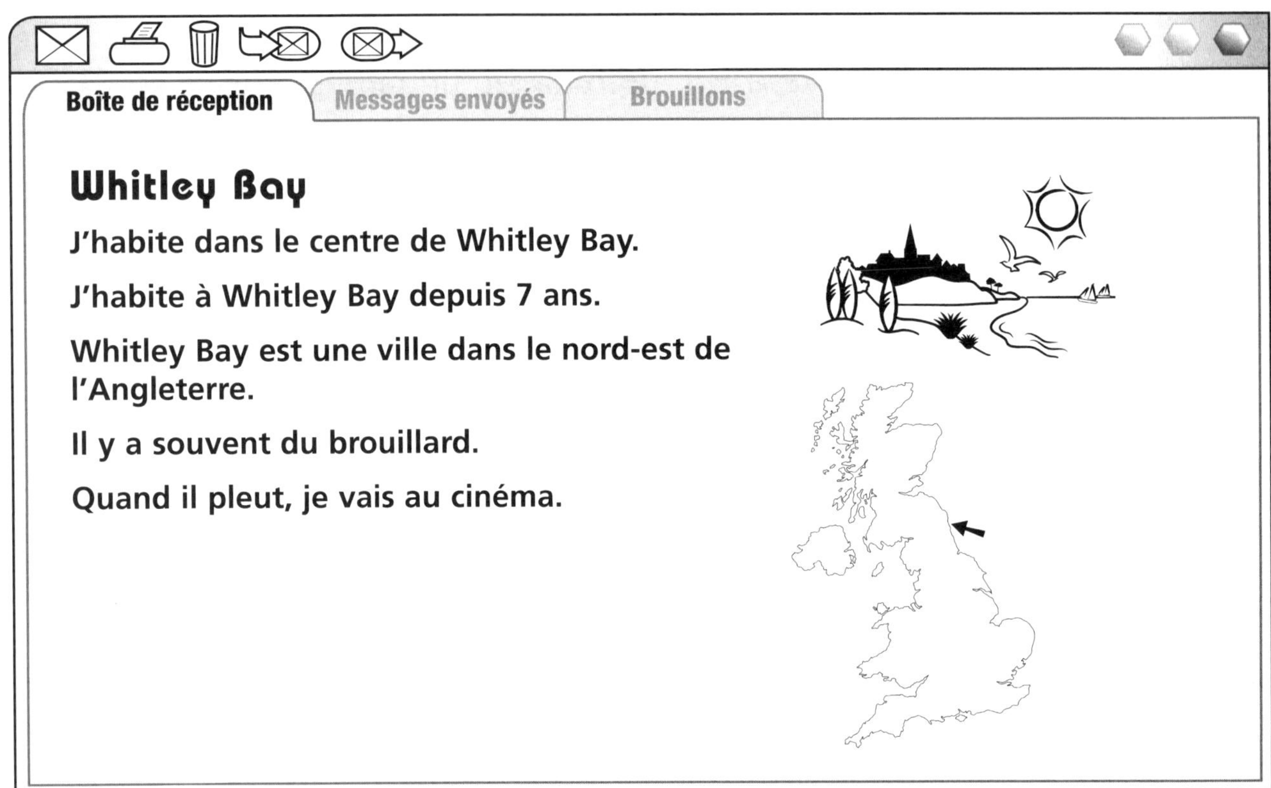

Whitley Bay

J'habite dans le centre de Whitley Bay.

J'habite à Whitley Bay depuis 7 ans.

Whitley Bay est une ville dans le nord-est de l'Angleterre.

Il y a souvent du brouillard.

Quand il pleut, je vais au cinéma.

B **Écris un paragraphe sur ta région. Utilise l'exemple pour t'aider. (Level 4)**

Level information	Pupil support	Example
You can show achievement at Level 3 or 4 depending on how you carry out the task.		
Level 3: Write three sentences, adapting the example supplied by using different details. (If you can include an opinion or a negative, you will be working towards Level 4.)	• Adapt the model so the sentences refer to you and where you live.	*J'habite dans le sud de Glasgow.* *J'habite dans une maison à Cardiff.*
Level 4: Write a short paragraph about where you live. Make your writing more interesting by including negatives, connectives, intensifiers and opinions.	• Say where you live and where it is located. • Say how long you have lived there. • Give your opinion of the place. • Say what the weather is often like. • Say what activities you do in two types of weather using *quand*.	*J'habite dans une très petite maison à Southport. J'aime Southport, mais je n'aime pas ma maison!*

Contrôle

Nom: ....

Écrire 2

A Imagine que tu es professeur. Écris un paragraphe sur ton métier et tes passe-temps. (Level 4)

B Ajoute de l'information sur ce que tu as fait le week-end dernier. (Level 5)

Level information	Pupil support	Example
You can show achievement at Level 4 or 5 depending on how you carry out the task.		
Level 4: Write a short paragraph about a teacher's typical day. Make your writing more interesting by including negatives, connectives, intensifiers and opinions.	• Say how long you have been a teacher and where you work. • Give an activity you do at work and when you start and finish. • Say what you do in your spare time, and what you do not like doing.	*Je suis professeur depuis 6 ans et je travaille dans un grand collège … Je n'aime pas le football parce que je ne suis pas très sportif.*
Level 5: As Level 4, but add a second section on what you did last weekend. Use the perfect tense with appropriate time expressions. Include reasons for your opinions.	• Give details of your daily routine (what you do and when). • When writing about your spare time activities and preferences, say how often and when you do certain activities. • Say what you did last weekend.	*J'aime mon travail parce que c'est intéressant et très varié. … Le week-end dernier, je suis allé au cinéma.*

Teacher's Notes

Contrôle Module 1

Listening assessment criteria
Mark scheme: 1 mark for each correct answer. Total for each task: 6 marks. For details of the sub-levels, see p. 167.

Écouter 1A [AT1 Level 3] 

This task tests understanding of a short passage in the context of describing people. The questions are multiple choice with pictures. Play the recording twice.

This task is similar to Asset Preliminary French Listening (external), p. 11, Part 1, Qs 1–5.

Go to p. 167

'a' This symbol can be found throughout the file and indicates tasks that can be used to practise for Asset assessments. See page 167 for further information.

Audioscript 2

Mon père s'appelle Georges. Il est grand et il a les cheveux noirs. Il travaille dans un grand hôtel depuis 12 ans. Il est serveur dans le restaurant. Sa passion est la musique. Il collectionne des CD. Il aime bien le soleil et il déteste la neige. Il n'est pas sportif, mais le week-end, il regarde le foot à la télé.

Réponses
1 C **2** C **3** B **4** B **5** A **6** A

Écouter 1B [AT1 Level 4]

This task tests understanding of a short passage in the context of families and activities. Pupils complete the statement for each member of the family, writing the appropriate letter. There are four distractors. Play the recording twice.

Audioscript  3

Salut, je m'appelle Nabila et voici ma famille! Moi, je suis très sportive. Mon père travaille dans un bureau et ma mère travaille dans un hôpital. Mon demi-frère n'aime pas le sport, mais il collectionne des cartes de joueurs de foot. Ma grande sœur adore manger, mais elle déteste la pizza. Sa grande passion est le tennis. Ma petite sœur n'aime pas les chats. Mais elle collectionne des araignées. Mon oncle vient souvent à la maison – il est très cool. Il aime le skate!

Réponses
1 E **2** B **3** H **4** C **5** A **6** I

Écouter 2A [AT1 Level 4]

This task tests understanding of details in a short text in the context of jobs. Pupils give one-word answers in French. Pupils should be told to give numbers as figures rather than to write out the words in French. Play the recording twice.

Audioscript  4

Les hôtels Expotel cherchent des serveurs ou serveuses pour travailler dans leurs hôtels dans le sud de la France. Beaucoup de leurs hôtels sont près de la plage. Le travail commence à 7h du matin et finit normalement à 16h. Le travail est assez facile, mais en été, quand il fait chaud, il y a beaucoup de clients. Si vous êtes intéressés, contactez-les sur leur site internet. Il faut avoir 18 ans et être intelligent. L'expérience n'est pas nécessaire.

Réponses
Mark for communication only.
A serveur(s) / serveuses **B** le sud (de la France)
C 7h **D** 16h **E** 18 **F** intelligent

Écouter 2B [AT1 Level 5]

This task tests understanding of main points in a longer passage (including the ability to distinguish between the present and future) in the context of future plans. Pupils tick the pictures mentioned. There are six distractors. Play the recording twice.

Audioscript 5

Salut, je m'appelle Roselyne. J'habite avec ma famille dans une grande maison à Saint-Laurent, dans le sud-est de la France. Je suis serveuse et je travaille dans un café au centre-ville. Je n'aime pas mon métier et bientôt je vais aller à Bordeaux pour être coiffeuse. Je vais habiter dans un appartement avec des amis. Je suis très sportive. Ici à Saint-Laurent, il neige en hiver et ma passion est le ski: je ne peux pas faire ça à Bordeaux. Mais Saint-Laurent est très petite: il y a un centre de sports et c'est tout. J'y vais tous les week-ends. Bordeaux est très grande et très jolie. S'il fait beau, je vais faire du vélo. S'il pleut, je vais aller au cinéma. Ma grand-mère habite près de Bordeaux et je vais la voir tous les week-ends. Bordeaux est près de la mer et en été je vais aller au bord de la mer.

Maintenant, Roselyne … F, H, E
Dans le futur, Roselyne … C, I, G

Speaking assessment criteria
See the Level information supplied on the Assessment sheet.

For detailed Assessment criteria (including sub-levels), see p. 168.

Level information and pupil support with examples are supplied on the assessment sheet. Encourage your pupils to use this to decide which Level they are aiming for. Point out that they should not copy the examples given, but use them as a guide.

Teacher's Notes

Contrôle Module 1

Parler 1 [AT2 Levels 3–4]

This task tests the ability to put together a conversation about a family member, his/her likes and dislikes and his/her job.

The best way to conduct the assessment is to listen to pairs of partners. Either the pupils can take turns in asking each other the questions, or confident pairs can turn the whole assessment into a more fluent conversation.

Parler 2 [AT2 Levels 3–5]

This task tests pupils' ability to put together a conversation about their region and what they do in different types of weather. Pupils aiming for Level 5 should also discuss what they are going to do this coming weekend if it is raining.

The best way to conduct the assessment is to listen to pairs of partners. Either the pupils can take turns in asking each other the questions, or more confident pairs can turn the whole assessment into a more fluent conversation.

Reading assessment criteria
Mark scheme: 1 mark for each correct answer. Total for each task: 6 marks.

For details of the sub-levels see p. 167.

Lire 1A [AT3 Level 3]

This task tests understanding of details in short extracts in the context of personal information. Pupils match the titles with the paragraphs. There are two distractors.

Réponses
1 C **2** H **3** A **4** G **5** D **6** I

Lire 1B [AT3 Level 4] 

This task tests the understanding of a short text in the context of personal information. Pupils answer the multiple choice questions.

This task is similar to Asset Preliminary French Reading (external), p. 8, Part 4, Qs 16–20.

Go to p. 167

Réponses
1 C **2** B **3** A **4** C **5** C **6** B

Lire 2A [AT3 Level 4]

This task tests understanding of a short text in the context of daily routine and jobs. Pupils read passage A on p. 25 and order the activities according to the text.

Réponses
1 G **2** E **3** F **4** B **5** C **6** D

Lire 2B [AT3 Level 5]

This task tests understanding of a longer text containing references to the future in the context of daily routine and jobs. Pupils read Passage A and Passage B on p. 25, then complete the sentences, choosing from the answers given. There are nine distractors.

Réponses
1 tard **2** se douche **3** le volley **4** à 12h
5 va faire du shopping **6** le mardi

Writing assessment criteria
See the Level information supplied on the Assessment sheet. For detailed Assessment criteria (including sub-levels) see p. 169.

First decide whether you want your pupils to complete *Écrire 1, Écrire 2* or both, depending on their ability and time available.

Level information and pupil assessment support with examples are supplied on the assessment sheet. Encourage your pupils to use this to decide which Level they are aiming for. Point out that they should not copy the examples given, but use them as a guide.

Écrire 1 [AT4 Levels 3–4]

This task tests the ability to write a short paragraph in the context of where pupils live. In Section A, pupils describe the area they live in by adapting the model text (Level 3). In Section B (Level 4), they describe their area at greater length, including negatives, connectives, quallifiers and opinions.

Écrire 2 [AT4 Levels 4–5]

This task tests the ability to write a paragraph about a day in the life of a teacher. It is divided into two sections. Pupils who feel more confident can complete both Sections A and B, the latter giving pupils the opportunity to reach Level 5 by requiring the use of the perfect tense, including appropriate time expressions.

Teacher's Notes

Contrôle Module 1

Target-setting section (pp. 17–18)

Before the module

Using their Year 7 attainments as a reference, pupils fill in the levels they would like to achieve by the end of Module 1 in the targets grid. In subsequent modules, they note the levels achieved in the module before.

With this aim in mind, pupils pick three or four focus targets for this module and put a mark against them in the **Before** column. Encourage some pupils to pick one or more bonus targets, which would show outstanding progress if achieved. Ask pupils to identify and add two Personal Targets. See the lists on pages 164–166 of this file for ideas to support this.

Mid-module review

Treat the Mini-test (for Module 1 Pupil Book, page 11) as a trigger to carry out the Mid-module target review. Using peer assessment, pupils work in pairs and decide how well they have done in each of the areas in the **Mid** column that have not been blocked out.

✓	I have achieved this target.
⁄	I have almost achieved this target, but I am not quite there.
○	I have not achieved this target.

End-of-module review

Pupils review the targets again, using the 'End' column. This review should be carried out while pupils still have enough time to improve before their assessment. When they have completed their assessment, you may like to use the **Attainment Grid** sheet to record their levels (page 170 of this file).

Answers to challenge, Activity A, page 12

1 F **2** D **3** G **4** B **5** H **6** C **7** A **8** F

Grammaire

Le passé composé avec *avoir*

If you want to talk about things that happened in the past, you use the **passé composé** (perfect tense). To form the **passé composé** you need three parts:

1 a subject pronoun: **je, il, nous**
2 the correct part of **avoir** for each subject pronoun: **ai, a, avons**
3 a past participle: **regardé, fini, perdu.**

Past participles are formed from regular infinitives as follows:

-er verbs: regard**er** – regardé — Hier, **j'ai regardé** un documentaire.
-ir verbs: fin**ir** – fini — Samedi soir, **il a fini** ses devoirs à 10h.
-re verbs: perd**re** – perdu — Nous avons joué au foot, mais **nous avons perdu.**

A **Put the past participles into the correct columns according to the infinitive. You can do this even if you don't know what the verbs mean.**

-er	-ir	-re

écouté, téléphoné, attendu, fini, perdu, joué, rougi, regardé, répondu, choisi, vendu, mangé

B **Complete the sentences in the *passé composé*, using the verbs in brackets. Use a dictionary to check the meaning of any new words.**

1 J'__________________ un CD. (acheter)
2 Le chien __________________ le garçon. (mordre)
3 Nous __________________ au basket. (jouer)
4 Tu __________________ ton stylo. (perdre)
5 Elles __________________ les bonbons. (cacher)
6 Vous __________________ le questionnaire? (remplir)

Some verbs have past participles which do not follow the normal rules. You have to learn these as you go along.

C **Match the irregular past participles with the correct infinitives.**

1 bu __________ 3 lu __________ 5 dit __________
2 fait __________ 4 pris __________ 6 vu __________

prendre **dire** **boire** **faire** **lire** **voir**

D **Complete the sentences with a past participle from C.**

1 J'ai __________ bonjour au professeur.
2 Vous avez __________ ce livre?
3 Ils ont __________ du coca.
4 Elle a __________ ses devoirs.
5 Tu as __________ le train?
6 Nous avons __________ un film.

Temps libre **2**

Thinking skills

Logic puzzle

Work with a partner. Read the information and complete the grid.

chaque = *each*

Juliette, Janine et Jamila ont regardé la télé hier soir.

Chaque fille a regardé deux émissions.

TV3

17h00: Scoubi-Doo (dessin animé)
17h30: Rue des copains (série)
18h00: Les animaux de l'Amazone (documentaire)
19h00: Poirot (série policière)

France 6

17h30: Je veux gagner! (jeu télévisé)
18h00: Informations
19h00: Film: Jurassic Parc

- **Juliette et sa sœur n'aiment pas regarder les informations.**
- **Deux filles ont regardé le film.**
- **La sœur de Janine a regardé le jeu télévisé.**
- **Une fille aime les séries policières.**
- **Une fille regarde toujours les informations.**
- **La sœur de Juliette adore les animaux, mais elle trouve les dinosaures ennuyeux.**
- **Jamila est fille unique et elle déteste les jeux télévisés.**

trouver = *to find, to think*

	Juliette	**Janine**	**Jamila**
Scoubi-Doo			
Je veux gagner!			
Rue des copains			
Informations			
Les animaux de l'Amazone			
Jurassic Parc			
Poirot			

Lesson starter

Revision of *au, à la, à l', aux*

A Work in a group. Make eight sentences using *au, à la, à l', aux* plus a noun.

au	au	au	à la
à la	à la	à l'	à l'
à l'	aux	aux	aux
piscine	centre de sport	magasins	maison
magasin de musique	hôtel	toilettes	office de tourisme

B Use the left-over words and write different place names on the blank squares to make four new sentences.

Temps libre **2**

Learning skills

Using a dictionary to look up verbs

- In a dictionary, French verbs are always listed in the infinitive: **aller**, **finir**, **vendre**.
- Some more detailed dictionaries also list the past participles of verbs and tell you what the infinitive is:

  bu / ptp de *boire*

  This means 'past participle of'.

- If you are working with a less detailed dictionary and you want to look up the verbs in French from their past participle, you need to be able to work out what the infinitive of the verb is.
- Regular **-er**, **-ir** and **-re** verbs are easy to work out from their past participles.

A **What are the infinitive endings if the past participles have these endings?**

1 -é ______________ **2** -i ______________ **3** -u ______________

B **Write down the infinitives of these verbs with their meanings. Use a dictionary, if necessary.**

Exemple: toussé
infinitive tousser / to cough
j'ai toussé I coughed

1 volé (two meanings)
infinitive __________/__________
____
j'ai volé __________/__________

2 apporté
infinitive __________/__________
Tu as apporté tes baskets?
____

3 rougi
infinitive __________/__________
Mon frère a rougi. ______________

4 fondu
infinitive __________/__________
La glace a fondu. ______________

With the past participles of irregular verbs, it's not so easy. For example, **écrit** is the past participle of **écrire** (to write). If your dictionary does not list past participles, you might need to take several guesses at the infinitive of an irregular verb, before you find it in the dictionary.

C **Work out the infinitives of these irregular past participles. Then look them up.**

1 entendu
infinitive __________/__________
J'ai entendu la musique.
____

2 compris
infinitive __________/__________
Tu as compris? ______________

3 couru
infinitive __________/__________
Le chat a couru dans la rue.
____

4 souri
infinitive __________/__________
Le professeur a souri.
____

Temps libre **2**

Grammaire

Le passé composé avec *être*

With some French verbs, the **passé composé** is formed with **être**, not **avoir**.

A **Match up these English and French sentences.**

1 Je suis allé(e).
2 Je suis arrivé(e).
3 Je suis resté(e).
4 Je suis entré(e).
5 Je suis tombé(e).
6 Je suis rentré(e)/retourné(e).
7 Je suis monté(e).
8 Je suis sorti(e).
9 Je suis parti(e).
10 Je suis venu(e).
11 Je suis descendu(e).

A I went in.
B I went out.
C I went back/returned.
D I went down.
E I left.
F I stayed.
G I went up.
H I went.
I I came.
J I arrived.
K I fell.

B **Put the verbs in A in pairs of opposites. This makes it easier to remember which verbs take *être*. You will be left with one verb on its own.**

Exemple: Je suis allé(e). Je suis venu(e).

____

____

C **Complete the sentences with the missing parts of *être*.**

1 Tu ____________ allé au cinéma?
2 Ils ____________ partis à 8h.
3 Il ____________ tombé.
4 Nous ____________ restés à la maison.
5 Je ____________ arrivé à 6h.
6 Elles ____________ sorties hier soir.
7 Quand ____________ vous rentrée?
8 Elle ____________ montée dans le bus.

D **Add agreements to these past participles, if you think they need them.**

Past participles sometimes need to add extra letter(s). Add:
- **e** if the subject pronoun is feminine
- **s** if the subject is masculine plural
- **es** if the subject is feminine plural.

Il est sorti. → Elle est sorti**e**.
Ils sont sorti**s**. → Elles sont sorti**es**.

1 Tu es venu ____ en bus, Valérie?
2 Bruno est entré ____ dans la maison.
3 Où es-tu descendu ____ de l'autobus, Julie?
4 Simon et Michel sont allé ____ en boîte.
5 Elles sont rentré ____ en taxi.
6 La fille est monté ____ dans le train.

A Use the words in the box to complete the grid with the parts of *avoir* and *être*.

	avoir	être
je/j'		
tu		
il		
elle		
on		
nous		
vous		
ils		
elles		

sort **as** **es** **ai** **est** **est**

avons **aimes** **avez** **sont** **sont** **suis**

êtes **est** **a** **ont** **allons** **a**

a **ont** **sommes**

B You should have three words left over. Which verbs do these come from?

____

____

____

Défi

Les grandes religions

A **Fill in the table using the words relating to the various religions below.**

	L'islam	Le judaïsme	L'hindouisme	Le christianisme
La personne				
Le(s) symbole(s) important(s)				
Le livre sacré				
Lieu de culte				
Clergé				

Musulman — la mosquée — Juif — l'étoile de David — la synagogue — la lune et l'étoile — le temple — Rabbin — Hindou — la Torah (l'Ancien Testament) — le Coran — Imam — Pandit — le lotus sacré — la croix — la Bible — Chrétien — le Mahabharata — l'église — Prêtre

top tip

After doing the ones you know, use reading strategies to work out the others. If you get stuck on these, check out the details on the Internet.

B **Read about what Emily does at the weekend. List her activities: (1) those which are primarily linked to her faith and (2) those which are not.**

Samedi matin, je vais souvent au supermarché avec ma mère, et puis je vais en ville avec des amis – j'aime faire du shopping. Normalement le soir, je regarde la télé ou je vais au cinéma. Après ça, je lis la Bible et je vais au lit. Dimanche matin, je vais à l'église et j'écoute le prêtre. Après ça, je fais de la natation à la piscine et je fais mes devoirs. Dimanche dernier, je suis allée à l'église pour la messe de Pâques – c'était intéressant.

1	2

top tip

What festivals or celebrations take place over the winter season for the different religions? Think about adding this to your presentation!

2 Défi

Les grandes religions

Assignment 2 Challenge

Imagine you are a young person for whom religion is important. Give information about daily life, including details of how you practise your faith.

Assignment 2 Support grid

Level 3	Give three pieces of information about what you do at the weekend (mentioning two things to do with your faith). Join them together where appropriate.	*Le week-end, je joue au football et je lis le Coran. Le samedi matin, …*
Level 4	Deliver a short presentation on what you do at the weekend, including references to faith (place of worship, what text you read, important symbols). Express likes and dislikes.	*Normalement le soir, je regarde la télé ou je vais au cinéma. Après ça, je lis la Bible et … J'aime …*
Level 5	As Level 4, but include details of what you did last weekend, using the perfect tense. Justify opinions. Use a dictionary to add something original when describing your religious practices.	*Samedi dernier, je suis allé(e) à la synagogue – j'étais vraiment touché(e), c'était un moment profond. Et puis …*

Assignment 2 Judging grid

Points for language level as shown plus 1 point for each of the other criteria.

(L3 = **1**, L4 = **2**, L5 = **3**)		References to faith are accurate.		
Spoken French is sufficiently loud and clear for the audience.		Small picture or artefact used to exemplify part of presentation.		
Pronunciation is accurate and confident.		Details on the religious festival are informative and interesting.		Total
Presentation learnt by heart and given confidently from prompt cards.		Imaginative response to what religion means when an important part of life.		/10

Les grandes religions: guidelines for teachers

For general guidelines on how to get the most out of the *Défi* sections, see page 14.

Use this activity alongside or instead of activities on page 38 of the Pupil's Book.

1 Hand out the activity sheet. Pupils work through the activities and use the Internet to find answers when the subject matter is less familiar to them.

2 Pupils then prepare and present a case study from a young person for whom religion is important, using the support and judging grids to help them.

Religious Education Programme of Study	1.2 Key concepts: practices and ways of life
Levels accessed	Levels 3–5
Key vocabulary	*Expo 2 Rouge* Pupil's Book, Module 2, pages 40–41

Temps libre

2 Vocabulaire

Le week-end dernier	***Last weekend***
J'ai joué au foot.	*I played football.*
J'ai regardé la télévision.	*I watched television.*
J'ai acheté des bonbons.	*I bought some sweets.*
J'ai mangé une pizza.	*I ate a pizza.*
J'ai écouté la radio.	*I listened to the radio.*
J'ai aidé mon père.	*I helped my father.*
J'ai téléphoné à mes copains.	*I phoned my friends.*
J'ai cassé une fenêtre.	*I broke a window.*
Je n'ai pas joué au tennis.	*I didn't play tennis.*
tout d'abord	*first of all*
puis/ensuite	*then*
après	*after*
et	*and*
enfin	*finally*

Hier soir	***Last night***
J'ai lu une BD.	*I read a comic book.*
J'ai vu un film d'horreur.	*I saw a horror film.*
J'ai bu un jus d'orange.	*I drank an orange juice.*
J'ai pris une douche.	*I had a shower.*
J'ai pris des photos.	*I took some photos.*
J'ai dit 'Bonne nuit'.	*I said 'Good night'.*
J'ai fait mes devoirs.	*I did my homework.*
J'ai fait la cuisine.	*I cooked.*
J'ai dormi.	*I slept.*
J'ai fini ...	*I finished ...*
J'ai vendu ...	*I sold ...*
J'ai choisi ...	*I chose ...*
J'ai perdu ...	*I lost ...*
J'ai attendu.	*I waited.*

Les émissions de télévision	***TV programmes***
une série	*a series*
un dessin animé	*a cartoon*
une série policière	*a police series*
un jeu télévisé	*a game show*
un documentaire	*a documentary*
les informations	*the news*
Ça passe quand?	*When is it on?*
C'était à quelle heure?	*What time was it on?*
C'était à 20h.	*It was at 8 o'clock.*
C'était comment?	*What was it like?*
Quelle est ton émission préférée?	*What is your favourite programme?*
avant	*before*
après	*after*
pendant	*during*

Les opinions	***Opinions***
C'était ...	*It was ...*
intéressant	*interesting*
passionnant	*exciting*
marrant	*funny*
bien	*good*
pas mal	*not bad*
ennuyeux	*boring*
affreux	*terrible*
nul	*rubbish*

Tu es sorti(e) samedi?	***Did you go out on Saturday?***
Je suis allé(e) ...	*I went ...*
à la piscine	*to the swimming pool*
au cinéma	*to the cinema*
à l'aéroport	*to the airport*
Je suis resté(e) à la maison.	*I stayed at home.*
Je suis parti(e).	*I went out.*
Je suis rentré(e).	*I came home.*
Je suis resté(e) 2 heures.	*I stayed for 2 hours.*

Vocabulaire

Mon week-end	*My weekend*
Je suis allé(e) en ville.	*I went to town.*
Nous avons pris le bus.	*We took the bus.*
J'ai retrouvé mes copains.	*I met my friends.*
samedi dernier	*last Saturday*
le soir	*in the evening*
malheureusement	*unfortunately*
pourtant	*however*
mais	*but*
donc	*so*

Les expressions de temps	*Time phrases*
ce matin	*this morning*
dimanche dernier	*last Sunday*
hier	*yesterday*
hier soir	*last night*
le soir	*in the evening*
le week-end dernier	*last weekend*
récemment	*recently*

Objectifs

Nom: ....

Module 1 Attainment			This module (M2) targets	
Listening			Listening	
Speaking			Speaking	
Reading			Reading	
Writing			Writing	

Before	Level 3 (Short sentences linked together, short conversations)	Mid	End
	Choose three free time activities and ask a partner whether he/she likes each of them. Respond to my partner's questions saying whether I like/don't like each activity.		
	Write sentences saying what I do at the weekend or in the evening. Mention at least six activities.		
	Ask a partner what his/her favourite TV programme is, what sort of programme it is and when it is on. Respond to my partner's questions.		
	Ask a partner what he/she does on a Saturday: where he/she goes, when he/she leaves home, when he/returns home. Respond to my partner's questions. **G** Use the appropriate form of *à*.		

Before	Level 4 (Short texts and longer conversations, short presentations)	Mid	End
	In a short paragraph, describe what I did last weekend (mention five activities). Include intensifiers, connectives and opinions.		
	G Use *j'ai* + past participle (e.g. *écouté*) to describe what I did, and *c'était* to give my opinions. Include at least one negative.		
	Give a short presentation about my television preferences and those of a family member (favourite programmes, the type of programme, time and day it is on). Include connectives, opinions and intensifiers. **G** Include at least one negative.		
	Ask a partner what TV programmes he/she watched last night. Respond to my partner, mentioning at least one programme, when it was on and my opinion of it. **G** Use *tu as regardé* and *c'était* in the questions. When replying, use *j'ai regardé* to say what I watched and *c'était* to say when it was on and what it was like.		

Objectifs

Nom: ....

Before	**Level 5 (Longer texts and more detailed conversations, longer presentations)**	Mid	End
	Write a text about two members of my family, saying what they usually do in their free time and what they did last weekend, using appropriate time expressions. For each give two activities that he/she did and one he/she didn't do. Include opinions with reasons. **G** Use the present tense and the perfect tense.		
	Interview a partner about his/her TV viewing habits: what his/her favourite programme is, what kind of programme it is and when it is on, what he/she watched last night, when it was on and what it was like. Respond to my partner's questions. Use appropriate time expressions and include connectives, intensifiers and opinions (with reasons). **G** Use the present tense and the perfect tense. Include at least two negatives.		
	Write a text about what I usually do in the evening and what I did last night, including what TV programmes I watched. Use time expressions in describing what I did before, during and after watching TV. Include connectives, intensifiers and the opinions (with reasons). **G** Use the present tense and the perfect tense. Include at least two negatives.		
	Write a text about a day trip. Include information about where I went, who I went with, when I left and when I returned, in addition to three activities I did while I was there. Include connectives, intensifiers and opinions (with reasons). **G** Use the present tense to say what I like doing on trips and the perfect tense of *avoir* and *être* verbs, as appropriate. Include some nous verb forms.		
	Choose a film star. Write an imaginative text describing him/her and saying what he/she did last weekend (where he/she went, where he/she stayed, four activities that he/she did). Use appropriate time expressions. Include connectives, intensifiers and opinions (with reasons). **G** Use the present tense and the perfect tense of *avoir* and *être* verbs, as appropriate.		

Personal Targets	**Mid**	**End**

Target Setting

Fill in the levels you reached in Module 1, then decide which level you are aiming for in Module 2 in each skill.

Go to the objective grid for your target level and decide which objectives you are going to focus on. You may want to include an objective from the level below or the level above, to help you make the transition from a lower to a higher level. Put a mark in the **Before** column for your chosen objectives.

To help you fill in your personal targets, you may like to refer to pages 164–166 for ideas.

Contrôle

Nom: ....

Écouter 1

A **What do the different people like to do with their friends? Listen and write a letter (A–J) in the box. (Level 3)**

A 

B 

C 

D 

E 

F 

G 

H 

I 

J 

Example: Clémentine  C

1 Jean-Pierre 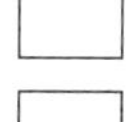

2 Amélie

3 Hugues

4 Soraya 

5 Kévin 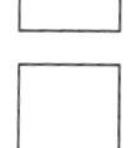

6 Véronique

Points	
Niveau	

B **Écoute et écris les bonnes lettres dans la case. (Level 4)**

A 

B 

C 

D 

E 

F 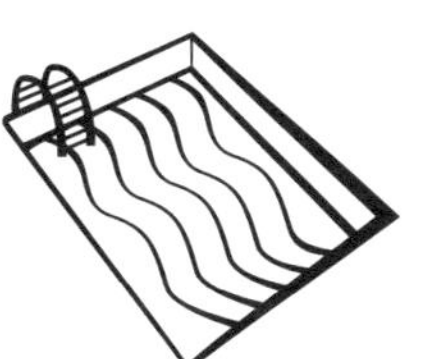

G 

H 

I 

J 

K 

☺	☹
Exemple: B	

Points	
Niveau	

Contrôle

Nom: ....

Écouter 2

A Lis la question et remplis la grille. (Level 4)

A

C

E

G

I

B

D

F

H

J

Qu'est-ce qu'ils regardent à la télé?

	émission	heure	opinion
Exemple:	C	18h	H
1			
2			

Points	
Niveau	

B Écoute et coche (✔) les bonnes réponses. (Level 5)

1 Qu'est-ce qu'ils vont regarder? Choisis l'émission.

A ☐

B

☐

C

☐

D

☐

E

☐

2 Pourquoi? Coche (✔) les cinq phrases correctes.

Exemple: Le jeu télévisé commence à 19h. ☑

A Ils n'aiment pas les jeux télévisés. ☐

B Le documentaire n'est pas intéressant. ☐

C Le documentaire finit trop tard. ☐

D Ils se couchent à minuit. ☐

E Il y a un film d'horreur à la télé. ☐

F Ils ont déjà vu le film. ☐

G La France joue au foot contre le Portugal. ☐

H Ils n'aiment pas le foot. ☐

I Ils n'aiment pas les programmes de musique. ☐

J L'émission de musique finit à 18h15. ☐

Points	
Niveau	

Nom: ....

Expo 2R Speaking

Parler 1

A Réponds aux questions de ton professeur ou de ton ami/amie. (Levels 3–4)

Qu'est-ce que tu fais normalement le samedi? Et le dimanche? (Level 3)

B Qu'est-ce que tu as fait le week-end dernier? C'était comment? (Level 4)

Level information	Pupil support	Example
You can show achievement at Level 3 or 4 depending on how you carry out the task.		
Level 3: Ask and answer the questions.	• Ask a partner what he/she usually does on Saturday. • Ask what he/she usually does on Sunday. • Respond to your partner's questions by giving two activities for each day, joining the sentences together appropriately.	■ *Qu'est-ce que tu fais normalement le samedi?* ● *Je joue à l'ordinateur et je regarde la télé.*
Level 4: Ask and answer questions. Put together a conversation with your partner. Include adjectives, intensifiers, connectives and negatives.	• Ask my partner what he/she did last weekend. • Respond by giving at least two activities for Saturday and two for Sunday, using *j'ai* + past participle (e.g. *écouté*). • Include details of who you did each activity with. • Ask how each activity was. • Respond by giving your opinion using *C'était*. • Include a negative opinion.	■ *J'ai joué au football avec mes amis dans le parc.* ● *C'était comment?* ■ *C'était très intéressant – ce n'était pas fatigant.*

Contrôle

Nom: ....

Parler 2 Pose des questions.

Réponds aux questions de ton professeur ou de ton ami/amie. Pose des questions à ton/ta partenaire aussi. (Levels 4–5)

- Quelle est ton émission préférée?
- C'est quelle sorte d'émission et ça passe quand?
- Quelle est l'émission préférée de tes amis/amies?
- Qu'est-ce que tu as regardé hier soir? C'était comment? (Level 5)
- Qu'est-ce que tu as fait après l'émission? (Level 5)

Level information	Pupil support	Example
You can show achievement at Level 4 or 5 depending on how you carry out the task.		
Level 4: Ask and answer questions. Put together a conversation with your partner. Include adjectives, qualifiers, connectives and negatives.	• Ask your partner what his/her favourite programme is, and respond. • Ask what sort of programme it is and when it is on, and respond. • Ask what a friend's favourite programme is.	■ *Quelle est ton émission préférée?* ● *Mon émission préférée est* Spooks. *C'est très passionnant et j'adore Adam Carter!*
Level 5: As Level 4, but your conversation needs to make reference to the past as well as the present, and use appropriate time expressions. Include reasons for your opinions.	• When discussing your favourite programmes, give reasons for your choices. • Ask each other what you watched on TV last night, using the perfect tense. • Ask each other what you did after watching TV last night, using the perfect tense.	■ *Qu'est-ce que tu as regardé hier soir? C'était comment?* ● *Hier, j'ai regardé* Shameless *avec mon frère. J'adore* Shameless *parce que c'est une série très marrante! Après ça nous avons regardé …*

Contrôle

Nom: ....

Lire 1

Points	
Niveau	

A Lis et écris les bons prénoms. (Level 3)

A *J'adore faire du vélo avec mes amis et je joue souvent au basket, trois fois par semaine et le samedi j'ai souvent des matchs. J'aime aussi lire, surtout les livres de science-fiction. Je collectionne des cartes de joueurs de foot. J'en ai 200.* *Ivan*

B *Je fais de la danse. Je suis membre d'un club – c'est le samedi après-midi. Je joue souvent à l'ordinateur. C'est passionnant! J'aime acheter des magazines sur les ordinateurs.* ***Ada***

C *Ma passion, c'est la musique. J'écoute toujours de la musique, j'ai toujours mon iPod sur moi. J'ai aussi une grande collection de cartes postales. J'aime aussi regarder la télé.* ***Alexis***

1 ____________

2  ____________

3  ____________

4  ____________

5  ____________

6  ____________

B Read and tick the correct answers. (Level 4)

Points	
Niveau	

Marcel Leclerc, 14 ans

Héros:	Je suis fana de Franck Ribéry, le joueur de foot.
Télévision:	J'adore les jeux télévisés. Je regarde les infos tous les jours parce que je crois que c'est important. Quelquefois les documentaires sont intéressants. Je n'aime pas les comédies. Elles ne sont pas marrantes.
Sport:	Je suis membre d'un club de foot. Je joue au foot le lundi, le mercredi et le samedi. Je fais de la natation une fois par semaine. De temps en temps, nous jouons au basket au collège.
Passe-temps:	Ma passion, c'est de parler au téléphone avec mes amis et chatter sur Internet. Je déteste lire.
Week-end idéal:	Retrouver mes amis, faire du shopping, aller au cinéma.
Week-end d'horreur:	Rester à la maison avec ma famille, aller à la pêche avec mon père, faire de la danse.
Ambitions:	Jouer pour l'équipe nationale de foot, faire de l'escalade.

1 On TV he prefers...
A game shows. ☐ **B** documentaries. ☐
C comedies. ☐

2 He watches the news...
A rarely. ☐ **B** sometimes. ☐ **C** often. ☐

3 He plays football...
A 3 times a week. ☐ **B** twice a week. ☐
C from time to time. ☐

4 He doesn't like...
A talking on the phone. ☐ **B** reading. ☐
C doing homework. ☐

5 On an ideal weekend, he likes...
A fishing with dad. ☐ **B** seeing friends. ☐
C staying at home ☐

6 He would like to try... **A** canoeing. ☐
B sailing. ☐ **C** climbing. ☐

Contrôle

Nom: ....

Lire 2

A Read Passage A on page 49, then read the statements and decide whether each is true (T), false (F) or not mentioned in the text (NM). (Level 4)

Example: Samy doesn't do much at the weekend. F

1 Samy has homework only at the weekend. ____
2 Samy prefers swimming to badminton. ____
3 Samy and Robert leave the sports centre at 4 o'clock. ____
4 On Saturday evenings Samy watches a film with his family. ____
5 Samy can't help his mother because he has homework. ____
6 Samy doesn't go to the cinema on Sunday evening. ____

Points	
Niveau	

B Lis Passage A et Passage B à la page 49. Écris les bonnes lettres dans la case. (Level 5)

A 

D 

G 

J 

B 

E 

H 

K 

C 

F 

I 

L 

Que fait Samy le week-end?

	normalement	le week-end dernier
samedi matin	*Exemple:* C	*Exemple:* E
samedi après-midi		
dimanche matin		
dimanche après-midi		

Points	
Niveau	

Temps libre **2**

Contrôle

Nom: ....

Expo 2R Reading

Lire 1

Points	
Niveau	

A Lis et écris les bons prénoms. (Level 3)

A *J'adore faire du vélo avec mes amis et je joue souvent au basket, trois fois par semaine et le samedi j'ai souvent des matchs. J'aime aussi lire, surtout les livres de science-fiction. Je collectionne des cartes de joueurs de foot. J'en ai 200.* *Ivan*

B *Je fais de la danse. Je suis membre d'un club – c'est le samedi après-midi. Je joue souvent à l'ordinateur. C'est passionnant! J'aime acheter des magazines sur les ordinateurs.* *Ada*

C *Ma passion, c'est la musique. J'écoute toujours de la musique, j'ai toujours mon iPod sur moi. J'ai aussi une grande collection de cartes postales. J'aime aussi regarder la télé.* *Alexis*

1 ____________ 2 ____________ 3 ____________ 4 ____________ 5 ____________ 6 ____________

B Read and tick the correct answers. (Level 4)

Points	
Niveau	

Marcel Leclerc, 14 ans

Héros:	Je suis fana de Franck Ribéry, le joueur de foot.
Télévision:	J'adore les jeux télévisés. Je regarde les infos tous les jours parce que je crois que c'est important. Quelquefois les documentaires sont intéressants. Je n'aime pas les comédies. Elles ne sont pas marrantes.
Sport:	Je suis membre d'un club de foot. Je joue au foot le lundi, le mercredi et le samedi. Je fais de la natation une fois par semaine. De temps en temps, nous jouons au basket au collège.
Passe-temps:	Ma passion, c'est de parler au téléphone avec mes amis et chatter sur Internet. Je déteste lire.
Week-end idéal:	Retrouver mes amis, faire du shopping, aller au cinéma.
Week-end d'horreur:	Rester à la maison avec ma famille, aller à la pêche avec mon père, faire de la danse.
Ambitions:	Jouer pour l'équipe nationale de foot, faire de l'escalade.

1 On TV he prefers...
A game shows. ☐ **B** documentaries. ☐
C comedies. ☐

2 He watches the news...
A rarely. ☐ **B** sometimes. ☐ **C** often. ☐

3 He plays football...
A 3 times a week. ☐ **B** twice a week. ☐
C from time to time. ☐

4 He doesn't like...
A talking on the phone. ☐ **B** reading. ☐
C doing homework. ☐

5 On an ideal weekend, he likes...
A fishing with dad. ☐ **B** seeing friends. ☐
C staying at home ☐

6 He would like to try... **A** canoeing. ☐
B sailing. ☐ **C** climbing. ☐

Temps libre

2 Contrôle

Nom: ....

Expo 2R Reading

Lire 2

A **Read Passage A on page 49, then read the statements and decide whether each is true (T), false (F) or not mentioned in the text (NM). (Level 4)**

Example: Samy doesn't do much at the weekend. F

1 Samy has homework only at the weekend. ____
2 Samy prefers swimming to badminton. ____
3 Samy and Robert leave the sports centre at 4 o'clock. ____
4 On Saturday evenings Samy watches a film with his family. ____
5 Samy can't help his mother because he has homework. ____
6 Samy doesn't go to the cinema on Sunday evening. ____

Points	
Niveau	

B **Lis Passage A et Passage B à la page 49. Écris les bonnes lettres dans la case. (Level 5)**

A 

D 

G 

J 

B 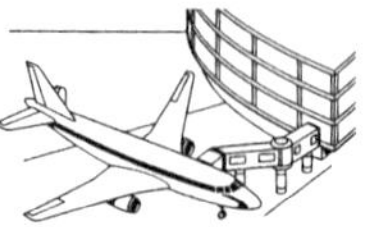

E 

H 

K 

C 

F 

I 

L 

Que fait Samy le week-end?

	normalement	le week-end dernier
samedi matin	*Exemple:* C	*Exemple:* E
samedi après-midi		
dimanche matin		
dimanche après-midi		

Points	
Niveau	

Nom: ....

Lire 2

Passage A

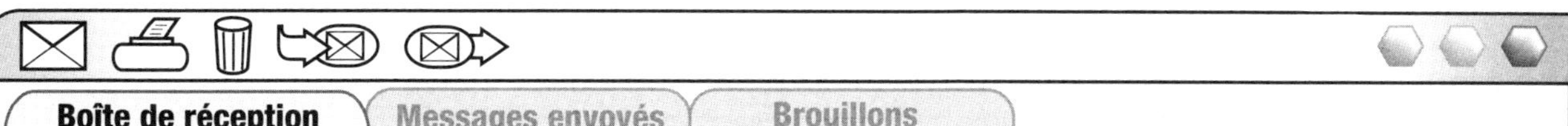

Normalement le week-end, je sors beaucoup et je fais beaucoup d'activités. Samedi matin, je vais au collège bien sûr, mais je finis à 10h. Je rentre chez moi et je fais mes devoirs tout de suite. Comme ça mes parents sont contents et je peux sortir. Je retrouve mes amis généralement vers 13h au centre de sports. Mes amis aiment nager, mais moi, je joue au badminton avec mon meilleur ami, Robert. On y reste normalement tout l'après-midi. Après je vais chez Robert. Le samedi soir, sa famille aime regarder un film à la télé, donc Robert et moi nous allons dans sa chambre et nous écoutons de la musique.

Dimanche matin, j'aide ma mère à la maison. Ma sœur n'aide pas parce qu'elle fait ses devoirs. Ce n'est pas juste! L'après-midi, je vais au parc avec mes amis. Le soir, mes amis vont au cinéma, mais je rentre chez moi et je regarde la télé. Je me couche à 21h.

Passage B

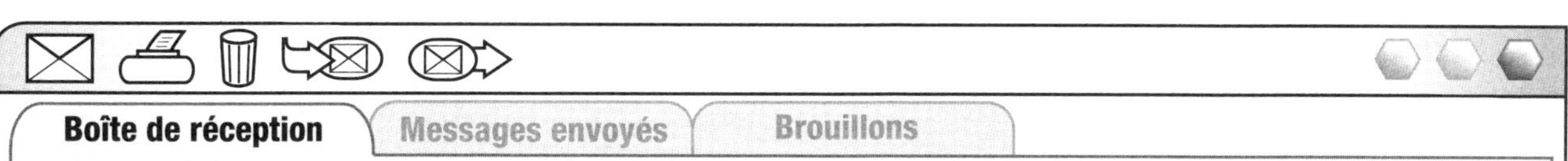

Le week-end dernier, il n'y avait pas de collège, donc je suis allé au stade avec mes amis. Nous avons joué au foot. L'après–midi, nous avons décidé d'aller au cinéma. On est arrivés au cinéma à 14h, mais c'était trop tard pour voir le film! J'ai invité mes amis chez moi et nous avons regardé un DVD.

Le dimanche matin, j'ai fait mes devoirs. J'ai passé deux heures à les faire. Mes parents sont allés à l'aéroport pour chercher ma grand-mère, qui passe une semaine chez nous. Je ne suis pas sorti avec mes amis l'après-midi parce que je suis allé avec ma famille au restaurant. Nous sommes restés trois heures au restaurant. On a bien mangé, mais c'était un peu ennuyeux.

Contrôle

Temps libre 2

Nom: ....

Écrire 1

A Copie et adapte les phrases pour toi et ta famille. (Level 3)

B Qu'est-ce que tu aimes comme émission? Ça passe quand? Qu'est-ce que tu n'aimes pas? Tu regardes souvent la télé? Et ta mère? (Level 4)

Level information	Pupil support	Example
You can show achievement at Level 3 or 4 depending on how you carry out the task.		
Level 3: Write three sentences, adapting the example supplied by using different details. (If you can change the details and include an opinion or a negative in the same sentence, you will be working towards Level 4.)	• Copy the sentences adapting the information to talk about TV programmes you watch.	Copy *Mon émission préférée est …* and change *Hollyoaks* to your favourite programme. Then change the type of programme and the details of when it is on. Try to include a negative or an opinion.
Level 4: Write a short text about your TV habits. Make your writing more interesting by including negatives, connectives, intensifiers and opinions.	• Say what type of programme you like, and give your favourite programme; include your opinions of other types of programme. • Say when your favourite programme is on. • Say how often you watch TV. • Include this information for a family member too.	*Moi, j'aime les dessins animés – mon émission préférée est* The Simpsons. *J'aime Bart – il est très marrant! Je regarde souvent ….*

Contrôle

Nom: ....

Écrire 2

A Qu'est-ce que tu as fait le week-end dernier? C'était comment? (Level 4)

top tip

Use the structure *j'ai …é* (e.g. *j'ai regardé*) to talk about the past.
Use *c'était …* to give your opinions.

B Tu es sorti(e) le week-end? Où es-tu allé(e)? (Level 5)

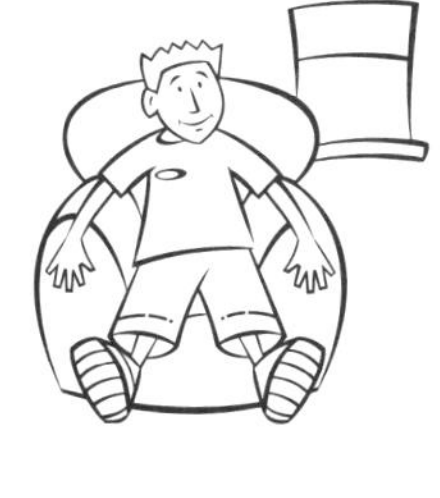

Level information	Pupil support	Example
You can show achievement at Level 4 or 5 depending on how you carry out the task.		
Level 4: Write a short text about what you did last weekend. Make your writing more interesting by including negatives, connectives and intensifiers.	• Talk about what you did last weekend (giving two activities for Saturday and two for Sunday). • Give your opinions on these activities using *c'était …* • Include information about where and with whom you did the activities. • Include appropriate time expressions.	*Samedi dernier, j'ai joué au football avec mes amis dans le parc. C'était très marrant. L'après-midi, j'ai …*
Level 5: As Level 4, but include details of where you went, and when you left and returned, using the perfect tense with *être*. Include details of what activities you like doing and/or usually do, using the present tense.	As for Level 4 but • Include information about an outing: where you went and when you returned, using the perfect tense with *être*. • Justify opinions. • Talk about activities that you like doing and/or usually do, using the present tense.	*Dimanche après-midi, je suis sorti avec John. Nous sommes allés en ville – j'aime aller en ville parce que j'aime les magasins…*

Teacher's Notes

Contrôle Module 2

Listening assessment criteria
Mark scheme: 1 mark for each correct answer. Total for each task: 6 marks. For details of the sublevels see p. 167.

Écouter 1A [AT1 Level 3] 

This task tests understanding of a short passage in the context of leisure time activities. Pupils identify the activity for each person, writing the correct letter. There are two distractors. Play the recording twice.

This task is similar to Asset Breakthrough French Listening (external), p. 14, part 3, Qs 11–15.

Go to p. 167

Audioscript 6

- *Alors, Clémentine, que fais-tu avec tes amis?*
- *Eh bien, le week-end, nous jouons au tennis.*
- *Et toi, Jean-Pierre?*
- *Mes amis viennent souvent chez moi et nous regardons des DVD.*
- *Amélie?*
- *On va au centre de sports. Nous jouons pour une équipe de volley.*
- *Hugues?*
- *Le mercredi avec mes amis, on va à la piscine. J'adore nager.*
- *Soraya?*
- *Nous ne sortons pas beaucoup, mais le samedi, je vais chez ma copine. Nous aimons écouter de la musique.*
- *Et toi, Kévin?*
- *Le Dimanche je rencontre mes amis et nous faisons du vélo. C'est super!*
- *Et finalement toi, Véronique?*
- *Moi et mes amies, nous aimons faire de la danse. C'est passionnant!*

Réponses
1 B **2** G **3** A **4** F **5** D **6** J

Écouter 1B [AT1 Level 4]

This task tests understanding of the main points of a short passage in the context of leisure time activities. Pupils identify the likes and dislikes, writing the appropriate letter in the correct box. There are four distractors. Play the recording twice.

Audioscript 7

Le samedi, j'aime retrouver mes amis. Le matin, nous faisons de la danse. J'adore ça! Et quelquefois nous allons en ville. J'aime ça – c'est marrant. Quelquefois nous jouons au basket. Moi, je n'aime pas ça – c'est affreux. Dimanche, je fais mes devoirs. Je déteste ça – c'est nul! Mon frère joue toujours à l'ordinateur. Je n'aime pas ça – c'est ennuyeux. Moi, j'aime bien lire. C'est passionnant.

Réponses

☺	☹
C, E, G	D, H, J

Écouter 2A [AT1 Level 4]

This task tests understanding of details in short passages in the context of leisure time. Pupils fill in the relevant information in the grid. There are four distractors. Play the recording twice.

Audioscript 8

- *Mon émission préférée s'appelle Columbo. C'est une série policière; c'est le mardi à 18h. C'est intéressant.*
- *Je n'aime pas beaucoup les documentaires. Je les trouve ennuyeux et je ne les regarde jamais. Mes parents regardent les informations tous les soirs à 20h – je déteste ça. Moi, j'écoute de la musique dans ma chambre! J'adore Questions pour un champion. C'est un jeu télévisé. C'est le lundi, je crois. Oui, c'est ça, le lundi à 19h30. C'est marrant.*
- *Moi, je ne regarde pas beaucoup la télé. Le week-end, je sors beaucoup mais le dimanche je reste à la maison avec ma famille. Nous mangeons à13h et l'après-midi nous regardons la télé. Il y a toujours une série qui s'appelle Les feux de l'amour. Ça commence à 15h45 et ma mère adore ça. Je la regarde avec elle, mais je trouve ça ennuyeux.*

Réponses
1 A, 19h30, G **2** E, 15h45, I

Écouter 2B [AT1 Level 5]

This task tests the understanding of a passage in the context of watching TV. In section 1 pupils tick which programme is chosen: there are four distractors. In part 2 they have to tick the five correct reasons: there are five distractors. Play the recording twice.

Audioscript 9

- *Qu'est-ce qu'il y a à la télé ce soir?*
- *Il y a un jeu télévisé qui commence à 19h. Personnellement, je n'aime pas les jeux télévisés.*
- *Moi, je les déteste! Il y a un documentaire sur TF1 à 21h. C'est sur la Chine – c'est très intéressant.*
- *Oui, mais ça finit à minuit! On doit se coucher à 22h30. Est-ce qu'il y a un film ce soir?*
- *Oui, sur A2 à 20h il y a Mission Impossible 3. C'est un film d'action.*
- *J'ai vu ça au cinéma.*
- *Moi, aussi. Il y a un match de foot, l'Écosse contre le Portugal – mais pour moi le foot est ennuyeux.*

Teacher's Notes

Contrôle Module 2

- *Moi, je n'aime pas ça. Il y a une émission de musique sur FR3.*
- *Oui, mais il est déjà 18h et l'émission finit à 18h15!*
- *À 19h il y a une série policière. C'est pas mal.*
- *J'aime bien les séries policières. Elles sont passionnantes. En plus, ça finit à 21h. Après on peut jouer à l'ordinateur.*
- *D'accord, on va regarder ça.*

Réponses

1 D **2** A, C, F, H, J

Speaking assessment criteria

See the level information supplied on the Assessment sheet.

For detailed Assessment criteria (including sublevels), see p. 168.

Level information and pupil support with examples are supplied on the assessment sheet. Encourage your pupils to use this to decide which level they are aiming for. Point out that they should not copy the examples given, but use them as a guide.

Use *Parler 1* in the first instance if you are unsure of which level to give a particular learner.

Parler 1 [AT2 Levels 3–4]

This task tests the ability to ask and answer questions in the context of talking about the weekend. At Level 4, this requires (exceptionally) the use of past tenses. Pupils do not have to manipulate the tenses: spider diagrams showing them the structures to use are supplied for support.

Parler 2 [AT2 Levels 4–5]

This task tests the ability to ask and answer questions in the context of television habits. Pupils are encouraged to add as much information as possible and to extend their answers, including information about the TV habits of a family member.

The last two questions give the opportunity to reach Level 5 by requiring use of the perfect tense to talk about what they watched/did last night.

The best way to conduct the assessment is to circulate as pupils are having their conversations, or indeed to ask pupils questions individually at the front of the class as the others complete other parts of the assessments.

Reading assessment criteria

Mark scheme: 1 mark for each correct answer. Total for each task: 6 marks.

For details of the sublevels see p. 167.

Lire 1A [AT3 Level 3]

This task tests understanding of the main points of short texts in the context of leisure time activities. Pupils identify who does each activity, writing down the correct name.

Réponses

1 Ada **2** Ivan **3** Alexis **4** Ada **5** Alexis **6** Ivan

Lire 1B [AT3 Level 4] 

This task tests understanding of the main points and some detail in a short text in the context of leisure time activities. The questions are multiple choice.

This task is similar to Asset Preliminary Reading (external), p. 8, part 4, Qs 16–20.

Go to p. 167

Réponses

1 A **2** C **3** A **4** B **5** B **6** C

Lire 2A [AT3 Level 4]

This task tests understanding of a short text in the context of weekend activities. Pupils read Passage A and decide whether the six statements about it are true (T), false (F) or contain information not given in the text (NM).

Réponses

1 NM **2** F **3** NM **4** F **5** F **6** T

Lire 2B [AT3 Level 5]

This task tests understanding of a longer text (including the ability to distinguish between past and present) in the context of weekend activities. Pupils read Passage A and Passage B. They identify the activities Samy did, writing in the letters in the correct part of the grid (by the appropriate time). There are four distractors.

Réponses

samedi après-midi	D, I
dimanche matin	F, G
dimanche après-midi	H, K

Writing assessment criteria

See the level information supplied on the Assessment sheet. For detailed Assessment criteria (including sublevels) see p. 169.

First decide whether you want your pupils to complete *Écrire 1, 2* or both, depending on their ability and time available.

Level information and pupil assessment support with examples are supplied on the assessment sheet. Encourage your pupils to use this to decide

Teacher's Notes

Contrôle Module 2

which level they are aiming for. Point out that they should not copy the examples given, but use them as a guide.

Écrire 1 [AT4 Levels 3–4]

Give this sheet to pupils who are working at levels 3–4. This task tests the ability to write a short paragraph in the context of television habits. It is divided into two sections. In Section A pupils describe their favourite programme by copying the model sentences and altering them accordingly. In Section B pupils write a similar paragraph giving more information, and including qualifiers, opinions, adjectives, negatives and adverbs of frequency in their writing.

Écrire 2 [AT4 Levels 4–5]

Give this sheet only to pupils who are working at Levels 4–5. If in doubt, give *Écrire 1* first.

This task tests the ability to write a paragraph in the context of describing last weekend. It is divided into two sections. In Section A pupils talk about what they did: exceptionally this involves the use of past tenses at Level 4. Pupils do not have to manipulate the tenses and they are given support on which structures to use. Pupils who feel more confident can complete both sections A and B, the latter giving them the opportunity to reach Level 5 by requiring the use of the perfect tense of both *avoir* and *être* verbs.

Thinking skills

Famous French people

A The four texts below about famous French people have each been cut into two and pasted together wrongly. Work with a partner or in a group. Use your powers of logic and reading strategies to work out the point in each text where the join has been made. Then cut and paste the texts together correctly.

Gustave Eiffel: *Cet architecte a construit la fameuse tour Eiffel, en 1889. Entre ses sujets fameux, il a beaucoup peint les nénuphars dans son joli jardin. On peut visiter la maison et le jardin de l'artiste à Giverny, près de Paris.*

Louis XIV: *'Le Roi Soleil', Louis, a commencé la construction du Château de Versailles en 1661. Leur bande dessinée est une des plus populaires du monde et on peut visiter un parc d'attractions consacré à leur création, juste au nord de Paris.*

René Goscinny et Albert Uderzo: *Ce sont les créateurs d'Astérix. Goscinny a écrit les histoires et Uderzo a fait les dessins. Les touristes adorent visiter ce beau palais royal, surtout pour voir ses jardins magnifiques et sa salle des glaces célèbre.*

Claude Monet: *Un des plus importants peintres impressionistes, Monet adorait la couleur et la lumière. Symbole de Paris et le plus célèbre monument de la France, elle mesure 324 mètres de hauteur et elle est visitée par plus de six millions de personnes par an.*

B Which of the famous people does each of the following statements refer to?

1. He was known as the Sun King. ____________
2. The characters he drew are famous throughout the world. ____________
3. Millions of visitors to Paris enjoy the view from his famous monument. ____________
4. His paintings of water lilies are some of the most valuable works of art in the world. ____________
5. Without his stories, one of France's most popular theme parks would not exist. ____________

C Find the following items in the texts above.

1. Four near-cognates which have one letter (or accent) different from English. ________ ________ ________ ________
2. Four non-cognates which have two letters different from English. ________ ________ ________ ________

Lesson starter
pouvoir and *devoir*

A **Work with a partner.**

- Which of the following do you think are the six forms of the verb *pouvoir* (to be able to)? Put a star next to them.
- Which are the six forms of the verb *devoir* (to have to)? Put a tick next to them.

Be careful! There are three words which are from completely different verbs.

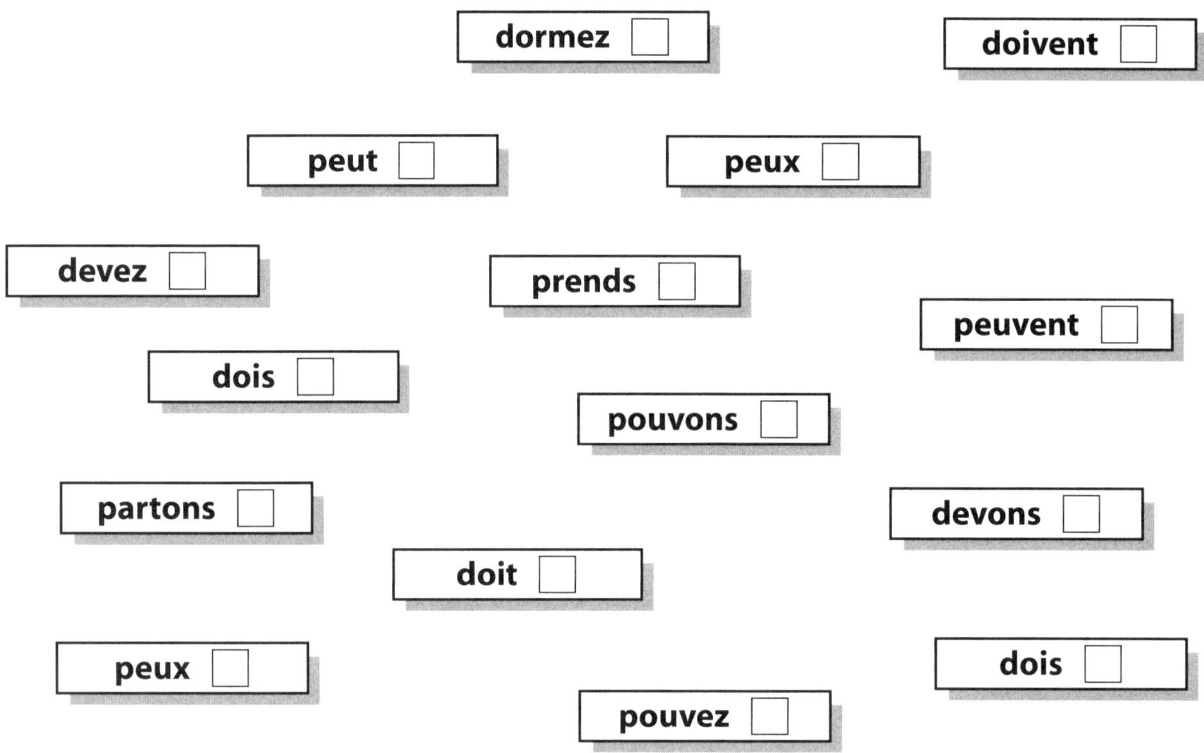

B **Complete the paradigms for *pouvoir* and *devoir*.**

pouvoir *to be able to*	**devoir** *to have to*
je ______________	je ______________
tu ______________	tu ______________
il/elle/on ______________	il/elle/on ______________
nous ______________	nous ______________
vous ______________	vous ______________
ils/elles ______________	ils/elles ______________

Grammaire

pouvoir, vouloir, devoir

vouloir, ***pouvoir*** and ***devoir*** are known as **modal verbs**. They are often used with another verb, which is always in the infinitive.

A **Complete the paradigms of *pouvoir*, *vouloir* and *devoir*.**

pouvoir *to be able to*	**vouloir** *to want to*	**devoir** *to have to*
je peux	je ________	je ________
tu ________	tu veux	tu dois
il/elle/on ________	il/elle/on ________	il/elle/on ________
nous ________	nous voulons	nous ________
vous pouvez	vous ________	vous ________
ils/elles ________	ils/elles ________	ils/elles doivent

veut **peuvent** **devons** **dois** **veux** **peut**

pouvons **devez** **veulent** **peux** **doit** **voulez**

B **Fill in the gaps with the correct part of a modal verb.**

1 Elles ________ venir.
2 Tu ________ acheter ce sweat?
3 Tu ________ faire tes devoirs.
4 Nous ________ aller en boîte.
5 Ils ________ aller en ville.
6 Je ________ aider mes parents.
7 Vous ________ voir un film.
8 Elles ________ écouter le prof.
9 Il ________ téléphoner à sa copine.
10 Nous ________ acheter des baskets.

C **Use the verbs *vouloir*, *pouvoir* and *devoir* with the infinitives below to make five positive and five negative sentences.**

Exemple: Nous devons arriver au collège à 9h.

Je ne veux pas faire mes devoirs.

____

____

____

____

manger du chewing-gum en classe **écouter le prof** **travailler en classe**

arriver au collège à 9h **porter des baskets au collège**

faire mes devoirs **danser en classe** **dormir en classe**

Lesson starter

Clothes

A **Work in a group. Look at the clothing words below. How many can you work out the meaning of, without using a dictionary?**

- Some French words are cognates (exactly the same as English words).
- Some French words are near-cognates (similar to, but not exactly the same as English words).

B **Write down what you think each word means and how you worked it out. Write 'cognate', 'near-cognate' or 'guess'. If you can't work a word out, mark it 'D' for dictionary.**

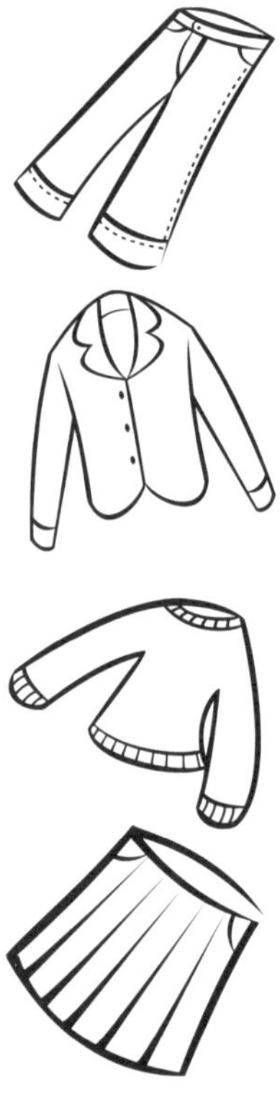

1 un haut ______________

2 un jean ______________

3 un jogging ______________

4 un maillot de foot ______________

5 un pantalon ______________

6 un polo ______________

7 un pull ______________

8 un sweat ______________

9 un tee-shirt ______________

10 une chemise ______________

11 une jupe ______________

12 une robe ______________

13 une veste ______________

14 des baskets ______________

15 des chaussures ______________

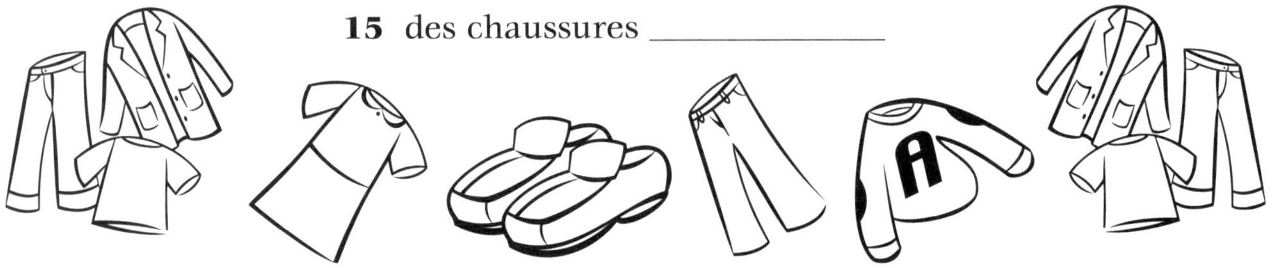

C **Which of the words are false friends – i.e. look like English words, but mean something different?**

____

Grammaire

Les adjectifs

In French, adjectives agree with the thing or person(s) they are describing. Most adjectives add -**e** in the feminine and -**s** or -**es** in the plural.

singular masculine	**feminine**	**plural masculine**	**feminine**
un pull bleu	une chemise bleu**e**	des pulls bleu**s**	des chemises bleu**es**
un maillot vert	une robe vert**e**	des maillots vert**s**	des robes vert**es**
un tee-shirt rouge	une jupe rouge	des tee-shirts rouge**s**	des jupes rouge**s**
un sweat blanc	une veste blanc**he**	des sweats blanc**s**	des vestes blanc**hes**
un joli pull	une joli**e** chemise	des joli**s** pulls	des joli**es** chemises
un jogging cool	une robe cool	des joggings cool	des robes cool

A Complete these sentences with *un*, *une* or *des*. Look at the adjective endings to help you.

Exemple: ____un____ stylo bleu

1 __________ voiture verte
2 __________ magasin démodé
3 __________ crayons blancs
4 __________ raquette blanche
5 __________ sandales vertes
6 __________ veste noire

B Fill in the gaps with the correct form of the adjectives given in brackets.

1 une jupe __________ (bleu)
2 des chaussures __________ (noir)
3 un pull __________ (rouge)
4 une robe __________ (vert)
5 des maillots de foot __________ (jaune)
6 une chemise __________ (blanc)

C Add colours to these clothes to describe your ideal school uniform. Remember to make agreements where necessary.

1 une veste __________
2 un pantalon __________
3 une jupe __________
4 une chemise __________
5 une robe __________
6 un pull __________
7 des chaussures __________
8 un sweat __________

Learning skills

Connectives and expression in text

A Match the French connectives to their English meanings.

avec	because
et	if
mais	which/who
ou	but
où	when
parce que/car	and
quand	where
si/s'	with
qui	or

B Which six of the connectives from task A are *not* used in this text from the Pupil's Book?

______ ______

______ ______

______

À Niort, il y a un centre commercial super où les jeunes vont le mercredi avec leurs copains. Là, il y a un magasin de sport, une librairie et un magasin de musique. En plus, il y a plusieurs magasins de vêtements et aussi un magasin de chaussures. Dans le centre commercial, on peut acheter plein de choses. Pour les adultes, il y a un supermarché, la poste bien sûr, une pharmacie, une boulangerie et une boucherie. Enfin, après les courses, on peut aller au café où on peut prendre un coca ou boire un café.

C Rewrite sentences from the text, to include three of the missing connectives.

Exemple: À Niort, il y a un centre commercial super où les jeunes vont le mercredi avec leurs copains, **parce que les magasins sont super**.

______

______

______

D The author uses other small words and expressions to enhance the text. Find the French for these expressions.

1 There (there is ...) ______

2 In addition ... ______

3 Of course ______

4 Finally, ... ______

E Here are some other expressions which could be used to enhance the text. Rewrite lines of the text to include two of them.

Non seulement ..., mais aussi ...	= Not only ..., but also ...
Le meilleur, c'est ...	= The best thing is ...
C'est formidable!	= It's great!
Quel paradis!	= What paradise!

______

______

______

______

Grammaire

Le comparatif et le superlatif

The comparative (**le comparatif**) is used to compare two people or things.

La France est **plus grande que** l'Angleterre. — *France is **larger than** England.*

Les chaussures sont **moins chères que** les baskets. — *The shoes are **less expensive than** the trainers.*

In English, you sometimes add **-er** to the adjective or put the word 'more' before the adjective. In French, you *always* use **plus … que** or **moins … que**.

A Complete the sentences about the outfits, using the adjectives in the box. Remember that the adjective has to agree with the noun as normal.

cool   joli(e)(s)   nul(le)(s)   démodé(e)(s)

1 La chemise est **plus/moins** ____________ que le pull.

2 Le jean est **plus/moins** ____________ que le pantalon.

3 Les baskets sont **plus/moins** ____________ que les chaussures.

B Write four more sentences comparing the clothes in task A, using the adjectives in the box.

élégant(e) – *elegant*	**moche** – *awful*
confortable – *comfortable*	**pratique** – *practical*

____

____

____

____

The superlative (**le superlatif**) is used to say who or which thing is the biggest, smallest, etc. To do this in French, use **le**, **la**, **les plus/moins** before the adjective.

C'est le jean **le plus cool**. → It's the **coolest** pair of jeans.

C'est la veste **la plus élégante**. → It's the **most elegant** jacket.

Ce sont les tee-shirts **les moins chers**. → They are the **cheapest** T-shirts.

Ce sont les baskets **les plus chères**. → They are the **most expensive** trainers.

C Write six sentences about the members of your family (or your teachers!) in the superlative, using the adjectives in the box. Watch out for agreements!

Exemple: *C'est ma mère qui est la plus amusante.*

amusant(e)	cool	sportif/-ive
jeune	grand(e)	élégant(e)

____

____

____

Défi

Les nouvelles technologies

A Look at the information in the grids and fill in the gaps in the sentences using the comparative/superlative forms of *vite* and *cher*.

Audi A3 cabriolet	Mazda MX5 coupé	Lotus Europa
236 kph	207 kph	246 kph
£20 750	£17 535	£33 945

top tip

Je suis plus grand(e) que Luc.
– I'm taller than Luc.
Je suis moins grand(e) que Pierre.
– I'm smaller than Pierre.
Amélie est la plus grande.
– Amélie is the tallest.

1 L'Audi est ________________________ la Mazda.
2 La Mazda est ________________________ la Lotus.
3 La Lotus est ________________________ l'Audi et l'Audi est ________________________ la Mazda – La Lotus est ________________________
4 À mon avis, la ________________________ est plus chic que la ________________________, mais la ________________________ est la plus chic.

Write four sentences about these cars, using the comparative/superlative forms of *vite* and *cher*.

Ford Kia Zetec	VW Polo	Skoda Octavia
167 kph	171 kph	192 kph
£6495	£7495	£15 795

B What was Dad's choice and why?

J'aime les voitures qui vont vite! La Lotus va très vite avec une vitesse de 246 kph, mais elle est chère. La Lotus est plus chère que la Mazda et l'Audi – elle coûte £33 945. La Mazda est moins chère que l'Audi, mais elle va moins vite, et la Mazda, c'est aussi la moins chic, à mon avis. La Mazda va à une vitesse de 207 kph. J'ai choisi l'Audi parce qu'elle va assez vite et elle est très chic. Elle n'est pas la moins chère, mais elle est moins chère que la Lotus!

C Choose three types of mobile phone and associated contract, fill in the grid and then write three sentences comparing the models.

Nom			
Nombre de textos			
Nombre de minutes			
Prix			
Durée du contrat			

Défi

Les nouvelles technologies

Assignment 3 Challenge

Working with a partner research and give a presentation comparing and contrasting three makes of car (or another consumer item featuring modern technology which makes daily life easier).

Assignment 3 Support grid

Level 3	Give three pieces of information about your items, including a comparison and at least one connective.	*La Lotus est plus chère que la Mazda, mais elle est chic et elle va vite!*
Level 4	Deliver a short presentation comparing and contrasting the items you have chosen, using both comparatives and superlatives. Include short descriptions and your opinions of the items. Use intensifiers, connectives and adjectives.	*J'aime les voitures qui vont vite! La Lotus va très vite avec une vitesse de 246 kph, mais elle est chère. La Lotus est la voiture qui va la plus vite!*
Level 5	As Level 4, but include information about someone you know who bought one of these items. Give details of his/her experience, using the perfect tense. Justify opinions. Use a dictionary to add something original.	*Mon père a choisi l'Audi parce qu'elle va vite et elle est très chic. Il a acheté une A3. Elle est moins chère que la Lotus!*

Assignment 3 Judging grid

Points for language level as shown plus 1 point for each of the other criteria.

(L3 = **1**, L4 = **2**, L5 = **3**)		Descriptions and reasons for preferences are plausible.		
Spoken French is sufficiently loud and clear for the audience.		The balance of activity between partners is good.		
Pronunciation is accurate and presentation is confident.		Presentation learnt by heart and given confidently from prompt cards.		Total
Visual support (e.g. Powerpoint or flashcards) is relevant, informative and interesting.		Persuasive arguments are used to recommend one item over the others.		/10

Les nouvelles technologies: guidelines for teachers

For general guidelines on how to get the most out of the *Défi* sections, see page 14.

Use this activity instead of activity 8 on page 49 of the Pupil's Book.

1 Hand out the activity sheet and ask pupils to do exercises A–C.

2 Pupils then work in pairs to research and give a short presentation comparing and contrasting three types of car (or another example of modern technology). They use PowerPoint or prepare flashcards to support their presentation.

Technology Programme of Study	Technology: 1.2 Key Concepts: cultural understanding
Levels accessed	Levels 3–5
Key vocabulary	*Expo 2 Rouge* Pupil's Book, Module 3, pages 58–59

Vocabulaire

Activités	***Activities***
Tu veux ...?	*Do you want to ...?*
aller en boîte	*go to a disco*
aller à un concert	*go to a concert*
aller à une fête	*go to a party*
faire du baby-sitting	*go baby-sitting*
faire du patin à glace	*go ice-skating*
faire une promenade	*go for a walk*
jouer au golf	*play golf*

Réactions	***Reactions***
Bonne idée!	*Good idea!*
Chouette!	*Great!*
D'accord.	*OK.*
Je veux bien.	*I'd like that.*
Bof, ...	*Well ... / So what?*
Ça m'est égal.	*I don't mind.*
Tu plaisantes!	*You must be joking!*
Ça ne me dit rien.	*I don't fancy that.*
Je n'ai pas envie.	*I don't want to.*

Des excuses	***Making excuses***
Désolé(e), mais ...	*I'm sorry, but ...*
Je dois ...	*I have to ...*
faire les courses	*go shopping for food*
faire mes devoirs	*do my homework*
laver la voiture	*wash the car*
promener le chien	*walk the dog*
ranger ma chambre	*tidy my room*
rester à la maison	*stay at home*
avec toi	*with you*
Je ne peux pas ...	*I can't ...*

Les problèmes de famille	***Family problems***
à l'âge de	*at the age of*
J'ai envie de ...	*I want to ...*
boire de l'alcool	*to drink alcohol*
dire	*to say*
fumer	*to smoke*
cher (chère)	*dear*
je t'écris	*I am writing to you*
Ce n'est pas juste!	*It's not fair!*
un problème	*a problem*
rencontrer	*to meet*

Les vêtements	***Clothes***
Je vais porter ...	*I'm going to wear ...*
des baskets (f)	*some trainers*
des chaussures (f)	*some shoes*
une chemise	*a shirt*
un haut	*a top*
un jean	*a pair of jeans*
un jogging	*a pair of tracksuit bottoms*
une jupe	*a skirt*
un maillot de foot	*a football top*
un pantalon	*a pair of trousers*
un polo	*a polo shirt*
un pull	*a jumper*
une robe	*a dress*
un sweat	*a sweatshirt*
un tee-shirt	*a T-shirt*
une veste	*a jacket*
une veste noire	*a black jacket*
un tee-shirt blanc	*a white T-shirt*

Les opinions	***Opinions***
à mon avis	*in my opinion*
franchement	*frankly*
je pense que	*I think (that)*
cool	*cool*
démodé(e)	*old-fashioned*
joli(e)	*pretty, nice*
moche	*awful*
nul(le)	*awful, rubbish*

Vocabulaire

Au centre commercial	*At the shopping centre*
Il y a ...	*There is ...*
une boucherie	*a butcher's*
une boulangerie	*a baker's*
un café	*a café*
un grand magasin	*a department store*
une librairie	*a book shop*
un magasin de chaussures	*a shoe shop*
un magasin de musique	*a music shop*
un magasin de sport	*a sports shop*
un magasin de vêtements	*a clothes shop*
une pharmacie	*a chemist's*
la poste	*the post office*
un supermarché	*a supermarket*

Dans un magasin	*In a shop*
Je peux vous aider?	*Can I help you?*
Je voudrais ...	*I would like ...*
Quelle taille?	*What size?*
Quelle couleur?	*What colour?*
la pointure	*shoe size*
la caisse	*the cash desk*
C'est combien?	*How much is it?*
Avez-vous ...?	*Have you got ...?*
quelque chose de (+ adj)	*anything*
Voilà.	*Here you are.*
De rien.	*You're welcome.*
cher (chère)	*expensive*
très	*very*
trop	*too*
plus cher	*more expensive*
moins cher	*cheaper*

Objectifs

Nom: ....

Module 2 Attainment			This module (M3) targets	
Listening			Listening	
Speaking			Speaking	
Reading			Reading	
Writing			Writing	

Before	Level 3 (Short sentences linked together, short conversations)	Mid	End
	Say what I want to do at the weekend, mentioning four activities or places I want to go. **G** Use *je veux* + infinitive.		
	Imagine I am at a theme park. Choose an activity and in a short role play, ask my partner if he/she wants to join in this activity. When my partner rejects the idea, give an alternative suggestion, which he/she accepts. Do the role play again, swapping roles.		
	Choose an activity for this evening, and in a short role play (as a call on my mobile), invite my partner to join in this activity. When my partner agrees, suggest a time and place to meet. Do the role play again, swapping roles.		
	Describe what I am wearing, giving four pieces of clothing, including colours and other adjectives. **G** Make adjectives agree.		
	Do a short role play with a partner (taking it in turns to be customer and sales assistant), set in a clothes shop. Ask and answer questions about colour, size and price.		

Before	Level 4 (Short texts and longer conversations, short presentations)	Mid	End
	In a short paragraph, describe what you want to do at the weekend (listing four activities). For each activity give reasons why you cannot do it, saying what chores you have to do instead. Include intensifiers and connectives. **G** Include modal verbs with infinitives and at least one negative.		
	Imagine I am Cinderella. In a short paragraph, describe what I have to do around the house, mentioning six activities. Include opinions, adjectives, intensifiers and connectives. Give examples of what my sisters do not do. **G** Include modal verbs with infinitives and at least two negatives.		
	In a short paragraph, describe what I wear for school (using *je porte* and mentioning at least four items) including details of colours. Give an opinion about each item of clothing. Include intensifiers and connectives. **G** Include at least one negative and make sure adjectives agree.		
	In a short paragraph, compare and contrast two outfits from a magazine. Include colours and give opinions. Include intensifiers and connectives. **G** Use comparatives. Include the words for 'this' and 'that'.		
	Do a role play with a partner (customer and sales assistant), set in a clothes shop. Ask questions about colour and size, but disagree with the sales assistant's suggestion both times, saying what is wrong. Finally select an item of clothing. **G** Use comparatives.		

Objectifs

Nom: ....

Before	Level 5 (Longer texts and more detailed conversations, longer presentations)	Mid	End
	Conduct an interview with a partner about what he/she usually wears and what he/she is going to wear at different events on holiday (trip to the cinema, night club, party). Use appropriate time expressions and include opinions. **G** Use the near future tense and the present tense. Include at least two negatives.		
	Write a text about the shops where I live. Give information about them and the other facilities in the area, saying what you can do there. Talk about what I did and bought last weekend. Use appropriate time expressions and include opinions. **G** Use *on peut* with the infinitive. Use the present tense and the perfect tense.		
	Give a presentation where I compare and contrast two places that I have visited. Say what there is in the two places, and what I did there. Use appropriate time expressions and include opinions. **G** Use the present tense and the perfect tense. Include the comparative and the superlative.		
	Write a text about a city-break. Talk about four places/sights I visited, giving information about what I did there. Use appropriate time expressions and include opinions. Use a dictionary to personalise my writing. **G** Use the present tense and the perfect tense. Include at least two negatives.		
	Write a text about a school trip. Talk about what I did and what two of my friends did on the trip. Compare the day of the trip to a normal school day. Use a dictionary to personalise my writing. **G** Use the present tense to talk about usual school routines and the perfect tense to describe the trip. Include the comparative and the superlative.		

Personal Targets	Mid	End

Target Setting

Fill in the levels you reached in Module 2, then decide which level you are aiming for in Module 3 in each skill.

Go to the objective grid for your target level and decide which objectives you are going to focus on. You may want to include an objective from the level below or the level above, to help you make the transition from a lower to a higher level. Put a mark in the **Before** column for your chosen objectives.

To help you fill in your personal targets, you may like to refer to pages 164–166 for ideas.

Contrôle

Nom: ....

Écouter 1

A Écoute et écris la bonne lettre. (Level 3)

Pourquoi ne peuvent-ils pas sortir?

A B C D E

F G H I

A.U.C.H.A.N

Exemple: Minette F

1 Thomas ☐ 2 Nicole ☐ 3 Rémy ☐

4 Kévin ☐ 5 Cécile ☐ 6 Michelle ☐

Points	
Niveau	

B 'a' Listen and tick the correct answers. (Level 4)

Example: Christelle rings ...

A Marie. ✓ **B** Nathalie. ☐ **C** home. ☐

1 Marie has to stay at home on ...

A Friday. ☐ **B** Saturday. ☐ **C** Sunday. ☐

2 They are going bowling on ...

A Friday. ☐ **B** Saturday. ☐ **C** Sunday. ☐

3 They are meeting ...

A at Marie's house. ☐ **B** at the bowling alley. ☐ **C** at the station. ☐

4 Christelle is going to wear ...

A a blue skirt and a white jacket. ☐ **B** jeans. ☐
C a green and white dress. ☐

5 How much did her outfit cost?

A 80€ ☐ **B** 85€ ☐ **C** 95€ ☐

6 Marie thinks Nathalie's outfit is ...

A old-fashioned. ☐ **B** cool. ☐ **C** pretty. ☐

Points	
Niveau	

Contrôle

Nom: ....

Écouter 2

A Écoute et mets les images dans le bon ordre. (Level 4)

A

B

C

D

E

F

G

H

I

Exemple: 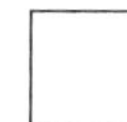

1 ☐ 2 ☐ 3 ☐ 4 ☐ 5 ☐ 6 ☐

Points	
Niveau	

B Écoute et écris les bonnes lettres dans la grille. (Level 5)

A

B

C

D

E
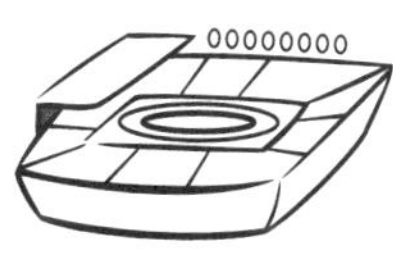

F

G

H

I

J

normalement	le week-end dernier
Exemple: B	F

Points	
Niveau	

Contrôle

Nom: ....

Écouter 3

A Écoute et coche (✓) la bonne case. (Level 4)

	☺	😐	☹
Exemple: Futuroscope	✓		
1 le bowling			
2 le cinéma			
3 le centre commercial			
4 le parc			
5 faire du patin			
6 faire une promenade			

Points	
Niveau	

B Écoute et coche les bonnes réponses. (Level 5)

1 Il est allé ...

A  ☐

B 

☐

C 

☐

2 Et il est allé ...

A 

☐

B 

☐

C 

☐

3 Il a acheté ...

A 

☐

B  ☐

C 

☐

4 Vendredi, il doit ...

A  ☐

B  ☐

C  ☐

5 Samedi, il va aller ...

A  ☐

B  ☐

C  ☐

6 Il va porter ...

A  ☐

B  ☐

C  

☐

Points	
Niveau	

Les sorties

3 Contrôle

Nom: ....

Fais une conversation avec ton professeur ou ton ami/amie. (Levels 3–5)

A	B	B	A	B
				17:00

Qu'est-ce que ton/ta partenaire va porter? (Level 5)

Level information	Pupil support	Example
You can show achievement at Level 3, 4 or 5 depending on how you carry out the task.		
Level 3: Ask and answer questions.	Take it in turns to make an invitation and to respond. • Invite your partner to do an activity. – Reject the suggestion, giving an excuse. – Offer an alternative suggestion. • Agree to the suggestion. – Suggest a time and place to meet.	■ *Tu veux jouer au baby-foot ce soir?* ● *Non. Je dois laver la voiture. Tu veux … demain soir?*
Level 4: As Level 3, but add more detail. Include adjectives, intensifiers, connectives and negatives.	• Extend your answers by giving opinions on the proposed activity and the household tasks that you have to do. • Mention one activity that you do not like.	■ *Tu veux jouer au baby-foot avec moi ce soir?* ● *Non. J'adore le baby-foot, mais je dois laver la voiture. Je n'aime pas laver la voiture. C'est très ennuyeux.*
Level 5: As Level 4, but your conversation needs to make reference to the future as well as the present, and use appropriate time expressions. Include reasons for your opinions.	• Ask your partner what he/she will be wearing, using the near future tense. Give details of what you will be wearing when you respond. • Justify any opinions given. • Lengthen your conversations by arranging two activities on two separate days and suggesting how to get there.	■ *Et qu'est-ce que tu vas porter?* ● *Je vais porter un jean bleu et ….* ■ *On va prendre le train?* ● *Oui. J'aime le train parce que c'est rapide et confortable.*

3 Contrôle

Nom: ....

Parler 2

A Décris les magasins et ce qu'on peut faire au centre-ville où tu habites. (Level 4)

B Dis ce que tu as fait le week-end au centre-ville. (Level 5)

Level information	Pupil support	Example
You can show achievement at Level 4 or 5 depending on how you carry out the task.		
Level 4: Prepare and deliver a presentation. Include adjectives, intensifiers, connectives and negatives.	• Talk about what shops and facilities there are in the town centre. • Include information about what you can do there. • Give your opinion of the town centre and the facilities: mention at least one thing that is missing.	*À Crumpsal, il y a quelques magasins. Il y a un magasin de sport, une pharmacie et la poste, mais il n'y a pas de cafés. On ne peut pas prendre un café!*
Level 5: As Level 4, but add details of what you did in town last weekend. Refer to the past as well as the present, and use appropriate time expressions. Include reasons for your opinions.	• Talk about your trip into the town centre last weekend: where you went, who you went with, what you did, what it was like. Include reasons for your opinions. • Include a comparison between your town and another, giving reasons for your opinions.	*Le week-end, je suis allé(e) au centre-ville avec mon copain, James. J'ai acheté un pull et …* *Manchester est plus grand et plus intéressant que Crumpsal parce que …*

Contrôle

Nom: ....

Expo 2R Reading

Lire 1

A **Lis et écris la bonne lettre. (Level 3)**

Voici mes amis. Kevin porte un short blanc, un tee-shirt et des baskets. Amélie porte une jolie jupe noire et une veste blanche et des chaussures noires. Thierry porte un pantalon, une chemise blanche et des chaussures – il est un peu démodé. Sandrine porte une très jolie robe, une veste, des chaussures. Fabien porte un jean avec un pull et des baskets. Samy aime être cool! Il préfère porter un pantalon et une veste. Moi, Chloé, je porte un jean, un tee-shirt et des baskets – très cool!

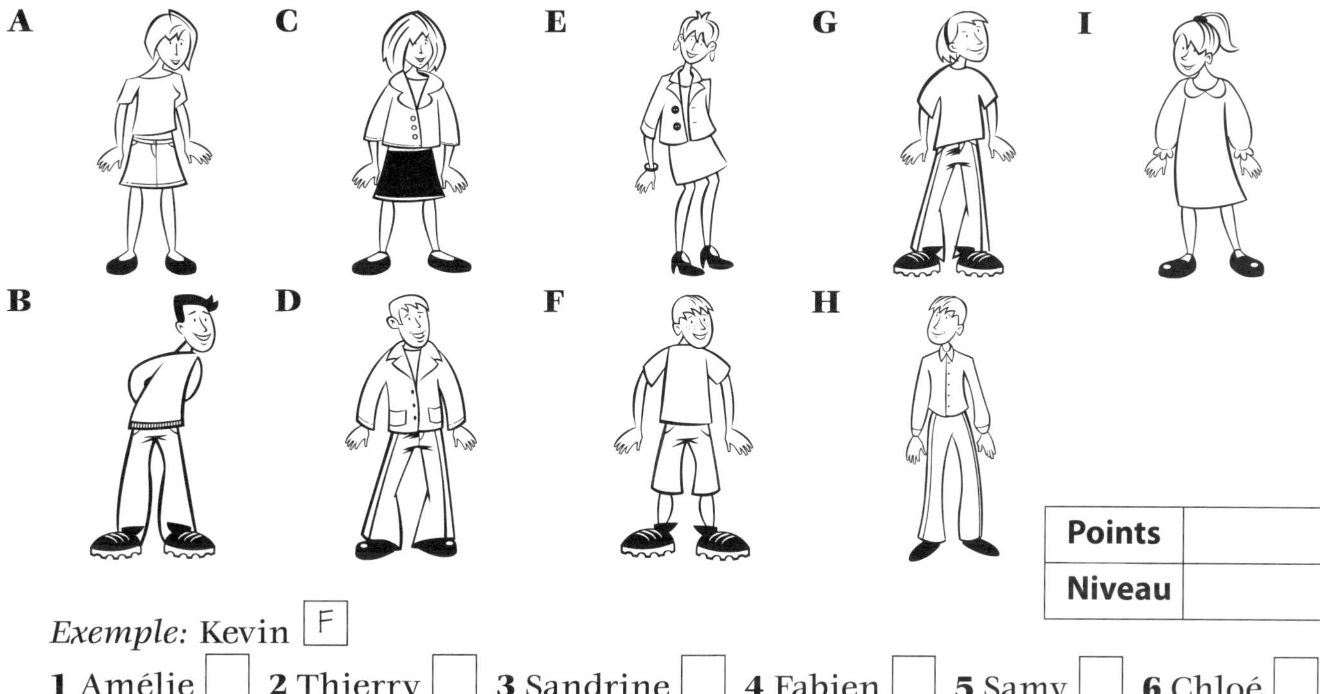

Points	
Niveau	

Exemple: Kevin [F]

1 Amélie [ ] **2** Thierry [ ] **3** Sandrine [ ] **4** Fabien [ ] **5** Samy [ ] **6** Chloé [ ]

B **Lis et écris les bons prénoms. (Level 4)**

Je suis grand, mais Philippe est plus grand que moi. Jérôme n'aime pas le sport, mais Roger joue au basket, au foot et au tennis. Vincent porte des beaux vêtements, mais Kamal porte des vêtements très chics, très à la mode. André porte toujours un jogging – il n'aime pas la mode. Sylvain parle beaucoup, mais Robert parle tout le temps, même en classe. Gérard travaille beaucoup. Le soir, il doit rester à la maison et il fait ses devoirs. Matthieu aussi doit rester à la maison, mais il joue toujours à l'ordinateur! Thierry est très gentil, il est très généreux et il aide tout le monde. Tout le monde l'aime. Vincent aime beaucoup sortir. Il va au cinéma, au bowling et au café chaque week-end.

Réponds aux questions.

Points	
Niveau	

Exemple: Qui est le plus grand? Philippe

Qui est ...

1 le plus cool? ____________________

2 le plus bavard? ____________________

3 le plus sportif? ____________________

4 le plus sérieux? ____________________

5 le plus démodé? ____________________

6 le plus sympa? ____________________

Les sorties **3**

Contrôle

Nom: ....

Lire 2

A **Read Passage A on page 75, then read the statements and decide whether each is true (T), false (F) or not mentioned in the text (NM). (Level 4)**

Example: Christian hates going to the cinema. F

1 Christian likes going out with his family. ___
2 Sylvie is going to Nathalie's party. ___
3 On Friday they're meeting up at 7 o'clock. ___
4 On Thursday Christian is going bowling. ___
5 Christian doesn't like swimming. ___
6 Christian isn't going out on Tuesday. ___

Points	
Niveau	

B **Lis Passage A et Passage B à la page 75. Écris les bonnes lettres dans la grille. (Level 5)**

A **B** **C** **D** **E**
F **G** **H** **I** **J**
K **L** **M**

	les projets de Christian	ce que Georges a fait
lundi	*Exemple:* B	
mercredi		
samedi		
dimanche		

Points	
Niveau	

Contrôle

Nom: ....

Lire 2

Passage A

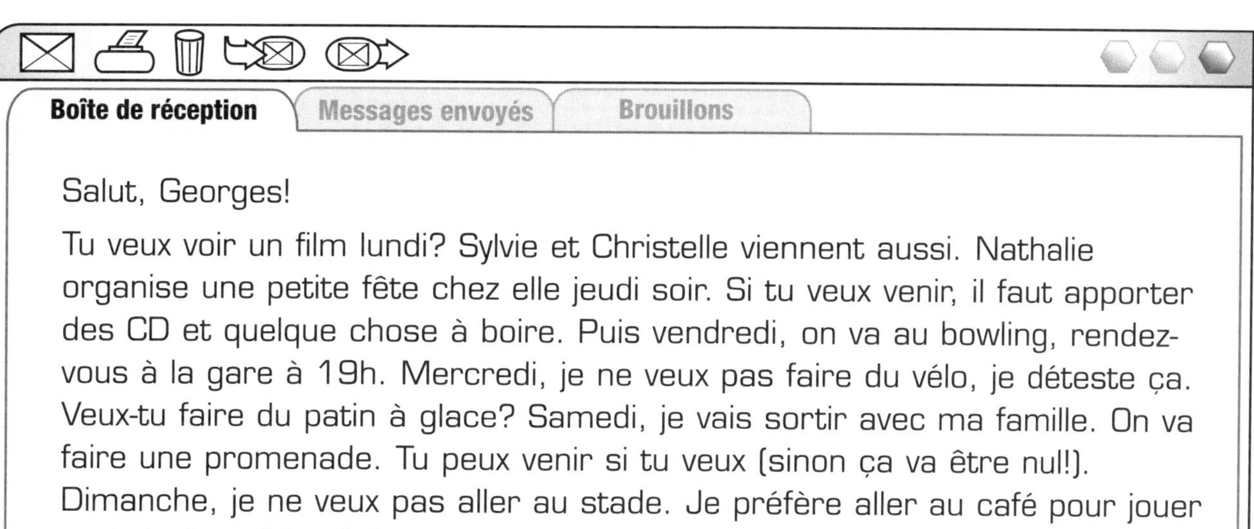

Boîte de réception | Messages envoyés | Brouillons

Salut, Georges!

Tu veux voir un film lundi? Sylvie et Christelle viennent aussi. Nathalie organise une petite fête chez elle jeudi soir. Si tu veux venir, il faut apporter des CD et quelque chose à boire. Puis vendredi, on va au bowling, rendez-vous à la gare à 19h. Mercredi, je ne veux pas faire du vélo, je déteste ça. Veux-tu faire du patin à glace? Samedi, je vais sortir avec ma famille. On va faire une promenade. Tu peux venir si tu veux (sinon ça va être nul!). Dimanche, je ne veux pas aller au stade. Je préfère aller au café pour jouer au baby-foot. Mardi, je ne peux pas sortir. Je dois rester à la maison. Tu peux venir si tu veux – on peut faire nos devoirs!

Christian

Passage B

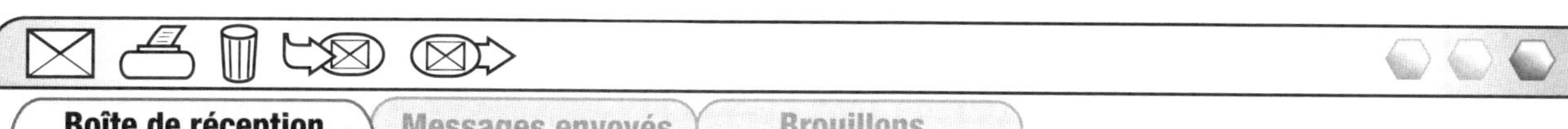

Boîte de réception | Messages envoyés | Brouillons

Chère Michelle,

Quelle semaine désastreuse! D'habitude le lundi, on joue au foot, mais cette semaine je n'y ai pas joué. J'ai rencontré mon ami Christian devant le cinéma. Mais on n'avait pas d'argent, donc nous sommes allés chez Christian et nous avons regardé un DVD. Le mercredi après-midi, je fais toujours du shopping, mais Christian m'avait invité à sortir. Mercredi matin, il m'a envoyé un texto: «Je ne peux pas sortir parce que je dois ranger ma chambre». Donc j'ai joué au foot avec mon petit frère.

Normalement le samedi matin, je fais mes devoirs, mais ce samedi les parents de Christian m'ont invité à faire une promenade avec eux. Malheureusement il pleuvait, donc je n'y suis pas allé. J'ai fait du shopping avec ma mère. Chaque dimanche, je vais chez ma grand-mère. Christian m'a encore invité à sortir, mais ma mère a dit non, donc j'ai visité ma grand-mère comme d'habitude. L'après-midi, mes parents et mon frère ont fait du vélo. Moi, aussi? Non, merci. Quelle horreur!

Georges

Contrôle

Nom: ....

Lire 3

A **Lis Passage A à la page 77. Coche (✓) les six bonnes images. (Level 4)**

Points	
Niveau	

Qu'est-ce qu'il y a au centre commercial?

A HACHETTE ☐
B MORGAN ☐
C ☐
D Chaussarama ☐
E MUSIQUE ☐
F PHARMACIE ☐
G ☐
H ☐
I BOUCHERIE ☐
J A.U.C.H.A.N ☐
K Café ☐
L Bureau de Poste ☐

B 'a' **Read Passage A and Passage B on page 77.**
Tick the correct answers. (Level 5)

Example: What does Sébastian like doing?

A going to the cinema. ✓ **B** going shopping for his mum. ☐
C washing the car. ☐

1 Who has to go to work on Saturday morning?

A his sister, Claudine. ☐ **B** his mum. ☐ **C** his dad. ☐

2 Where is the nearest chemist's?

A in his village. ☐ **B** in the town. ☐ **C** in the shopping centre. ☐

3 Why does Sébastien have to go shopping in town?

A to buy shoes. ☐ **B** to go to the supermarket. ☐
C to buy books for school. ☐

4 Who went shopping yesterday?

A Sébastien. ☐ **B** his brother. ☐ **C** his mum. ☐

5 Who went to the cinema yesterday?

A Sébastien. ☐ **B** his mum. ☐ **C** his dad. ☐

6 Who stayed at home yesterday?

A Sébastien. ☐ **B** Claudine. ☐ **C** Patricia. ☐

Points	
Niveau	

Contrôle

Nom: ....

Lire 3

Passage A

J'habite à Wattignies, un petit village dans le nord de la France. Il n'y a pas beaucoup de distractions dans mon village. Moi, j'adore le cinéma, mais pour ça il faut aller au centre commercial. Heureusement, il y a un centre commercial tout près et il est facile d'y aller. Au centre commercial, il y a beaucoup de grands magasins. Il y a deux magasins de sport et plusieurs magasins de vêtements.

J'aime bien aller au centre commercial avec mes amis. On y va souvent le samedi. On aime bien aller au café et jouer au baby-foot. Il y a aussi un bowling. On y va de temps en temps. J'adore ça, c'est génial! Parfois je dois aller au supermarché pour ma mère. Ça, par contre, c'est ennuyeux!

Dans mon village, il n'y a pas beaucoup de magasins: Il y a une boucherie, un magasin de chaussures et une petite boulangerie (où travaille ma sœur Claudine). Il n'y a pas de pharmacie. Il faut aller en ville pour ça. Il y a aussi un grand magasin de musique au village, où j'achète tous mes CD. Malheureusement il n'y a pas de librairie, donc pour les livres scolaires je dois aller en ville. La poste, elle aussi est au centre commercial.

Sébastien

Passage B

Hier, c'était samedi et je ne suis pas allé au centre commercial. Je suis resté à la maison, et tout le monde est sorti. Ma sœur aînée est partie pour le travail à 6h30. Normalement le samedi matin, mon père fait les courses. Il va sur la grande place du village. Mais ce samedi, il a lavé la voiture et puis il est allé chez ma grand-mère. Normalement, c'est ma mère qui va toujours chez ma grand-mère le samedi, mais sa copine a téléphoné et a invité ma mère à voir un film. Mon frère, Antoine, est allé en ville. Normalement il joue au foot, mais il n'y avait pas de match ce week-end. Il est allé à la librairie et puis à la pharmacie et à la boulangerie. Ma petite sœur, Patricia, est allée à la piscine, puis à un cours de danse. D'habitude, elle reste à la maison avec mon père. J'étais tout seul à la maison! J'ai révisé pour mon examen d'anglais.

Sébastien

Contrôle

Nom: ....

Écrire 1

A **Copie et adapte les phrases pour le mannequin. (Level 3)**

Amélie

Anne porte une jolie robe rose et une chemise bleue.

Elle porte aussi des chaussures rouges.

La robe est cool, mais la chemise est démodée et les chaussures sont nulles.

____

____

____

B **Écris un paragraphe sur tes vêtements. Qu'est-ce que tu portes au collège? (Level 4) Qu'est-ce que tu vas porter ce soir? (Level 5)**

Level information	Pupil support	Example
You can show achievement at Level 3, 4 or 5 depending on how you carry out the task.		
Level 3: Write three sentences, adapting the example supplied by using different details. (If you can change the details and include an opinion or a negative in the same sentence, you will be working towards Level 4.)	• Copy the sentences adapting the information so that it refers to the picture of Amélie.	Change the name to Amélie and copy porte. Change the words for items of clothing to reflect the details in the picture; invent colours and use other adjectives. Try to include a negative or an opinion.
Level 4: Write a short paragraph about what you wear for school. Make your writing more interesting by adding negatives, connectives, intensifiers and opinions.	• Give information about four items of clothing. • Give the colour and another adjective for each item. • Mention one item of clothing that you do not wear at school. • Give your opinion about what you wear at school.	*Au collège, je porte un pantalon gris. À mon avis, le pantalon est très démodé. Je ne porte pas de jean au collège …*
Level 5: As Level 4, but include details of what you are going to wear this evening. Use the near future tense, with appropriate time expressions. Include reasons for your opinions.	• Talk about what you are going to wear to go out this evening, giving colours and other adjectives. • Compare what you are going to wear this evening to what you wear at school or what you usually wear in the evening. Include opinions with reasons.	*Ce soir, je vais porter un jogging noir et … J'aime mon jogging parce que c'est plus cool que le pantalon.*

Contrôle

Nom: ....

Écrire 2

A Compare ce que tu fais le week-end avec ce que David Beckham fait. (Level 4)

B Qu'est-ce que tu as fait samedi dernier? Et David? Qui a fait des activités plus intéressantes? (Level 5)

Level information	Pupil support	Example
You can show achievement at Level 4 or 5 depending on how you carry out the task.		
Level 4: Write a short description of what you and David Beckham (or a different famous person) do at weekends. Make your writing more interesting by including negatives, connectives, intensifiers and opinions.	• Give three activities you do at weekends, where you like to do them, and who you like to do them with. • Give three activities that David Beckham does at weekends. • Include some activities that you do not do, using negatives.	*Normalement le week-end, je vais en ville avec mes copains … David joue au football dans son grand jardin.*
Level 5: As Level 4, but include details of what you and David (or a different famous person) did last Saturday, comparing your experiences. Use the perfect tense, with appropriate time expressions. Include reasons for your opinions.	• Compare your typical Saturday and David's typical Saturday, using the comparative and the superlative. Justify opinions. • Describe what you did last Saturday. • Describe what David did last Saturday: be inventive!	*David joue au football le week-end et c'est plus intéressant que ce que je fais. Moi, je préfère le sport mais mes amis vont toujours en ville. Samedi matin, je suis resté(e) à la maison et j'ai regardé un film à la télé. David est allé à Monaco avec Posh – c'est beaucoup plus cool.*

Teacher's Notes

Contrôle Module 3

Listening assessment criteria
Mark scheme: 1 mark for each correct answer. Total for each task: 6 marks. For details of the sublevels see p. 167.

Écouter 1A [AT1 Level 3]

This task tests understanding of a short passage in the context of arranging to go out. Pupils identify why each person can't come to the party, writing down the letter of the appropriate activity. There are two distractors. Play the recording twice.

Audioscript 10

- *Salut, Michelle. C'est Patrick. Est-ce que tout le monde vient à ma fête samedi?*
- *Minette ne peut pas. Elle doit faire du shopping avec sa mère.*
- *Alors, est-ce que Thomas et Nicole vont venir?*
- *Thomas doit aller chez sa grand-mère et Nicole doit laver la voiture de son père.*
- *Et Rémy?*
- *Rémy doit faire ses devoirs.*
- *Alors Kévin?*
- *Il doit promener le chien.*
- *Cécile?*
- *Elle doit faire le ménage.*
- *Et toi, Michelle?*
- *Désolée, je dois rester à la maison.*

Réponses
1 H **2** A **3** E **4** B **5** G **6** D

Écouter 1B [AT1 Level 4] 'Q'

This task tests understanding of a short passage in the context of arranging to go out. The questions are multiple choice. Play the recording twice.

This task is similar to Asset Preliminary French Listening (external), p. 14, Part 2, Qs 6–10.

Go to p. 167

Audioscript 11

- *Tu veux aller au bowling samedi, Marie?*
- *Désolée, Christelle, mais samedi, je ne peux pas. Je dois rester à la maison.*
- *Alors, dimanche? Nathalie vient aussi.*
- *D'accord.*
- *Rendez-vous à 15h30 à la gare.*
- *D'accord. Qu'est-ce que tu vas porter, Christelle?*
- *Ma jupe bleue et ma veste blanche.*
- *J'aime bien ta veste. Elle est très cool.*
- *Oui, mais c'était cher – ma mère a payé 95 euros.*
- *Oui, mais c'est très joli.*
- *Nathalie va porter sa robe jaune et verte.*
- *Je n'aime pas sa robe. Elle est démodée et moche. Nathalie doit porter un jean. Elle est plus jolie en jean. Je la préfère en jean.*

Réponses
1 B **2** C **3** C **4** A **5** C **6** A

Écouter 2A [AT1 Level 4]

This task tests understanding of a passage in the context of shopping/weekend activities. Pupils put the pictures in the order they hear them, writing down the correct letters. There are two distractors. Play the recording twice.

Audioscript 12

Voici ta liste pour faire les courses ce matin. D'abord, va à la boulangerie et prends deux baguettes. Puis va au marché et achète deux kilos de pommes. Ensuite, va à la poste pour envoyer la lettre à ta grand-mère. Puis à la pharmacie, achète des aspirines pour ton père. Après ça, va à la librairie et choisis un livre pour ta sœur. Voilà 15 euros pour toi. Va au magasin de musique et achète un CD. On va se retrouver à midi au café.

Réponses
1 A **2** E **3** I **4** G **5** F **6** B

Écouter 2B [AT1 Level 5]

This task tests understanding of a passage (including the ability to distinguish between past and present) in the context of weekend activities. Pupils identify the pictures mentioned, writing down the letters in the appropriate part of the grid. There are two distractors. Play the recording twice.

Audioscript 13

Le vendredi soir, je vais au cinéma, mais ce vendredi je suis resté à la maison et j'ai fait mes devoirs. Le Samedi matin, je me lève à 7h30 pour aller à la boulangerie et acheter des croissants. Mais ce samedi, je suis allé au stade pour jouer au foot. D'habitude l'après-midi, je retrouve mes amis en ville et on va à la piscine, mais nous avons fait du shopping. J'ai acheté un pantalon – il est très cool! Dimanche matin, j'ai lavé la voiture de mon père. Normalement, j'aide ma mère à faire le ménage, mais elle est allée en ville pour faire des courses.

Réponses

normalement	le week-end dernier
H, C, A	E, I, D

Écouter 3A [AT1 Level 4]

This task tests understanding of a passage in the context of arranging to go out. Pupils identify the response to each invitation, ticking the appropriate column. Play the recording twice.

Teacher's Notes

Contrôle Module 3

Audioscript 14

- *Alors, on va faire beaucoup de choses cette semaine. Veux-tu aller au Futuroscope samedi?*
- *Oui, je veux bien!*
- *Dimanche, veux-tu aller au bowling?*
- *Ah oui, bonne idée.*
- *Lundi, il y a un film de kung-fu au cinéma. Tu veux aller le voir?*
- *Je n'ai pas envie.*
- *Alors, mardi, on peut aller au centre commercial pour faire du shopping.*
- *Bof, si tu veux.*
- *Mercredi, tu veux aller au parc?*
- *Alors ça, ça ne me dit rien.*
- *Jeudi, on peut faire du patin à glace.*
- *Chouette!*
- *Vendredi, veux-tu faire une promenade?*
- *Ça m'est égal.*

Réponses

1 ☺ **2** ☹ **3** 😐 **4** ☹ **5** ☺ **6** 😐

Écouter 3B [AT1 Level 5]

This task tests understanding of a longer passage featuring more detail and a variety of tenses (present and perfect). The questions are multiple choice with pictures. Play the recording twice.

Audioscript 15

- *Salut, Thierry! Ça va? Qu'est-ce que tu as fait samedi?*
- *Salut, Nadine. Samedi, je suis allé au centre commercial. Je voulais un nouveau maillot de foot. Malheureusement, dans le magasin les maillots étaient démodés et moches. Par contre, les baskets étaient super cool et je vais y retourner la semaine prochaine pour en acheter une paire. Je suis aussi allé à la librairie pour acheter un livre. C'est pour mon cours de français.*
- *Tu veux aller en boîte vendredi?*
- *Je veux bien, mais je ne peux pas. Je dois rester à la maison pour finir mes devoirs avant le week-end.*
- *Alors samedi, il y a une fête chez Cécile. Tu veux bien y aller?*
- *Chouette! Je veux bien. Qu'est-ce que tu vas porter?*
- *Un jean, un sweat et un tee-shirt – très relaxe. Et toi?*
- *Je veux porter un jean, mais ma mère m'a acheté un nouveau pantalon gris et une chemise et je dois les porter. Il est affreux, le pantalon et la chemise n'est pas confortable!*

Réponses

1 B **2** B **3** B **4** A **5** B **6** A

Speaking assessment criteria

See the level information supplied on the Assessment sheet.

For detailed Assessment criteria (including sublevels), see p. 168.

Level information and pupil support with examples are supplied on the assessment sheet. Encourage your pupils to use this to decide which level they are aiming for. Point out that they should not copy the examples given, but use them as a guide.

Use *Parler 1* in the first instance if you are unsure of which level to give a particular learner.

Parler 1 [AT2 Levels 3–5]

This task tests the ability to put together a conversation in the context of organising social activities. Pupils have the chance to be the person making the invitation and the person responding.

The last question gives the opportunity to reach Level 5 by requiring use of the near future tense to talk about what they are going to wear.

The best way to conduct the assessment is to listen to pairs of partners. Pupils can take turns in playing each role.

Parler 2 [AT2 Levels 4–5]

This task tests the ability to prepare and deliver a presentation in the context of describing a town centre and saying what there is to do there. The second question gives the opportunity to reach Level 5 by requiring use of the perfect tense to talk about a recent visit to the town centre.

The best way to conduct the assessment is to listen to individuals, either at the front of the class or as the others continue other aspects of the assessments. Pupils could record these as podcasts for marking also.

Reading assessment criteria

Mark scheme: 1 mark for each correct answer.
Total for each task: 6 marks.

For details of the sublevels see p. 167.

Lire 1A [AT3 Level 3]

This task tests understanding of a short passage in the context of clothes/friends. Pupils identify the people described, writing down the letters of the correct pictures. There are two distractors.

Réponses

1 C **2** H **3** E **4** B **5** D **6** G

Lire 1B [AT3 Level 4]

This task tests understanding of the main points in a short passage in the context of friends. Pupils identify the person being described, writing down the correct name. There are two distractors.

Teacher's Notes

Contrôle Module 3

Réponses
1 Kamal **2** Robert **3** Roger **4** Gérard **5** André **6** Thierry

Lire 2A [AT3 Level 4]

This task tests understanding of the main points in a text in the context of arranging to go out. Pupils read Passage A and decide whether the six statements about it are true (T), false (F) or contain information not given in the text (NM).

Réponses
1 F **2** NM **3** T **4** F **5** NM **6** T

Lire 2B [AT3 Level 5]

This task tests understanding of the main points in a text (including the ability to distinguish between past and present) in the context of arranging to go out. Pupils read Passage A and Passage B and fill in the grid with the appropriate letter. There are six distractors.

Réponses

les projets de Christian	ce que Georges a fait
mercredi E, samedi C, dimanche K	mercredi J, samedi H, dimanche G

Lire 3A [AT3 Level 4]

This task tests understanding of a text in the context of shopping/weekend activities. Pupils read Passage A and tick the six correct pictures. There are six distractors.

Réponses
B, G, H, J, K, L

Lire 3B [AT3 Level 5] 

This task tests understanding of the main points of a text featuring a wider range of language and two tenses (perfect and present) in the context of shopping and leisure activities. Pupils read Passage A and Passage B. The questions are multiple choice.

This task is similar to Asset Preliminary French Reading (external), p. 10, Part 5, Qs 21–25.

Go to p. 167

Réponses
1 A **2** B **3** C **4** B **5** B **6** A

Writing assessment criteria
See the level information supplied on the Assessment sheet. For detailed Assessment criteria (including sublevels) see p. 169.

First decide whether you want your pupils to complete *Écrire 1, 2* or both, depending on their ability and time available.

Level information and pupil assessment support with examples are supplied on the assessment sheet. Encourage your pupils to use this to decide which level they are aiming for. Point out that they should not copy the examples given, but use them as a guide.

Écrire 1 [AT4 Levels 3–5]

Give this sheet only to pupils who are working at Levels 3–5. If in doubt, give Écrire 1 first.

This task tests the ability to write a short paragraph in the context of clothes. It is divided into two sections. In Section A pupils describe the person pictured by changing the model sentences accordingly (Level 3). In Section B (Levels **4–5**) pupils describe their own clothes: this section contains two question prompts, the second giving pupils the opportunity to reach Level 5 by requiring the use of the near future tense, including appropriate time expressions.

Écrire 2 [AT4 Levels 4–5]

This task tests the ability to write a paragraph in the context of weekend activities. Pupils are asked to compare their own weekends with those of a famous person (David Beckham is suggested). It is divided into two sections. Pupils who feel more confident can complete both sections A and B, the latter giving them the opportunity to reach Level 5 by requiring the use of the perfect tense, including appropriate time expressions.

Lesson starter

Battleships

Work in pairs.
Keep your grid hidden from your partner. Put one tick in each line of the top grid. This shows which item of food each person likes.
Now play Battleships. Take turns to ask a question, e.g. ***Ahmed aime le fromage?***
Use the bottom grid to keep a record of what you have already asked your partner and the correct answers you find out.

Ahmed					
Céline					
Jean-Luc					
Suzanne					
Thomas					

Ahmed					
Céline					
Jean-Luc					
Suzanne					
Thomas					

Lesson starter

Word puzzle

Find the words. Insert them in the grid. What is the secret word?

1
2
3
4
5
6
7
8
9
10
11

1 Deux _ _ _ _ _ de pommes, s'il vous plaît.
2 Une _ _ _ _ _ _ _ _ _ de coca.
3 Un _ _ _ _ _ _ _ de biscuits.
4 Une _ _ _ _ _ de thon.
5 Cinq _ _ _ _ _ _ _ _ de jambon.
6 C'est tout, _ _ _ _ _ .
7 Deux cents _ _ _ _ _ _ _ de fromage.
8 Un l _ t _ _ de lait.
9 Cinq _ _ _ _ _ grammes de raisins.
10 Un demi-kilo de p ê _ _ _ _ .
11 Un paquet de c _ _ _ .

Grammaire
Le partitif

The grammatical term for 'some' is the **partitive article**.

the	**le**	**la**	**l'**	**les**
some	**du**	**de la**	**de l'**	**des**

Au petit déjeuner, je mange **du** pain avec **de la** confiture. Le dimanche, je mange **des** croissants. Je bois **de l'**eau.

A Change 'the' to 'some'.

1 les haricots verts ________________

2 la saucisse ________________

3 le jus d'orange ________________

4 le yaourt ________________

5 la soupe ________________

6 le coca ________________

7 les fruits ________________

8 la limonade ________________

9 les spaghettis ________________

10 l'omelette ________________

B Complete the text by putting *du*, *de la*, *de l'* or *des* in the gaps.

Aujourd'hui, pour le déjeuner, j'ai mangé **1** ________ salade de tomates avec **2** ________ pain. Comme plat, j'ai mangé **3** ________ viande avec **4** ________ petits pois et **5** ________ pommes de terre. Comme dessert, j'ai mangé **6** ________ tarte aux pommes et **7** ________ glace. Le soir, j'ai mangé **8** ________ poisson avec **9** ________ pâtes et **10** ________ riz. Puis j'ai mangé **11** ________ fromage, et ensuite **12** ________ fraises.

In English you can miss out the words for 'the' and 'some', but in French you must always put them in!

J'aime **la** confiture.	*I like (the) jam.*	J'aime **les** frites.	*I like (the) chips.*
Je mange **de la** confiture.	*I eat (some) jam.*	Je mange **des** frites.	*I eat (some) chips.*

C Underline the correct words in the sentences.

Exemple: J'aime les/**des** fraises.

1 Il adore **les**/**des** frites.

2 Je mange souvent **la**/**de la** viande.

3 Il boit **l'**/**de l'**eau à la cantine.

4 Je vais acheter **les**/**des** pommes.

5 **La**/**De la** glace est délicieuse.

6 Je vais manger **la**/**de la** glace en dessert.

Expressions of quantity are followed by **de** or **d'**.

un kilo **de** pommes → une bouteille **d'**eau minérale → une canette **de** coca

Learning skills

Not literally!

A **You cannot always translate French words literally. Look at the following list of foods from a restaurant menu. Guess what each one might mean and write it down. Then look it up in a dictionary. Were you right?**

	My guess	Dictionary definition
1 steak bleu		
2 salade composée		
3 œuf sur le plat		
4 thé nature		
5 fruits de mer		

B **Some words for food and drink items have a second meaning, which is completely different. What do the underlined words mean in each of these pairs of sentences?**

1 Il y a un café dans le centre commercial. ________________
Je bois un café dans le centre commercial. ________________

2 À midi, je mange une pêche. ________________
À midi, je vais à la pêche. ________________

3 J'ai vu une araignée dans la glace. ________________
J'ai vu mon reflet dans la glace. ________________

How do you know which is the correct meaning of the underlined words in the sentences above? ________________________

C **Pair up the French and English sayings. Check in a dictionary to see if you were right. They will probably be listed under the noun – the item of food – in a fairly detailed dictionary.**

> Food is often used in colloquial expressions, both in English and French. In these expressions, food words are not used literally. For example, when we say 'She's full of beans', we don't mean she's been eating beans, we mean she is full of energy.
> Often, French sayings which use words for food are expressed in a different way in English. You've already met one in the Pupil's Book: **Ce ne sont pas mes oignons.** (It's none of my business.)

1 Tu es trempé comme une soupe.
2 Il a un œil au beurre noir.
3 Je m'occupe de ma pomme.
4 N'en fais pas tout un fromage!
5 Poisson d'avril!
6 C'est pas du gâteau.

A Don't make such a fuss!
B It's no picnic.
C He has a black eye.
D April Fool!
E You're soaked to the skin.
F I'm looking after number one.

Thinking skills
Making connections

Work in a group. For each set of words, look at the relationship between the two example words. Then complete the next sets of words following the pattern.

Exemple: un poulet: le — une viande: la

poulet is a masculine word, so the definite article is **le**.

viande is a feminine word, so the definite article is **la**.

1 un poulet: le

une viande: ______la______

un œuf: ____________

des carottes: ____________

2 le lait: du lait

la salade: ____________

les beignets: ____________

l'Orangina: ____________

3 fraises: fraise

pommes de terre: ____________

eaux minérales: ____________

ananas: ____________

4 fromage: fromages

poisson: ____________

jus: ____________

gâteau: ____________

5 soupe: entrée

mousse au chocolat: ____________

jus d'orange: ____________

poulet rôti: ____________

6 je mange: j'ai mangé

tu bois: ____________

nous achetons: ____________

il prend: ____________

7 blanc: blanche

végétarien: ____________

cher: ____________

délicieux: ____________

8 petit déjeuner: matin

déjeuner: ____________

goûter: ____________

dîner: ____________

9 adorer: détester

beaucoup: ____________

il faut: ____________

bon pour la santé: ____________

10 carotte: orange

citron: ____________

fraise: ____________

petits pois: ____________

Défi

Tout à un Euro?

A Which spreadsheet calculations would you use? Decide and then input the information in a spreadsheet package and work out the answers.

	A	B (£)	C (€)
1	le lait	0.68	
2	le beurre	1.29	
3	la confiture	0.69	
4	le pain	0.69	
5	le jus d'orange	0.58	
6	Total cost		

- Most of the large supermarkets in the UK have price check facilities on their website: use these to research prices.
- You need the prices in the same currency. You can either convert UK prices to euros or vice versa. Work out the formula to convert French prices to pounds.
- Check online to find the actual exchange rates today!

To get the total cost of the shopping:

1 =sum (B1:B5) 2 =sum (A1:A6) 3 =sum (A1:A5:B1:B5) 4 =sum (B1:B6)

To get the cost of an item in euros, assuming £1 is equal to 1,40 €:

1 = sum (B1*Euro) 2 = sum (B1*1.4) 3 = sum (B1, B2, B3, B4, B5)
4 = sum (C1*1.4)

What would the calculation be for the following cells?

1 C4 ____________ 2 C6 ____________

B Compare the cost of food items in France and the UK: use a spreadsheet and the following information (£1 = 1,40 €).

À *Champion* en France, le beurre coûte 1,45€ et à *Tesco* en Grande-Bretagne, il coûte £1.29 (ça fait ________ €). Le beurre est plus cher en Grande-Bretagne. La confiture à *Champion* est plus chère. Ça coûte 2,05€, mais à *Tesco* ça coûte 69p (ça fait ________ €). À *Champion*, le jus d'orange coûte 1,10€ et à *Tesco* ça coûte 58p (ça fait ________ €). Moi, j'aime la confiture, surtout la confiture à la framboise. J'ai mangé du pain grillé avec de la confiture à la framboise ce matin pour le petit déjeuner. Alors, à mon avis, la France est un peu plus chère que la Grande-Bretagne, mais il faut bien chercher parce qu'on trouve des supermarchés moins chers et plus chers dans les deux pays.

Défi

Tout à un Euro?

Assignment 4 Challenge

Using the Internet, research the prices of picnic food and drink in a UK and a French supermarket. Then create a simple spreadsheet to log prices and work out the total cost. Add a description comparing prices in France and the UK.

Assignment 4 Support grid

Level 3	Produce a simple spreadsheet and write three sentences comparing the prices of picnic items in France and the UK	*À Champion en France, le beurre coûte 1,45 € et à Tesco en Grande-Bretagne le beurre coûte £1.29 (ça fait 1,80 €).*
Level 4	Produce a spreadsheet and attach a paragraph comparing and contrasting food items you would buy for a picnic in a supermarket in France and the UK. Give your opinions on the food items and the comparative costs. Include intensifiers, adjectives and at least one negative.	*La confiture coûte 2,05 € mais à Tesco ça coûte 69p (ça fait 0,96 €). Moi, j'aime la confiture, surtout la confiture à la framboise.*
Level 5	As Level 4, but also justify any opinions. Include an example of when you bought/ate a particular item and how much it cost, using the perfect tense. Use a dictionary to say something original. Come to a conclusion on whether it costs more to have a picnic in France or the UK.	*J'ai acheté de la confiture à la framboise la semaine dernière. C'était une offre spéciale, donc … Alors à mon avis, la Grande-Bretagne est un peu plus chère que la France, mais …*

Assignment 4 Judging grid

Points per level reached as shown plus 1 point for each of the other criteria.

L3 = **1**, L4 = **2**, L5 = **3**		Spreadsheet is clearly laid out, using fonts and colours to good effect.		
Sums on spreadsheet are correct.		Text is presented in the body of the spreadsheet document.		
Prices in pounds converted to euros correctly (or vice versa).		Graph showing price comparison included.		Total
Prices researched accurately, with comparable items chosen.		A conclusion on the comparative cost of living in France and the UK is given.		/10

Tout à un Euro?: guidelines for teachers

For general guidelines on how to get the most out of the *Défi* sections, see page 14.

Use this activity alongside or instead of exercise 3 on page 67 of the Pupil's Book.

1 Hand out the activity sheet and work through the simple exercises with the pupils, preferably using a spreadsheet package on a computer.

2 Pupils then plan a picnic and research French and UK prices online.

3 They enter the information into a spreadsheet, total the amounts and convert them into euros/pounds as necessary. They attach a written French description as outlined in the support grid and modelled in activity B, including a conclusion about the cost of picnics in the UK and France.

ICT Programme of Study	1.1 Key Concepts: capability
Levels accessed	Levels 3–5
Key vocabulary	*Expo 3 Rouge* Pupil's Book, Module 4, pages 76–77

Vocabulaire

La nourriture	***Food***
J'aime …	*I like …*
Je n'aime pas …	*I don't like …*
Je préfère …	*I prefer …*
le fromage	*cheese*
le poulet	*chicken*
le poisson	*fish*
le pain	*bread*
le beurre	*butter*
la viande	*meat*
les pommes de terre	*potatoes*
les œufs	*eggs*
les fruits	*fruit*
les frites	*chips*
en général	*generally*
surtout	*especially*
par exemple	*for example*
ça dépend	*it depends*
beaucoup	*a lot*
pas vraiment	*not really*
pas tellement	*not really*
c'est délicieux	*it's delicious*

Le petit déjeuner	***Breakfast***
au petit déjeuner	*for breakfast*
je mange …	*I eat …*
un croissant	*a croissant*
un petit pain	*a bread roll*
une tranche de pain grillé	*a slice of toast*
des céréales	*cereals*
Je ne mange rien.	*I don't eat anything.*
je bois …	*I drink …*
du café	*coffee*
du thé	*tea*
du chocolat chaud	*hot chocolate*
du jus d'orange	*orange juice*
du lait	*milk*
Je ne bois rien.	*I don't drink anything.*

Le déjeuner	***Lunch***
je mange/prends …	*I have …*
une salade de tomates	*a tomato salad*
des crudités	*raw chopped vegetables*
des carottes	*carrots*
des petits pois	*peas*
une mousse au chocolat	*chocolate mousse*
un yaourt	*a yoghurt*
Je bois …	*I drink*
un verre de vin blanc	*a glass of white wine*

On prépare une fête	***Preparing for a party***
Il faut acheter …	*We need to buy …*
un gâteau	*a cake*
des biscuits	*biscuits*
des crêpes	*pancakes*
des beignets	*doughnuts*
des saucisses	*sausages*
des tomates	*tomatoes*
des chips	*crisps*
une salade	*salad*
des raisins	*grapes*
un ananas	*a pineapple*
des fraises	*strawberries*
du fromage	*cheese*
du thon	*tuna*
Il faut apporter des boissons.	*You must bring drinks.*
Tu peux venir à mon anniversaire?	*Can you come to my birthday party?*

Vocabulaire

Faire les courses	***Going shopping***
un kilo de ...	*a kilo of ...*
un demi-kilo/500 grammes de ...	*half a kilo of ...*
poires	*pears*
pêches	*peaches*
un litre de ...	*a litre of ...*
une bouteille de ...	*a bottle of ...*
une boîte de ...	*a tin/can of ...*
un paquet de ...	*a packet of ...*
un pot de ...	*a jar of ...*
une tranche de ...	*a slice of ...*
C'est combien?	*How much is it?*
s'il vous plaît	*please*
C'est tout.	*That's all.*

Au restaurant	***At a restaurant***
Je voudrais ...	*I would like ...*
Je prends ...	*I'll have ...*
un coca	*a Coke*
une eau minérale	*a mineral water*
un jus de fruit	*a fruit juice*
la soupe	*soup*
le pâté	*pâté*
le steak	*steak*
avec ...	*with ...*
des frites	*chips*
du riz	*rice*
des carottes	*carrots*
Je prends ...	*I'll have ...*
la crème caramel	*crème caramel*
la tarte aux pommes	*apple pie*
la glace	*ice cream*
le menu	*the menu*
les entrées	*starters*
les plats	*main courses*
les desserts	*desserts*
l'addition	*the bill*
s'il vous plaît	*please*
tout de suite	*straight away*
Vous avez terminé?	*Have you finished?*

Objectifs

Nom: ....

Module 3 Attainment	
Listening	
Speaking	
Reading	
Writing	

This module (M4) targets	
Listening	
Speaking	
Reading	
Writing	

Before	Level 3 (Short sentences linked together, short conversations)	Mid	End
	Choose three items of food. Ask a partner if he/she likes each item. Respond to these questions. **G** Include the definite article with likes.		
	Choose two types of food. Ask a partner which item he/she prefers. Respond to this question. **G** Include the definite article with preferences.		
	Ask a partner when and what he/she usually eats for breakfast and in the evening. Respond to these questions.		
	In a short role play about an invitation, where we take it in turns to play each part, invite my partner to a birthday party. When he/she responds, asking for details of when, at what time and where it is happening, give these details.		
	In a short role play in a food shop, where we take it in turns to be the shop assistant and customer, ask the customer what he/she wants and respond each time; at the end give the total price. As the customer, ask for two different foods; say thank you and goodbye.		

Before	Level 4 (Short texts and longer conversations, short presentations)	Mid	End
	In a short paragraph, give information about my eating habits, saying what I like and dislike and what I prefer, mentioning eight items of food/drink in total. Include connectives and intensifiers. **G** Include the definite article with likes and preferences. Include at least one negative.		
	Give a short presentation about what I have for breakfast, comparing mornings during the week and at the weekend/on special occasions. Include adverbs of frequency, connectives and intensifiers. **G** Include at least one negative.		
	Give a short presentation about evening meals at home. Give details of when we usually eat during the week and at weekends, and what we usually eat and drink. Include adverbs of frequency, connectives and intensifiers. **G** Use *du/de la/de l'/des* with food/drink items. Include at least one negative.		
	In a short paragraph, describe what foods I need to buy and what activities we need to do at a party for an older relative. Include connectives and intensifiers. **G** Use *il faut* and the infinitive. Use *du/de la/de l'/des* with food/drink items. Include at least one negative.		
	Working with a partner (one waiter, one customer), decide what we want to order in a restaurant. As the waiter, ask what the customer wants for each course and to drink; ask if he/she wants a particular item included. As the customer, answer the waiter's questions.		

Objectifs

Nom: ....

Before	Level 5 (Longer texts and more detailed conversations, longer presentations)	Mid	End
	Choose a cartoon character. Write a text about the eating habits of this character (what he/she likes and dislikes and what he/she prefers to eat). Give examples of what he/she ate and drank yesterday using the perfect tense. Include opinions, connectives and a variety of adjectives.		
	Write a food diary for yesterday. Say what I ate and drank for each meal, when I ate and with whom, using appropriate time expressions. Compare this with my normal routine. Include and justify opinions. **G** Use the perfect tense and the present tense. Include at least two negatives.		
	Imagine I am organising a school reunion. Write a short invitation for a friend, including ideas of what to wear and what we will have to eat and drink at the reunion. Say what I need to do to prepare for the party. Include appropriate time expressions. Give opinions and justify them. **G** Use the present tense and the near future tense.		
	Give a presentation about a family trip to a restaurant. Describe what we ate (at least two courses) and drank, using appropriate time expressions, and give opinions of the food. Include information about what we usually eat in a restaurant. Include intensifiers and connectives. **G** Use the perfect tense and the present tense. Include expressions of frequency and at least two negatives.		

Personal Targets	Mid	End

Target Setting

Fill in the levels you reached in Module 3, then decide which level you are aiming for in Module 4 in each skill.

Go to the objective grid for your target level and decide which objectives you are going to focus on. You may want to include an objective from the level below or the level above, to help you make the transition from a lower to a higher level. Put a mark in the **Before** column for your chosen objectives.

To help you fill in your personal targets, you may like to refer to pages 164–166 for ideas.

Contrôle

Nom: ....

Écouter 2

A Écoute et coche (✔) les six bonnes cases. (Level 3)

Exemple:  ✓

A 

☐

B  ☐

C  ☐

D  ☐

E 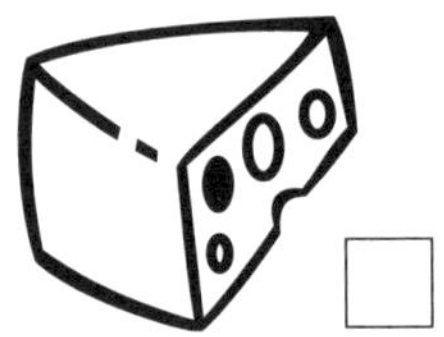 ☐

F 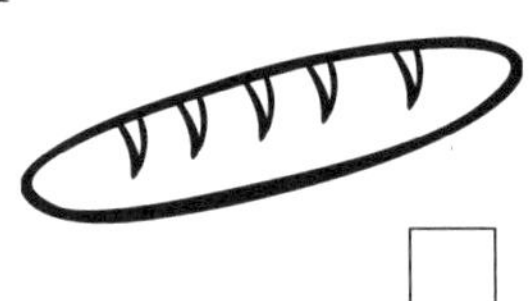 ☐

G 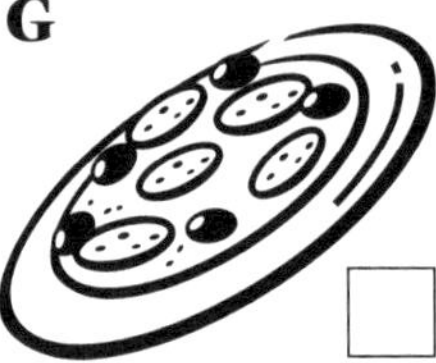 ☐

H  ☐

I 

☐

J  ☐

K  ☐

L  ☐

Points	
Niveau	

B Écoute et note les bons prix. (Level 4)

Exemple:  1,10€

1  ______________

2  ______________

3  ______________

4  ______________

5  ______________

6  ______________

Points	
Niveau	

Manger et boire **4**

Contrôle

Nom: ....

Expo 2R
Listening

Écouter 2

A Écoute et écris les bonnes lettres dans la case. (Level 4)

Qu'est-ce que Kemal aime manger? Qu'est-ce qu'il n'aime pas manger?

A

B 

C 

D 

E 

F petits pois

G 

H 

I 

☺	☹
Exemple: C	

Points	
Niveau	

B Listen and tick the correct answers. (Level 5)

Example: Sonya's family went to the restaurant because it was ...

A Sonya's birthday. ☐
B her mum's birthday. ☐
C her dad's birthday. ☑

1 Her mum chose ...
A the steak. ☐
B the chicken. ☐
C mushroom omelette. ☐

2 Her dad chose ...
A the steak. ☐
B pasta. ☐
C quiche. ☐

3 Her brother normally likes ...
A fish. ☐
B burgers. ☐
C pizza. ☐

4 Her brother had ... with his meal.
A chips ☐
B green beans ☐
C carrots ☐

5 For dessert, her mum ...
A didn't have anything. ☐
B had strawberry ice cream. ☐
C had chocolate mousse. ☐

6 Sonya's favourite meal is ...
A burger. ☐
B steak. ☐
C pizza. ☐

Points	
Niveau	

Contrôle

Nom: ....

Écouter 3

A Écoute et écris les bonnes lettres. (Level 4)

Où est la fête?

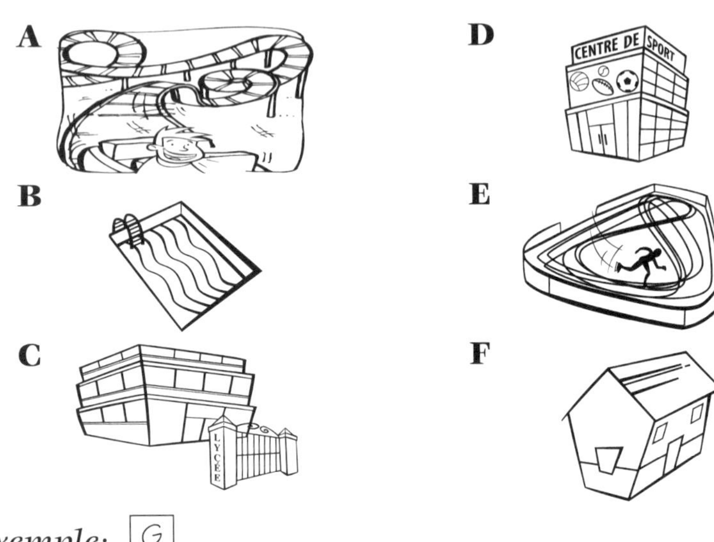

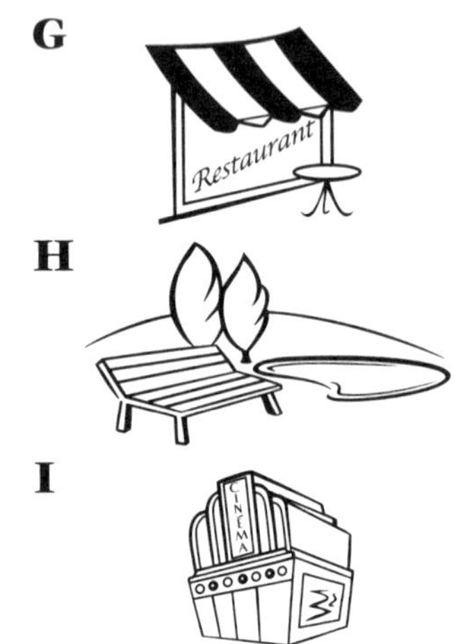

Exemple: G

1 ☐ 2 ☐ 3 ☐ 4 ☐ 5 ☐ 6 ☐

Points	
Niveau	

B Écoute et écris les bonnes lettres dans la grille. (Level 5)

Pour la fête de Serge

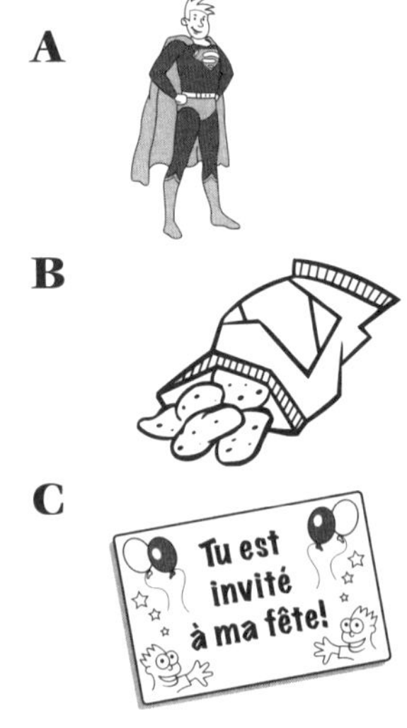

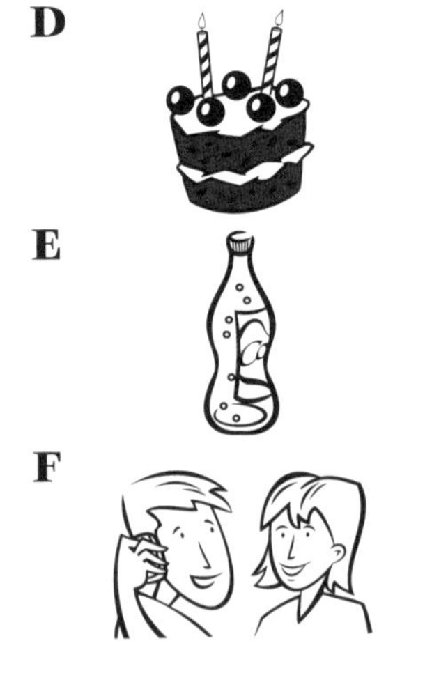

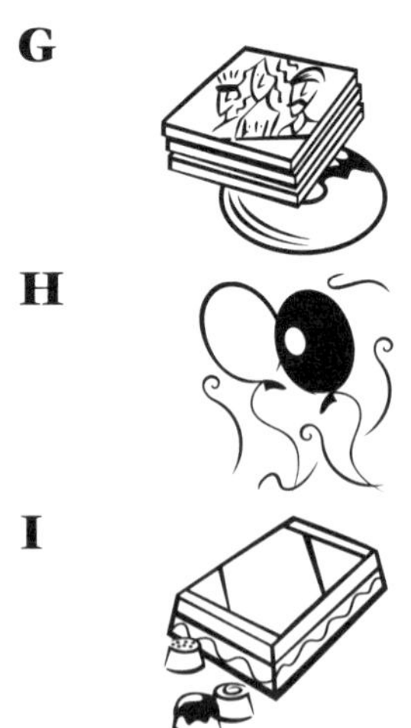

déjà organisé	il faut ...
Exemple: C	

Points	
Niveau	

Contrôle

Nom: ....

Parler 1

Réponds aux questions de ton professeur ou de ton ami/amie. Pose des questions à ton/ta partenaire aussi. (Levels 3–5)

- Qu'est-ce que tu aimes manger et boire?
- Qu'est-ce que tu préfères?
- Qu'est-ce que tu manges et bois au petit déjeuner?
- Qu'est-ce que tu n'aimes pas manger et boire? (Level 4)
- Qu'est-ce que tu as acheté au supermarché? (Level 5)

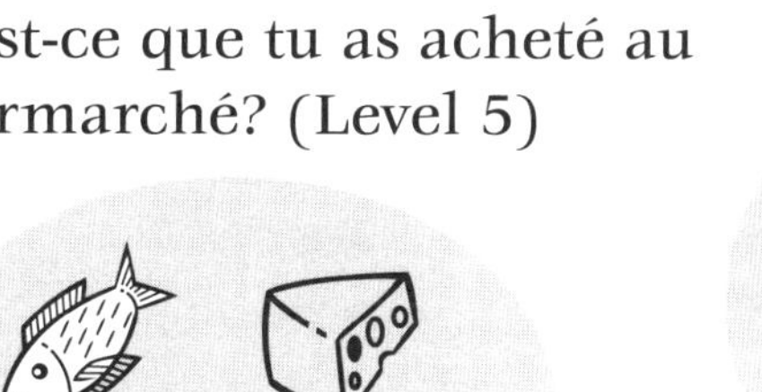

Level information	Pupil support	Example
You can show achievement at Level 3, 4 or 5 depending on how you carry out the task.		
Level 3: Ask and answer the questions.	• Ask each other what you like to eat and drink, and respond. • Ask each other what food/drinks you prefer, and respond. • Ask each other what you eat and drink for breakfast, and respond.	■ *Qu'est-ce que tu aimes manger et boire?* ● *J'aime le fromage et les œufs …*
Level 4: As Level 3, but include adjectives, intensifiers, connectives and negatives in your answers.	Also ask each other what you do not like eating and drinking, and respond. Include at least two negatives. Include expressions of frequency when talking about what you eat and drink for breakfast.	■ *Qu'est-ce que tu n'aimes pas manger et boire?* ● *Je n'aime pas du tout le fromage. C'est dégoûtant!*
Level 5: As Level 4, but your conversation needs to make reference to the past as well as the present, and use appropriate time expressions. Include reasons for your opinions.	• When discussing what food and drinks you like/dislike, say why. • When discussing what you usually eat for breakfast, include details of what you had today as an example, using the perfect tense. • Ask each other what you bought at the supermarket last time you went, and respond.	■ *Qu'est-ce que tu as acheté au supermarché?* ● *Je suis allé(e) au supermarché mercredi soir avec mon père. J'ai acheté des biscuits, des chips et un gâteau pour l'anniversaire de ma mère.*

Contrôle

Nom: ....

Parler 2

A Tu es joueur/joueuse de tennis célèbre. Qu'est-ce que tu manges et bois? Qu'est-ce qu'il faut manger et boire? Pourquoi? (Level 4)

B Décris ce que tu as mangé et bu le week-end dernier – avant le match et après le match. (Level 5)

AVANT

APRÈS

Level information	Pupil support	Example
You can show achievement at Level 4 or 5 depending on how you carry out the task.		
Level 4: Prepare and deliver a presentation as a famous tennis player (or other sports star). Include adjectives, intensifiers, connectives and negatives.	• Talk about what you eat and drink during the week for breakfast and dinner, including expressions of frequency. • Talk about what you have to eat so that you keep fit and perform well. • Give your opinions about different items of food and drink, including what you dislike.	*Bonjour! Au petit déjeuner, je mange souvent … et je bois … J'aime le … mais je préfère le … Je dois manger des légumes.*
Level 5: As Level 4, but add a second section on what you ate and drank before and after the match last weekend. Use the perfect tense, with appropriate time expressions. Include reasons for your opinions.	• Talk about what you ate before the match you played last Saturday (energy foods). • Talk about what you ate afterwards to celebrate/console yourself. • Justify opinions.	*Le week-end dernier, j'ai joué contre Roger Federer. Avant le match, j'ai mangé … et j'ai bu … Je (n')ai (pas) gagné … C'était … parce que …*

Contrôle

Nom: ....

Expo 2R Reading

Lire 1

Points	
Niveau	

A Lis cette invitation. Coche (✔) la bonne réponse. (Level 3)

Samedi, c'est mon anniversaire. Viens fêter mes quatorze ans. Rendez-vous au centre de sport à 15h30. On va jouer au volley et il y a une piscine. Moi, j'adore nager. Après on va manger. Maman va préparer une salade de tomates et puis on va manger du poulet et des frites. C'est mon plat préféré. Pour terminer, il y a du gâteau, un grand gâteau au chocolat. Délicieux!

Exemple: Annie a **A** 12 ans ☐ **B** 13 ans ☐ **C** 14 ans ☑

1 La fête est **A**  ☐ **B**  ☐ **C** CENTRE DE SPORT ☐

2 Activité 1 **A**  ☐ **B**  ☐ **C**  ☐

3 Activité 2 **A**  ☐ **B**  ☐ **C**  ☐

4 L'entrée **A**  ☐ **B**  ☐ **C**  ☐

5 Plat **A**  ☐ **B**  ☐ **C**  ☐

6 Dessert **A**  ☐ **B**  ☐ **C**  ☐

B Lis et écris les bons prénoms. (Level 4)

Points	
Niveau	

Qui c'est? 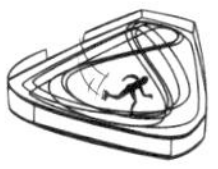 Daniel

1 Restaurant ____________

2 ____________

3 ____________

4 ____________

5 ____________

6 ____________

C'est mon anniversaire samedi. J'organise une fête chez moi, de 15h à 19h. Viens déguisé! Le thème, c'est les dessins animés. Si tu veux m'acheter un cadeau, je voudrais un CD! Corinne

Tu es invité à ma fête d'anniversaire, mercredi. On va au centre de loisirs. On peut faire du patinage ou de la natation. Après, on va manger au fast-food. N'oublie pas d'arriver pour 18h. Daniel

Viens fêter mes 13 ans chez moi dimanche. Robert et Thomas viennent aussi. On va écouter de la musique et danser. Maman va préparer des snacks et un grand gâteau. Apporte tes CD. Mathilde

Jeudi, c'est mon anniversaire. Maman organise une sortie au restaurant pour toute la famille – mes grands-parents et mes deux frères, quelle horreur! Il faut venir si tu peux! Sinon, ça va être ennuyeux. Après, tu peux venir chez moi pour regarder un DVD. Téléphone-moi pour me donner ta réponse. Jérôme

Contrôle

Nom: ....

Lire 2

A Lis Passage A à la page 101. Coche (✔) les six phrases correctes. (Level 4)

Exemple: Sylvie essaie de bien manger. ☑

1 Elle mange un croissant tous les jours. ☐
2 Elle ne boit pas de café. ☐
3 Quelquefois, elle mange un fruit au petit déjeuner. ☐
4 Elle prend le déjeuner à la maison une fois par semaine. ☐
5 À la cantine, il n'y a rien pour les végétariens. ☐
6 Elle mange toujours un gâteau comme dessert à midi. ☐
7 Son plat préféré est le poulet rôti. ☐
8 Les repas à la cantine ne sont pas bons. ☐
9 Le soir, elle mange avec tous les membres de sa famille. ☐
10 Son père fait bien la cuisine. ☐
11 Elle aime la cuisine française. ☐
12 Elle est végétarienne. ☐

Points	
Niveau	

B Lis Passage A et Passage B à la page 101. Mets les lettres dans les bonnes cases. (Level 5)

A

B

C CRÊPES

D

E

F

G

H

I

J

Ce que Sylvie mange normalement le jeudi	Ce que Sylvie a mangé jeudi dernier
Exemple: J	

Points	
Niveau	

Nom: ....

Passage A

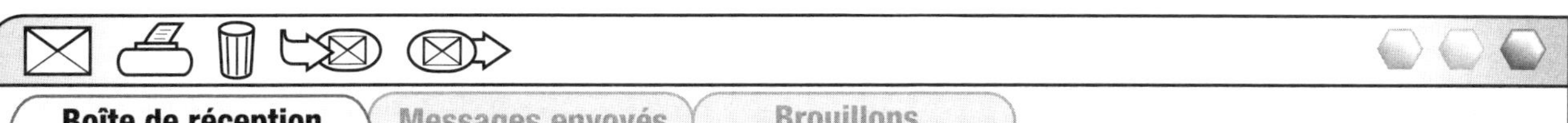

Moi, je m'appelle Sylvie et je suis en cinquième. J'essaie de bien manger parce que c'est bon pour la santé. Au petit déjeuner, je mange toujours un yaourt puis des tartines et je bois du lait. Mes parents boivent du café, mais je n'aime pas ça. Si j'ai faim, je mange aussi une banane ou une poire. Le week-end, mon père va à la boulangerie pour chercher des croissants. Je les adore!

Pendant la semaine, je mange à la cantine au collège (sauf le mercredi quand je rentre à la maison). En général on mange bien. Il y a toujours une entrée, un plat principal et un dessert. Pour commencer, je prends une salade de tomates ou de la soupe. Comme plat, il y a toujours de la viande ou du poisson, et un plat pour les végétariens comme des pâtes. Moi, je prends toujours de la viande. Jeudi, c'est mon jour préféré parce que je mange du poulet rôti avec des frites. C'est très bon. J'adore ça. Comme dessert, on a toujours un yaourt ou de la glace. Moi, je choisis toujours de la glace! Une fois par semaine, on nous prépare une tarte à la pomme.

Le soir à la maison, on mange vers 20h quand mon père rentre et tout le monde est là. Ma mère adore faire la cuisine et elle prépare beaucoup de spécialités françaises. Elles sont délicieuses.

Passage B

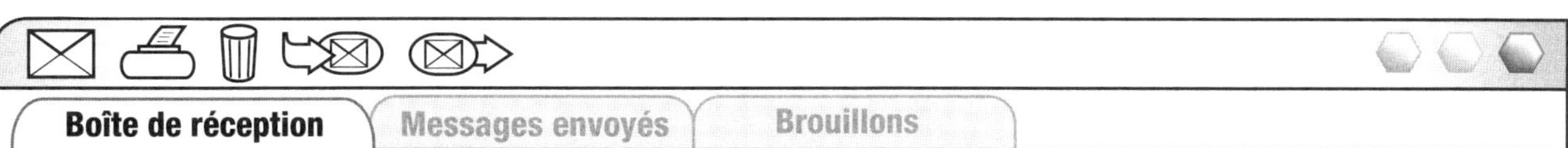

Le jeudi, maman rentre tard et elle n'a pas beaucoup de temps, alors nous mangeons souvent une omelette avec du riz. Jeudi dernier était un peu différent parce que ma grand-mère est venue passer quelques jours chez nous. Elle vient de Bretagne et pour le petit déjeuner elle a fait des crêpes. Elles étaient délicieuses, surtout avec de la confiture aux fraises.

Parce que ma grand-mère était à la maison, je suis rentrée à midi. Elle aime bien préparer les plats bretons et normalement elle prépare de la viande avec des légumes. Mais ce jour-là on a mangé du poisson avec une sauce à la crème. C'était très bon! Le soir, on est allés au restaurant. C'était un restaurant italien. On y va de temps en temps parce que les pâtes sont très bonnes. D'habitude, je prends des pâtes, mais je n'avais pas très faim, donc j'ai choisi une pizza. À vrai dire, j'ai beaucoup mangé au petit déjeuner et à midi, alors j'avais un peu mal au ventre!

Lire 3

A **Read the texts in Passage A on page 103. Answer the questions by writing the correct letter. (Level 4)**

Example: Who likes pizza? [A]

1 Who doesn't eat chocolate? [ ]

2 Who likes cakes? [ ]

3 Who likes French dishes? [ ]

4 Who eats cheese every day? [ ]

5 Who's not keen on eating vegetables? [ ]

6 Who says you shouldn't eat too much? [ ]

Points	
Niveau	

B **Lis les Passages A et B à la page 103. Coche (✔) les bonnes cases. (Level 5)**

Qui a dit ça?

	Alexandre	**Delphine**	**Didier**	**Rachid**	**Margot**
Exemple: J'aime le chocolat.	✔				
1 Je suis végétarien(ne).					
2 Je ne mange pas de fromage.					
3 Je préfère tout ce qui est sucré.					
4 Récemment je suis allé(e) au restaurant avec mes amis.					
5 La dernière fois au restaurant, j'ai trop mangé.					
6 J'aime les hamburgers.					

Nom: ....

Expo 2R
Reading

Lire 3

Passage A

A

Je pense qu'il faut bien manger, et ne pas trop manger, pour être en bonne santé. Personnellement, je mange un peu de tout. J'adore les fruits, la viande et les légumes, mais j'adore aussi la pizza, le chocolat et le fromage. Le fromage français est délicieux. J'en mange tous les jours. Le soir après le plat, maman apporte un choix de fromages. On mange ça avec du pain. Pour moi, l'important est de ne pas trop manger. Même quand je vais au restaurant, j'essaie de ne pas trop manger.

Alexandre

B

Moi, j'adore les glaces, toutes les sortes de gâteaux et les pâtisseries. J'adore la tarte aux pommes! Je préfère manger un gâteau à un steak. Mais j'adore les hamburgers! Malheureusement, je dois manger des légumes. Tous les soirs, ma mère prépare un bon repas avec de la viande ou du poisson et beaucoup de légumes! Je crois franchement que j'en mange trop! Je vais souvent au café avec mes amis. On aime bien les fast-food.

Delphine

C

Moi, j'aime bien manger. J'aime les plats français comme le coq-au-vin et le bœuf bourguignon. J'adore aussi le fromage, mais malheureusement je suis allergique aux produits laitiers: le lait, le fromage et les yaourts. Je ne peux pas en manger, sinon je deviens malade. Je ne peux pas manger de gâteaux ni de chocolat non plus!

Didier

Passage B

Je ne mange ni de viande ni de poisson. Je mange bien et je suis en bonne santé. Je vais assez souvent au restaurant et il y a toujours beaucoup de choix pour moi. Le week-end dernier, je suis allé à un restaurant italien avec mes amis. J'ai mangé des pâtes avec une sauce à la tomate, c'était bon. Ensuite, j'ai mangé une glace. Normalement, je ne mange pas de glace, mais la glace italienne est délicieuse.

Rachid

Moi, j'adore la cuisine italienne. Ma mère prépare des pâtes à la maison, mais j'adore aller au restaurant italien avec ma famille. La dernière fois, je n'ai pas pris de pâtes. J'ai essayé une nouvelle pizza. C'était très bon! J'en ai mangé deux … et après j'ai vomi! J'ai dû courir aux toilettes et malheureusement j'ai renversé mon dessert sur la jupe de ma mère. Elle n'était pas contente …

Margot

Contrôle

Nom: ....

Écrire 1

A Copie et adapte les phrases pour une fête pour ta mère. (Level 3)

Il faut acheter des légumes.

Il faut écouter de la musique techno.

Il faut porter un masque de Dalek.

Il faut inviter ton professeur de français.

Menu

B Écris un email. Invite ton ami/amie à ta fête d'anniversaire.

- C'est quand?
- C'est où?
- Qu'est-ce qu'il faut acheter/faire? (Level 4)
- Qu'est-ce qu'on va manger/boire/faire? (Level 5)

samedi 15h00

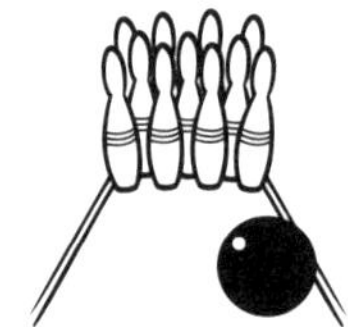

Level information	Pupil support	Example
You can show achievement at Level 3, 4 or 5 depending on how you carry out the task.		
Level 3: Write two or three sentences, adapting the example supplied by using different details. (If you can change the item/activity and include an opinion or a negative in the same sentence, you will be working towards Level 4.)	• Copy the sentences adapting the information to relate to a party for your mother.	Copy Il faut acheter and change légumes to a type of food your mother would appreciate. Try to include a negative or an opinion.
Level 4: Write a short invitation to your party. Make your writing more interesting by including negatives, connectives, intensifiers and opinions.	Invite my friend to the party: • Say when and where the party will take place. • Say what I have to buy for the party. • Mention one other thing that needs to be done in preparation for the party.	*Salut! Je fête mon anniversaire samedi prochain à la plage. Il faut acheter des pizzas. J'adore les hamburgers, mais je préfère les pizzas. Il faut porter …*
Level 5: As Level 4, but include details of what you are going to eat/drink/do. Use the near future tense, with appropriate time expressions. Include reasons for your opinions.	Give reasons for any opinions given. Using the near future tense, give information about what you are going to eat, drink and do at the party.	*À la plage, on va jouer au volley et on va manger … et boire … parce que j'aime le coca.*

Contrôle

Nom: ....

Écrire 2

A **Qu'est-ce que tu manges et bois au petit déjeuner/déjeuner? Qu'est-ce que tu aimes manger et boire? (Level 4)**

B **Une visite récente au restaurant. Qu'est-ce que tu as mangé et qu'est-ce que tu as bu? (Level 5)**

Level information	Pupil support	Example
You can show achievement at Level 4 or 5 depending on how you carry out the task.		
Level 4: Write a short description of what you usually have for breakfast or lunch, and what items of food and drink you like. Make your writing more interesting by including negatives, connectives, intensifiers and opinions.	• Give information about what you usually have for breakfast/lunch (food and drink). • Include details of what you have for breakfast/lunch on Sundays. • Give details of your favourite meal, listing at least three items of food. Give an example of a food you dislike.	*Normalement, je mange le déjeuner à 13h avec mes amis au collège. Je mange … et je bois …* *J'aime … mais je préfère …*
Level 5: As Level 4, but include a section describing a recent visit to a restaurant, using the perfect tense, with appropriate time expressions. Include reasons for your opinions.	• Say when you went to the restaurant and who you went with. • Describe what you ate and drank. • Describe what another person you went with had to eat and drink. • Justify any opinions given.	*Samedi dernier, je suis allé(e) au restaurant chinois avec mon oncle et ma tante. J'ai mangé … et j'ai bu …* *C'était excellent parce que j'adore le poulet.*

Teacher's Notes

Contrôle Module 4

Listening assessment criteria

Mark scheme: 1 mark for each correct answer. Total for each task: 6 marks. For details of the sublevels see p. 167.

Écouter 1A [AT1 Level 3]

This tasks tests understanding of the main points of a short text in the context of shopping. Pupils identify the food/drink mentioned, ticking the six items on the shopping list. There are six distractors. Play the recording twice.

Audioscript 16

Alors, pour l'anniversaire de maman, il faut un gâteau. Il nous faut aussi des beignets. Maman adore les beignets! Puis il faut beaucoup de fromage et de jambon. Il ne faut pas oublier d'acheter de la glace, tout le monde aime la glace. À boire, on va acheter du jus d'orange pour les enfants et du café pour les adultes.

Réponses

B, D, E, H, J, K

Écouter 1B [AT1 Level 4]

This task tests understanding of detail in a short extract in the context of shopping. Pupils write down the prices of the items. Play the recording twice.

Audioscript 17

Fils: *Alors, qu'est-ce qu'il faut acheter?*
Père: *Tout d'abord, il ne faut pas oublier le pain.*
Fils: *C'est combien?*
Père: *1,10 euro. Attends que je regarde ma liste. La voilà. Alors, une tarte aux pommes pour le dessert. Elle a l'air délicieuse et regarde le prix: 12,40 euros. Ce n'est pas cher.*
Fils: *Qu'est-ce qu'on va manger pour le déjeuner?*
Père: *Grand-père vient, donc on va manger du poulet. C'est son plat préféré et il y a des offres spéciales en ce moment. Un poulet, c'est 9,90 euros.*
Fils: *Qu'est-ce qu'on va manger comme légumes?*
Père: *Attends, je vais regarder la liste … un kilo de pommes de terre. Tu prends un kilo à 3,80 euros.*
Fils: *Est-ce qu'il faut autre chose?*
Père: *Oui, de l'eau, six bouteilles d'eau. Tu vois l'eau là-bas? Six bouteilles pour 4,90 euros.*
Fils: *C'est tout?*
Père: *Non. Il faut des chocolats pour maman. Elle adore le chocolat et cette semaine il y a des boîtes de chocolats à 11,70 euros la boîte.*
Fils: *On prend des chips. Regarde – seulement 60 centimes d'euros le paquet.*
Père: *Oui, mais là on a fini!*

Réponses

1 12,40 € **2** 9,90 € **3** 3,80 € **4** 4,90 € **5** 11,70 € **6** 0,60 €

Écouter 2A [AT1 Level 4]

This task tests understanding of the main points of a text in the context of food likes and dislikes. Pupils identify the foods Kemal likes/doesn't like, writing the letters of the correct pictures in the appropriate boxes. There are two distractors. Play the recording twice.

Audioscript 18

J'adore les spaghettis, surtout à la sauce tomate. Je n'aime pas tellement la viande, mais j'aime le poulet. Quand je vais au restaurant, je prends toujours un poulet avec des frites. Les frites sont délicieuses, mais elles ne sont pas bonnes pour la santé. Je n'aime pas beaucoup les légumes, mais ma mère dit qu'il faut manger des légumes. Je déteste les petits pois, beurk! Ce n'est pas bon! Comme dessert, j'adore les crêpes, surtout les crêpes avec un peu de crème. Ce que je n'aime pas, c'est le fromage. Le fromage français est très bon, mais personnellement je déteste ça. Je ne mange jamais de fromage. Je déteste aussi le poisson. Ma mère en fait une fois par semaine. Je ne l'aime pas du tout.

Réponses

Likes: A, E, I
Dislikes: F, G, B

Écouter 2B [AT1 Level 5] 

This task tests understanding of a passage (including the ability to distinguish between past and present) in the context of food likes/dislikes and choices. The questions are multiple choice. Play the recording twice.

This task is similar to Asset Preliminary French Listening (external), p. 14, Part 2, Qs 6–10.

Go to p. 167

Audioscript 19

Récemment, on est allés au restaurant pour fêter l'anniversaire de mon père. Ma mère prend normalement le poulet, mais c'était dans une sauce aux champignons et elle déteste les champignons. Alors elle a pris le steak. Mon père par contre ne mange pas de steak, il est végétarien. Il préfère les pâtes, mais il n'y avait pas de pâtes. Donc il a choisi une quiche au fromage et à l'oignon. C'était la spécialité du restaurant. Mon frère a pris le poisson. Normalement, il n'aime pas ça, (il préfère le fast-food), mais le poisson était avec des frites. Mes parents ont mangé des carottes et des haricots verts. D'habitude, ma mère ne prend pas de dessert, mais elle a mangé une mousse au chocolat. Moi, je déteste ça! J'ai pris une glace à la fraise. Comme plat, j'ai choisi le steak. À vrai dire, je préfère une pizza ou quelquefois un hamburger, mais il n'y avait pas ça au menu!

Réponses

1 A **2** C **3** B **4** A **5** C **6** C

Teacher's Notes

Contrôle Module 4

Écouter 3A [AT1 Level 4]

This task tests understanding of a short passage in the context of parties/special events. Pupils write down the correct letter. There are two distractors. Play the recording twice.

Audioscript 20

Exemple: Ma mère a organisé une soirée au restaurant pour fêter l'anniversaire de ma grand-mère. Toute la famille est venue!

1 *Pour l'anniversaire de Miriam on va voir un film. C'est un film d'horreur, donc viens déguisé! Moi, j'ai un costume de Dracula!*

2 *Les profs ont organisé une fête pour l'équipe de foot pour fêter toutes nos victoires! C'est dans la salle de gym. Il faut venir pour 19h.*

3 *J'espère qu'il va faire beau. On va jouer au tennis et on peut faire du vélo. Ma mère prépare un pique-nique. N'oublie pas mon cadeau!*

4 *J'ai organisé une fête chez moi samedi soir. On va danser et écouter de la musique. Apporte tes CD!*

5 *On va à Cyberworld parce que j'adore la science-fiction. On va aussi jouer aux jeux vidéo à la Cité du Numérique.*

6 *Tu veux venir à ma fête dimanche? On va monter au mur d'escalade – c'est super cool. On va aussi jouer au badminton et au squash. Il faut porter un jogging et n'oublie pas tes baskets.*

Réponses
1 I **2** C **3** H **4** F **5** A **6** D

Écouter 3B [AT1 Level 5]

This task tests understanding of a passage (including the ability to distinguish between past and present) in the context of organising a party. (There are also instances of the near future tense, but this is not tested.) Pupils write the correct letters in the appropriate box. There are two distractors. Play the recording twice.

Audioscript 21

Salut, c'est Serge. J'espère que tu peux venir tôt à ma fête d'anniversaire samedi. J'ai déjà envoyé les invitations à tout le monde. Il faut venir déguisé. Le thème, c'est les dessins animés. Je sais que tu veux un costume de Mickey, mais je t'ai choisi un costume – tu vas aimer ça! On m'a donné beaucoup de CD comme cadeaux, donc il ne faut pas en apporter.

On va manger de la pizza et des chips. Est-ce que tu peux apporter des chips? Ma mère a acheté un grand gâteau au chocolat. C'est mon gâteau favori. Je l'ai remercié, mais est-ce que tu peux m'acheter des chocolats pour donner à ma mère? Je n'ai pas le temps d'aller au magasin. Et je n'ai pas eu le temps de téléphoner à Marthe. Est-ce que tu peux lui téléphoner pour l'inviter? C'est tout, je crois. Je ne vais pas décorer la maison. Ma mère n'aime pas ça et ça prend beaucoup de temps. À bientôt!

Réponses
déjà organisé: G, A, D
il faut: B, F, I

Speaking assessment criteria
See the level information supplied on the Assessment sheet.

For detailed Assessment criteria (including sublevels), see p. 168.

Level information and pupil support with examples are supplied on the assessment sheet. Encourage your pupils to use this to decide which level they are aiming for. Point out that they should not copy the examples given, but use them as a guide.

Use *Parler 1* in the first instance if you are unsure of which level to give a particular learner.

Parler 1 [AT2 Levels 3–5]

This task tests the ability to put together a simple conversation in the context of food preferences.

Pupils who can include information on what they bought at the supermarket last time they went (showing use of the perfect tense in addition to the present tense) can attain Level 5.

The best way to conduct the assessment is for pupils to listen to each other's conversations while you circulate, or to listen to individual learners at the front of the class, while pupils continue with other parts of the assessments.

Parler 2 [AT2 Levels 4–5]

This task tests the ability to prepare and deliver a presentation in the context of describing the eating habits of a famous sports personality (here a tennis player). The second question gives the opportunity to reach Level 5 by requiring use of the perfect tense to talk about what he/she ate before and after the match.

The best way to conduct the assessment is to listen to individuals, either at the front of the class or as the others continue other aspects of the assessments. Pupils could record these as podcasts for marking also.

Reading assessment criteria
Mark scheme: 1 mark for each correct answer. Total for each task: 6 marks.

For details of the sublevels see p. 167.

Lire 1A [AT3 Level 4]

This task tests understanding of the main points of a short passage in the context of invitations. The

Teacher's Notes
Contrôle Module 4

questions are multiple choice with pictures. Pupils tick the correct answers.

Réponses
1 C **2** B **3** B **4** A **5** B **6** A

Lire 1B [AT2 Level 4]

This task tests understanding of the main points of a text in the context of invitations. Pupils identify whose party activity is shown in each picture, writing the appropriate name.

Réponses

1 Jérôme	**2** Corinne	**3** Mathilde
4 Corinne	**5** Jérôme	**6** Daniel

Lire 2A [AT3 Level 4]

This task tests understanding of the main points of a passage in the context of food. Pupils read Passage A and tick the six correct sentences. There are six distractors.

Réponses
2, 3, 4, 7, 9, 11

Lire 2B [AT3 Level 5]

This task tests understanding of a passage (including the ability to distinguish between past and present) in the context of food. Pupils read Passage A and Passage B. They identify the foods Sylvie mentions, writing the correct letters in the appropriate box according to whether she usually has them on a Thursday/she had them last Thursday. There are three distractors.

Réponses
normalement: B, E, G
jeudi dernier: C, D, I

Lire 3A [AT3 Level 4] 'Q'

This task tests the understanding of the main points in short passages in the context of food likes and dislikes. Pupils read Passage A. They identify who is being described, writing the letter of the correct paragraph.

This task is similar to Asset Preliminary French Reading (external), p.5, part 2, Qs 6–10.

Go to p. 167

Réponses
1 C **2** B **3** C **4** A **5** B **6** A

Lire 3B [AT3 Level 5]

This task tests the understanding of texts featuring a wider range of language and two tenses (perfect/imperfect and present) in the context of food. Pupils read Passage A and Passage B. They identify the person who says each statement, ticking the correct column.

Réponses
1 Rachid **2** Didier **3** Delphine **4** Rachid
5 Margot **6** Delphine

Writing assessment criteria
See the level information supplied on the Assessment sheet. For detailed Assessment criteria (including sublevels) see p. 169.

First decide whether you want your pupils to complete *Écrire 1, 2* or both, depending on their ability and time available.

Level information and pupil assessment support with examples are supplied on the assessment sheet. Encourage your pupils to use this to decide which level they are aiming for. Point out that they should not copy the examples given, but use them as a guide.

Écrire 1 [AT4 Levels 3–5]

Give this sheet only to pupils who are working at Levels 3–5. If in doubt, give Écrire 1 first.

This task tests the ability to write a short paragraph in the context of planning a birthday party. It is divided into two sections. In Section A pupils describe what is appropriate for their mother's party by changing the model sentences accordingly (Level 3). In Section B (Levels 4–5) pupils write an invitation to a friend for their own beach birthday party: this section gives pupils opportunity to reach Level 5 by requiring the use of the near future tense, including appropriate time expressions.

Écrire 2 [AT4 Levels 4–5]

This task tests the ability to write a paragraph in the context of eating habits (usual breakfast or lunch, likes and dislikes, recent visit to a restaurant). It is divided into two sections. Pupils who feel more confident can complete both sections A and B, the latter giving pupils the opportunity to reach Level 5 by requiring the use of the perfect tense, including appropriate time expressions.

Answers to Challenge, page 88
A 1, 2, C4 = (B4*1.4), C6 = (B6*1.4)
B UK prices in euros – butter 1,81 €; jam 0,97 €; orange juice 0,81 €

Lesson starter
Questions for the stars

Choose one of the stars (1–4) on the sheet and prepare three or four questions about holiday preferences to ask that person in French.

When you are ready, go and find a partner. Point to the star you have chosen, and ask your questions. Your partner must invent possible answers to your questions, imagining they are the person in the picture.

? ? ? ? ?

juin

1

2

août

3

4

juillet

juin

? ? ? ? ? ? ? ? ? ? ? ? ?

Voyages et vacances

5 Grammaire

Comment poser une question

There are three different ways of asking a question in French.

1 By raising your voice: **Tu passes tes vacances en France?**
2 By using **Est-ce que** (or **Est-ce qu'** + vowel) in front of a sentence: **Est-ce que tu passes tes vacances en France?**
3 By using inversion (the verb form and the subject): **Passes-tu tes vacances en France?**

A Ask the questions in a different way.

1 Tu aimes jouer au foot? ____
2 Est-ce que vous allez à la plage? ____
3 Vas-tu en vacances avec ta famille? ____
4 Est-ce que tu préfères rester en France? ____
5 Parles-tu espagnol? ____
6 Vous restez un mois? ____
7 Est-ce que tu fais du vélo? ____
8 Passes-tu tes vacances au bord de la mer? ____
9 Joues-tu au tennis en vacances? ____
10 Est-ce que vous aimez nager? ____

B Match the English question words with the French.

1 When? **2** Where? **3** How? **4** At what time? **5** What? **6** How long? **7** Who? **8** Why? **9** Who with?

A Combien de temps? **B** Où? **C** Qui? **D** À quelle heure? **E** Avec qui? **F** Quand? **G** Pourquoi? **H** Comment? **I** Que/qu'?

C Use inversion to complete the questions. Use the verb and subject given in brackets.

Exemple: Avec qui ____voyages-tu____? (tu voyages)
1 Combien de temps ____? (tu restes)
2 Où ____ tes vacances? (tu passes)
3 Quand ____? (tu pars)
4 Que ____ en vacances? (tu fais)
5 Pourquoi ____ en train? (vous voyagez)
6 Avec qui ____ au tennis? (vous jouez)
7 Comment ____ passer vos vacances? (vous préférez)
8 À quelle heure ____? (vous partez)

Learning skills

Predicting and looking for expression

In a moment, you are going to see an advert in French for a hotel in the Alps. It is often helpful, if you know what sort of text you are going to read, to predict what might be in it.

A **Answer the questions in English.**

1 Do you think the advert will be written in formal or informal language? Will it address the reader as **tu** or **vous**? Why? ______________________

2 What sort of information do you think the advert might include?
Exemple: ____accommodation____

____

3 Choose two of your categories from Question 2 above. List three words for each category, which you think might appear in the advert.
Exemple: ____accommodation: chambres, lits____

Category 1:

__________ __________ __________

Category 2:

__________ __________ __________

4 Look at the advert below. How many words did you predict correctly?

____

Au cœur des Alpes:

L'Hôtel de l'Aigle

Situé en pleine montagne, à 10 kilomètres de Chamonix, le pittoresque Hôtel de l'Aigle vous offre un séjour parfait.

Nos chambres

Le confort, c'est notre spécialité. Toutes nos chambres (à 2 ou 4 lits) sont tranquilles et équipées de douche, télévision satellite et mini-bar. Des chambres avec balcon sont aussi disponibles. Et quelle vue!

Manger et boire

2 restaurants et notre fameux 'Bar Chamois' sont à votre disposition. Goûtez notre fondue traditionnelle! Elle est délicieuse!

Activités

- Vous aimez les sports d'hiver? De décembre à février on vous propose: le ski, le snowboard (service de car gratuit aux pistes) et le patin à glace.
- Vous venez en été? On a le ski sur herbe, les randonnées de montagne et l'alpinisme.
- La nature vous intéresse? Il y a notre tour pour voir les marmottes (petits cousins alpins du cochon d'Inde).

5 Look at the advert again. In what ways has the writer tried to make the hotel sound exciting and attractive to the reader? (Clue: look for adjectives and punctuation.) ______________________

____

6 How many non-cognates can you find in the text, which you can guess or work out from the context? Underline them.

Grammaire

Le passé composé – un peu de révision!

A **Write out the auxiliaries *avoir* and *être* in full.**

avoir *to have*		être *to be*	
j'______	nous ______	je ______	nous ______
tu ______	vous ______	tu ______	vous ______
il/elle/on ______	ils/elles ______	il/elle/on ______	ils/elles ______

To form the **passé composé** use the present tense of **avoir** or **être** plus the past participle of the verb.
-er verbs take off the **-er** and add **-é**
-ir verbs take off the **-ir** and add **-i**
-re verbs take off the **-re** and add **-u.**
The past participle agrees with the subject after verbs which take **être.**

B **Complete the sentences with the correct form of *avoir* or *être*.**

1 Hier, il ________ regardé la télé.
2 Tu ________ allé à la plage.
3 Je ________ resté à la maison.
4 Nous ________ voyagé en avion.
5 Vous ________ fait du jet-ski.
6 Tu ________ acheté des souvenirs.
7 Ils ________ rentrés à 10h.
8 Elle ________ fini ses devoirs.
9 Nous ________ joué au tennis.
10 Il ________ nagé.

C **Rewrite the sentences in the perfect tense.**

1 Je voyage en train. ____________________
2 Tu joues aux boules. ____________________
3 Nous restons un mois. ____________________
4 Vous écoutez la radio. ____________________
5 Je vais à la plage. ____________________
6 Ils achètent une glace. ____________________
7 Elle rentre à 11h. ____________________
8 Tu fais tes devoirs. ____________________

D **Complete the text in the perfect tense. Check the meaning of any verbs you don't know and put them into the perfect tense by following the rules at the top of the page.**

Ce matin, Patrice **1** ____________ (oublier) son sac et puis, il **2** ____________ (arriver) en retard. À la récréation, il **3** ____________ (jouer) au foot avec ses amis et malheureusement il **4** ____________ (casser) une fenêtre. Puis, à la cantine, il **5** ____________ (perdre) son argent et il **6** ____________ (ne pas manger) et finalement, il **7** ____________ (manquer) le car et il **8** ____________ (rentrer) à la maison à pied.

Lesson starter

Quick change!

A Look at the questions. Can you work out what they mean?

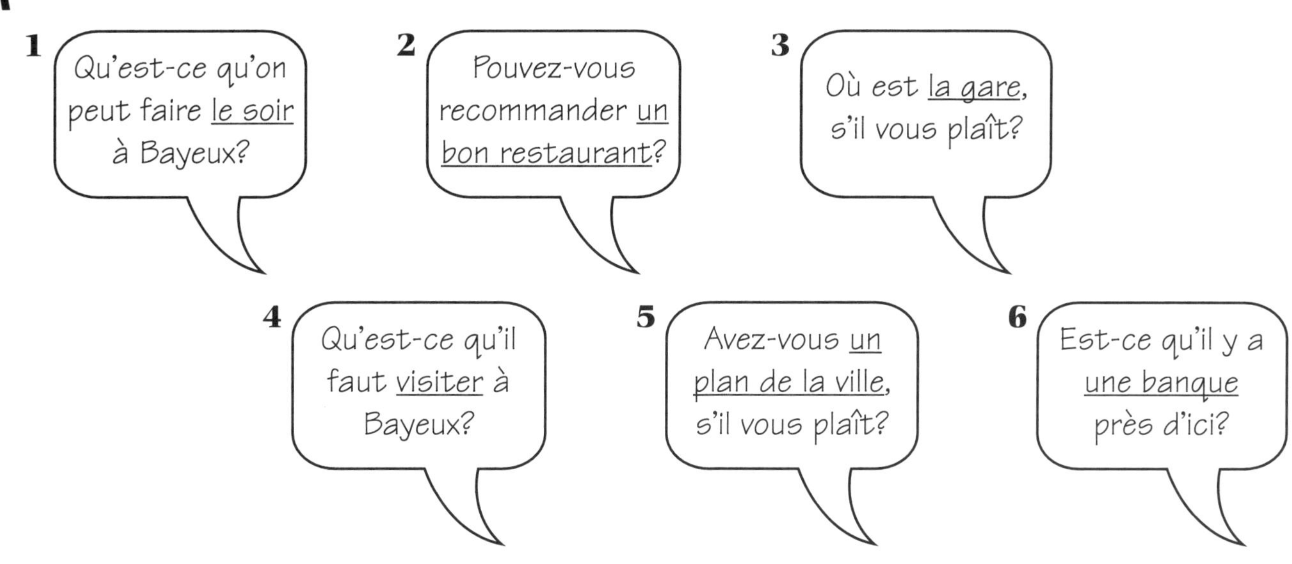

B Work with a partner. Choose three questions from A above. Find two alternatives from the box below which could be used in place of the underlined words. Write down your six new questions.

faire
un livre sur Bayeux
un hôtel pas cher
voir
des magasins
en juillet
le marché
la poste
comme sports
le dimanche
un camping
l'Hôtel Soleil
une liste des restaurants
des toilettes

C Come up with your own ideas for changing each of your questions once more. Write down your three new questions.

5 Thinking skills

A history lesson

A **Work with a partner or in a group. Read the text.**

Si on visite Bayeux, on peut voir la fameuse Tapisserie de Bayeux. C'est une sorte de bande dessinée historique. L'histoire, c'est la défaite de l'Angleterre par la France à la bataille d'Hastings en 1066.

B **Read about some key events in French history and work out the date of each one.**

1 Huit cent soixante-treize ans après la bataille d'Hastings, la France est occupée par les Allemands, pendant la Deuxième Guerre Mondiale. ____________

2 Sept cent vingt-trois ans après la bataille d'Hastings, il y a une révolution et la France devient une république. ____________

3 Neuf cent trente-deux ans après la bataille d'Hastings, la France est championne du monde de football. ____________

4 Sept cent trente-huit ans après la bataille d'Hastings, Napoléon Bonaparte se déclare Empereur de la France. ____________

5 Huit cent vingt-trois ans après la bataille d'Hastings, on construit la fameuse tour à Paris. ____________

6 Neuf cent trente-trois ans après la bataille d'Hastings, la France introduit l'euro. ____________

C **Write in the dates of these important French events and put them in historical order.**

French Revolution	*Exemple:* 1066 Battle of Hastings
Eiffel Tower built	____________
France wins the Football World Cup	____________
Napoleon becomes Emperor	____________
Battle of Hastings	____________
German occupation	____________
Introduction of the euro	____________

Défi
Expo-sur-Eure

A **Sketch a simple labelled plan of the holiday centre, which includes all of the facilities described in the text.**

Bienvenue au centre de vacances

Expo-sur-Eure

Ici on vous offre des activités pour toute la famille. Nos appartements sont spacieux et ils ont un salon avec coin cuisine et deux chambres.

À votre disposition sur place, il y a deux restaurants et quatre petites boutiques. On peut nager au paradis aquatique tropical, aller au sauna ou jouer dans la salle de jeux. Pour les actifs, il y a beaucoup de possibilités! Il y a deux circuits de jogging et une patinoire. On peut jouer au golf, faire du tennis (il y a deux courts de tennis chez nous) et on peut même faire du tir à l'arc. N'oubliez pas de visiter le salon de beauté!

Nous vous souhaitons de très bonnes vacances chez nous.

B **Match the questions and answers to create an interview with a visitor to the holiday centre.**

top tip

Use colour and/or a key to make the plan more user-friendly.

1 Qu'est-ce que tu penses du centre de vacances? ☐
2 Qu'est-ce qu'il y a au centre? ☐
3 Et qu'est-ce qu'on peut y faire? ☐
4 Est-ce qu'il y a assez d'activités pour les sportifs? ☐
5 Qu'est-ce que tu as fait hier? ☐
6 Et est-ce que vous avez des projets pour demain? ☐

A On va profiter des restaurants le soir. Je vais essayer la cuisine de la région.

B Il y a des restaurants et des boutiques, mais je préfère le paradis aquatique tropical.

C Moi, j'ai joué au golf avec mon frère et après je suis allé(e) au sauna.

D À mon avis, il est excellent, car il est très bien situé et il y a beaucoup de choses à faire pour toute la famille.

E On peut faire du sport ou nager au paradis aquatique tropical.

F Oui, je pense qu'il y a beaucoup de choses. Il y a un golf à neuf trous, deux circuits de jogging et assez de courts de tennis.

top tip

What could you add to these answers to make them more varied and interesting?

Défi
Expo-sur-Eure

Assignment 5 Challenge

Design your own holiday centre. Either on paper or using ICT, present annotated diagrams and pictures to show and describe facilities. Include a short newspaper report written one year after the centre has opened, containing visitor comments.

Assignment 5 Support grid

Level 3	Label your design in French and give three facts about what there is/what you can do. Include a connective.	*On peut nager au paradis aquatique tropical ou … Il y a deux restaurants.*
Level 4	Create a newspaper article including information, a labelled design and an interview with a visitor about what you can do and what it is like. Include short descriptions and opinions. Use intensifiers, connectives and adjectives.	*On peut jouer au golf, faire du tennis (il y a deux courts de tennis chez nous), et on peut même faire du tir à l'arc. C'est très bien et il y a beaucoup d'activités!*
Level 5	As Level 4, but include details of the visitor's experiences there, using the perfect tense. Justify opinions. Use a dictionary to say something original.	■ *Qu'est-ce que tu as fait hier?* ● *Moi, j'ai joué au golf avec mon frère et je suis allé(e) au sauna. C'était fantastique. Le centre est très animé.*
Level 6	As Level 5, but use a broader range of vocabulary and structures. Use the near future tense to include details of what the visitor is planning to do tomorrow. Include *assez/trop*, negatives and comparatives/superlatives.	■ *Et est-ce que vous avez des projets pour demain?* ● *Oui. On va faire du tir à l'arc le matin, et après …*

Assignment 5 Judging grid

Points for language level as shown plus 1 point for each of the other criteria.

(L3 = **1**, L4 = **2,** L5 = **3**, L6 = **4**)		Details included are appropriate and of interest to a possible visitor.		
The activity centre is well planned.		Newspaper style used.		
A key or symbols are used to make the plan user-friendly.		The visitor comments contain an original observation/detail.		Total
Colour is used effectively in the design.				/10

Expo-sur-Eure: guidelines for teachers

For general guidelines on how to get the most out of the *Défi* sections, see page 14.

Use this activity instead of activities 5 and 6 on page 83 of the Pupil's Book.

1 Hand out the activity sheet. Pupils do activities A and B. Show some good sketches from activity A to the class and invite constructive comments. Ask for pupils' suggestions on how they would make the interview answers more interesting.
2 Pupils then design their own holiday centre (either on paper or using an ICT design package) and produce a short newspaper report (description of the centre together with visitor interview).

Art and Design Programme of Study	1.2 Key Concepts: competences
Levels accessed	Levels 3–6
Key vocabulary	*Expo 2 Rouge* Pupil's Book, Module 5, pages 94–95

Vocabulaire

Les pays	***Countries***
l'Allemagne	*Germany*
l'Angleterre	*England*
l'Autriche	*Austria*
l'Écosse	*Scotland*
l'Espagne	*Spain*
la France	*France*
la Grèce	*Greece*
l'Irlande	*Ireland*
l'Irlande du Nord	*Northern Ireland*
l'Italie	*Italy*
le Pays de Galles	*Wales*
le Portugal	*Portugal*
Elle habite à Stuttgart.	*She lives in Stuttgart.*
J'habite en Espagne.	*I live in Spain.*
Il habite au Portugal.	*He lives in Portugal.*
J'ai visité l'Allemagne.	*I visited Germany.*
On va aller en Grèce.	*We're going to go to Greece.*
Je voudrais visiter l'Écosse.	*I'd like to go to Scotland.*

Les langues	***Languages***
allemand	*German*
anglais	*English*
espagnol	*Spanish*
français	*French*
gallois	*Welsh*
grec	*Greek*
italien	*Italian*
portugais	*Portuguese*
Il parle anglais.	*He speaks English.*

Les vacances	***Holidays***
Où passes-tu les vacances?	*Where do you spend your holidays?*
D'habitude, ...	*Usually ...*
à l'étranger	*abroad*
au bord de la mer	*at the seaside*
Combien de temps y restes-tu?	*How long do you go there for?*
J'y reste un mois.	*I go for a month.*
J'y reste quinze jours.	*I go for a fortnight.*
Avec qui passes-tu les vacances?	*Who do you go on holiday with?*
Je passe mes vacances ...	*I spend my holiday ...*
Je vais à la plage.	*I go to the beach.*
Je me baigne.	*I swim.*
J'adore bronzer.	*I love to sunbathe.*
Je rencontre des gens.	*I meet people.*
Je vais à des concerts.	*I go to concerts.*
L'année dernière, je suis allé(e) ...	*Last year I went ...*

Pour poser une question	***Question words***
combien de temps?	*how long?*
comment?	*how?*
pourquoi?	*why?*
où?	*where?*
quand?	*when?*
que/qu'est-ce que?	*what?*
qui?	*who?*

Au centre de vacances	***At the holiday centre***
un appartement	*a flat, apartment*
une boutique	*a shop*
une chambre	*a bedroom*
un coin-cuisine	*a kitchen area*
un court de tennis	*a tennis court*
un terrain de golf	*a golf course*
un lit	*bed*
la location de vélos	*bikes for hire*
la pêche sur lac	*fishing on the lake*
un restaurant	*a restaurant*
une salle de bains	*a bathroom*
une salle de jeux	*a games room*
un salon	*a living-room*
un terrain de boules	*a place to play boules*
le tir à l'arc	*archery*
Est-ce qu'on peut ... ?	*Can you ... ?*

Le règlement	***Rules***
il faut ...	*you must ...*
laisser votre voiture	*leave your car*
quitter votre appartement	*leave your flat*
il ne faut pas ...	*you mustn't ...*
faire de bruit	*make any noise*

Vocabulaire

Les opinions	***Opinions***
penser de	*to think of*
qu'est-ce que tu penses de ...?	*what do you think of ...?*
à mon avis	*in my opinion*
je pense que	*I think (that)*
je trouve que	*I think (that)*
il y a ...	*there is/are ...*
il n'y a pas ...	*there isn't/aren't ...*
assez de	*enough*
beaucoup de	*lots of*
trop de	*too many*

Les vacances passées	***Past holidays***
J'ai passé mes vacances au/en ...	*I spent my holidays in ...*
Je suis allé(e) avec ...	*I went with ...*
l'hôtel était ...	*the hotel was ...*
il y avait ...	*there was/were ...*
J'ai fait des excursions en car/bateau.	*I went on coach/ boat trips.*
J'ai fait de la plongée.	*I went diving.*
J'ai fait du ski nautique.	*I went water-skiing.*
J'ai fait du tir à l'arc.	*I did archery.*
C'était ...	*It was ...*
magnifique	*magnificent*
chouette	*great*

Être touriste	***Being a tourist***
avez-vous ...?	*have you got ...?*
une carte de la région	*a map of the area*
un plan de la ville	*a town plan*
est-ce qu'il y a ...?	*is there ...?*
ici	*here*
qu'est-ce qu'il faut voir?	*what must we see?*
qu'est-ce qu'on peut faire à ...?	*what can you do in ...?*

On réfléchit	***Thinking time words***
alors ...	*well, ...*
eh bien, ...	*well, ...*
euh, tu sais/vous savez	*mmm, you know*
mmm, voyons ...	*mmm, let's see ...*

Objectifs

Nom: ....

Module 4 Attainment			This module (M5) targets	
Listening			Listening	
Speaking			Speaking	
Reading			Reading	
Writing			Writing	

Before	Level 3 (Short sentences linked together, short conversations)	Mid	End
	Choose three different countries in Europe. Ask a partner where he/she lives. Respond to this question with a different country each time.		
	G Think of a family friend or pen friend. Write three sentences about where he/she lives (country and location) and what language(s) he/she speaks.		
	G Write three sentences about what there is at a holiday centre and what you can do there using *il y a* and *on peut*.		
	Choose two places in a town. Ask my partner if these places exist in his/her town. Respond to my partner's questions negatively and mention instead a different place that there is in my town each time.		
	Choose two activities you can do in town. Ask my partner if you can do these activities in his/her town. When my partner asks these questions, respond negatively and mention instead a different activity each time.		

Before	Level 4 (Short texts and longer conversations, short presentations)	Mid	End
	Imagine I have three friends on a social networking site from different countries in Europe. In a short paragraph, describe where my friends live and what languages they speak. Also include a different detail about each friend. Include connectives and intensifiers. **G** Use the appropriate word/expression for 'in'. Include at least one negative.		
	Have a conversation about holidays. Ask my partner where he/she usually goes (country and location), how long he/she stays, who he/she goes with, how he/she gets there, what he/she prefers doing there. Respond to my partner's questions. Include connectives and intensifiers.		
	In a short paragraph, describe my favourite holiday. Say where I go, how long I stay, how I get there, what I like about the destination, what I like doing, and what I do if it is sunny or cold. Include connectives and intensifiers. **G** Include at least one negative.		
	Have a conversation about a holiday centre. Ask my partner what he/she thinks about it and what he/she prefers doing there. In my responses include information on what there is and what you can do there. Include adjectives and opinions. **G** Use *on peut* + infinitive. Include at least one negative.		
	Have a conversation in a tourist information office (as tourist and sales assistant). As the sales assistant, greet the tourist and respond to his/her queries. As the tourist, ask for a map and for information about what there is to do in the area. Ask specifically about two facilities that interest you. Include connectives, intensifiers and opinions.		

Objectifs

Nom: ....

Before	**Level 5 (Longer texts and more detailed conversations, longer presentations)**	Mid	End
	Give a presentation about a family trip to a holiday centre. Say where I went, who I went with, how I got there, where I stayed and what I did there. Include information about facilities and what you can do in the area, and give opinions on these. Include appropriate time expressions. **G** Use the perfect and present tenses.		
	Choose a rich celebrity. Do an interview with a partner (as interviewer and celebrity) about a recent holiday. Ask where he/she spent the holiday, how he/she got there, what he/she did there, and his/her opinion of the destination, what he/she usually does when he/she is not on holiday. Respond, giving reasons for my opinions. Include appropriate time expressions. **G** Use the perfect and present tenses.		
	Describe a recent holiday in Senegal in a short presentation, including information about travel and activities and what there is to do and see there. Include and justify opinions. Include appropriate time expressions. **G** Use the perfect and present tenses.		

Before	**Level 6 (Longer texts and short talks/more detailed conversations using known language and structures in new contexts)**	Mid	End
	Give a presentation about family holidays. Say where I went last year, what I typically do on holiday and where I am going next year, using appropriate time expressions. Say where I would like to visit one day. Be ready to answer simple prepared questions about the presentation. **G** Use the present, perfect and near future tenses as appropriate, and the conditional *je voudrais*. Use *quand* and *si* to extend sentences.		
	Write an email while on holiday to a friend. Give information about the journey and what I did yesterday, and what I am going to do for the rest of my time away, using appropriate time expressions. Include and justify opinions in more detail. **G** Use the present, perfect and near future tenses as appropriate. Include a variety of negatives.		
	Write a text about a trip to a holiday centre from hell. Describe what facilities there are and what you can do. Give information about what went wrong/I didn't like. Add details of what I usually like doing on a holiday and what I am going to do next year. Use appropriate time expressions. **G** Use the present, perfect and near future tenses. Include at least one comparative and superlative form.		
	Leave a long voicemail message for a French friend when on a weekend break in the UK. Give information about what I did yesterday, what I am doing today and what I am planning to do tomorrow, giving lots of detail and including and justifying opinions. **G** Use the present, perfect and near future tenses as appropriate. Include a variety of negatives.		

Personal Targets	Mid	End

Target Setting

Fill in the levels you reached in Module 4, then decide which level you are aiming for in Module 5 in each skill. To help you fill in your personal targets, you may like to refer to pages 167–168 for ideas.

Contrôle

Nom: ....

Écouter 1

A 'a' **You will hear six conversations. What are they about? Match each to the appropriate heading by writing a letter (A–I) in the box. (Level 3)**

A How they get there
B Where they go on holiday
C Who they prefer to go with
D Where they stay
E How long they go on holiday for
F What they like doing on holiday
G What they don't like doing on holiday
H Places they would like to visit
I Where they don't like going on holiday

Example:	B
1	
2	
3	
4	
5	
6	

Points	
Niveau	

B **Écoute et coche (✔) les bonnes réponses. (Level 4)**

		A		B		C	
Exemple: Elle part avec	A 		☐	B 	✔	C 	☐
1 Elle reste	A 		☐	B 	☐	C 	☐
2 Elle préfère aller	A 		☐	B 	☐	C 	☐
3 Elle voyage en	A 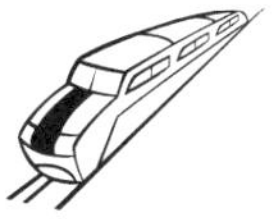		☐	B 	☐	C 	☐
4 Elle aime	A 		☐	B 	☐	C 	☐
5 Elle n'aime pas	A 		☐	B 	☐	C 	☐
6 Elle voudrait visiter	A 	MADRID	☐	B 	ROME ☐	C 	☐

Points	
Niveau	

Contrôle

Voyages et vacances 5

Nom: ....

Expo 2R Listening

Écouter 2

A Écoute et coche (✔) la bonne image. (Level 4)

Que fait la famille d'Henri?

	A	B	C	D	E	F	G	H	I
Exemple: toute la famille	✔								
1 son père									
2 sa mère									
3 Rachelle									
4 Kévin									
5 Nathalie									
6 Henri									

Points	
Niveau	

B Écoute et coche (✔) les six bonnes cases. (Level 5)

Qu'est-ce que Chloë a fait?

Exemple:   ✔

A ☐

B  ☐

C 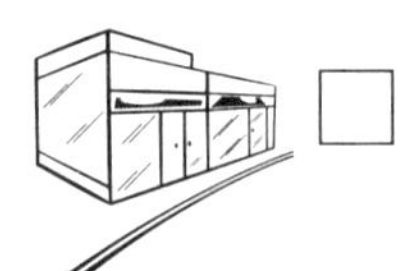 ☐

D  ☐

E  ☐

F  ☐

G  ☐

H  ☐

I  ☐

J  ☐

K  ☐

L  ☐

Points	
Niveau	

Voyages et vacances

5 Contrôle

Nom: ....

Expo 2R
Listening

Écouter 3

A Écoute et coche (✔) les six phrases correctes. (Level 5)

Exemple: Cécile est allée en vacances avec son amie. ☑

1 Elle est partie un mois. ☐
2 Sa copine est bavarde. ☐
3 Il a fait chaud. ☐
4 Elle est allée au bord de la mer. ☐
5 Elle aime faire la cuisine. ☐
6 Il y avait des magasins dans le centre de vacances. ☐
7 Elle a nagé. ☐
8 Elle a fait du vélo. ☐
9 Elle a rencontré des Anglais. ☐
10 Il y avait beaucoup à faire. ☐
11 Elle a adoré ses vacances. ☐
12 L'année prochaine, elle veut aller dans un pays chaud. ☐

Points	
Niveau	

B Listen and choose the correct answer. (Level 6)

1 For his holidays Ahmed ...
A always stays in France. ☐
B sometimes goes abroad. ☐
C always goes to the same place. ☐

2 Last year his hotel ...
A was near a holiday centre. ☐
B offered very little to do. ☐
C offered a range of activities. ☐

3 Last year on holiday he ...
A did a lot of sightseeing. ☐
B did a lot of diving. ☐
C did lots of different sports. ☐

4 He tried ... for the first time.
A water skiing ☐
B fishing ☐
C boat trips ☐

5 He ...
A has often been to England. ☐
B doesn't want to go to England. ☐
C is going to England this year. ☐

6 This year he plans to ...
A do a lot of sightseeing. ☐
B do a lot of shopping. ☐
C go to a beach resort. ☐

Points	
Niveau	

Contrôle

Nom: ....

Parler 1

Réponds aux questions de ton professeur ou de ton ami/amie. Pose des questions à ton/ta partenaire aussi. (Levels 3–5)

- Qu'est-ce qu'il y a au centre de vacances?
- Qu'est-ce qu'on peut faire au centre?
- Qu'est-ce que tu préfères faire en vacances?
- C'est comment? C'est quoi ton opinion? (Level 4)
- Décris ta visite au centre de vacances l'année dernière. (Level 5)

Level information	Pupil support	Example
You can show achievement at Level 3, 4 or 5 depending on how you carry out the task.		
Level 3: Ask and answer the questions.	• Ask each other what there is at the holiday centre, and respond (mention at least two things). • Ask each other what you can do there, and respond (mention at least two things). • Ask each other what you prefer to do on holiday, and respond (mention at least two things).	■ *Qu'est-ce qu'il y a au centre de vacances?* ● *Il y a beaucoup de restaurants et des courts de tennis.*
Level 4: As Level 3, but include adjectives, intensifiers, connectives and negatives in your answers.	• Say what you cannot do at the centre. • Ask each other your opinion of the centre, and respond by saying what you think there is too much of/is missing.	■ *C'est comment? C'est quoi ton opinion?* ● *C'était un peu ennuyeux. Il y a trop de restaurants et il n'y a pas assez de salons de beauté. J'aime les salons de beauté!*
Level 5: As Level 4, but your conversation needs to make reference to the past as well as the present, and use appropriate time expressions. Include reasons for your opinions.	• Use expressions such as *à mon avis* to introduce your opinions. • Describe a visit you made to the centre last year (when you went, who you went with, what you did), using the perfect tense and *c'était* to give your opinions.	■ *Décris ta visite.* ● *L'année dernière je suis allé(e) au Center Parcs France avec mon oncle. Nous avons fait … et nous avons visité … À mon avis, c'était …*

Contrôle

Nom: ....

Parler 2

Prépare et fais une présentation (Levels 4–5) et réponds aux questions de ton professeur ou de ton ami/amie. (Level 6)

Mentionne:
- où tu vas d'habitude en vacances.
- ce que tu fais d'habitude.
- ce que tu as fait hier et comment c'était. (Level 5)
- ce que tu vas faire demain. (Level 6)

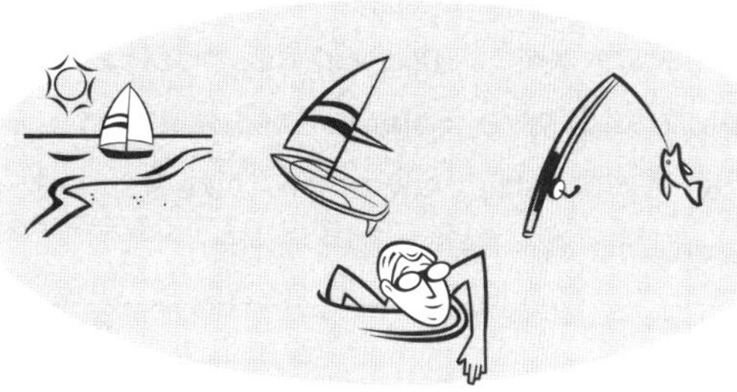

Level information	Pupil support	Example
You can show achievement at Level 4, 5 or 6 depending on how you carry out the task.		
Level 4: Prepare and deliver a presentation. Include adjectives, intensifiers, connectives and negatives.	• Talk about your usual holiday (where you go, who with, how you get there, where you stay). • Talk about what you usually do on holiday. • Give information about what you like and don't like doing on holiday. • Say what activities you are doing today.	*D'habitude, je vais en France avec ma famille; ma mère, mon père et ma sœur. Nous allons en voiture et en train …*
Level 5: As Level 4, but add a second section including details of what you did yesterday. Use the perfect tense, with appropriate time expressions. Include reasons for your opinions.	• Include information about what you did yesterday (three activities). • Give your opinions of these activities and justify them with reasons.	*Hier soir, je suis allé(e) au restaurant avec mon père. J'ai mangé … et j'ai bu … C'était … parce que …*
Level 6: As Level 5, but include descriptions and extra detail. Extend the presentation where appropriate, adapting grammatical structures. Be prepared to answer simple questions on your presentation.	• Include information about what you are going to do tomorrow (three activities). • Use thinking time expressions to buy time and to sound authentic. • Use a variety of structures to describe activities including *assez de* and *trop de*.	*Demain matin, je vais faire du vélo avec ma sœur. J'aime faire du vélo parce qu'il n'y pas trop de voitures dans le parc. Euh, après ça …*

Voyages et vacances

5 Contrôle

Nom: ....

Lire 1

A Lis et écris les bonnes lettres. (Level 3)

Qu'est-ce qu'ils font?

Christelle: Je vais toujours au bord de la mer. J'aime être active. Je nage tous les jours. Ce que j'aime aussi, c'est le banana-riding. C'est rigolo!

Michael: J'aime bien aller à la campagne parce que c'est calme. Nous faisons beaucoup de sport. J'adore faire du vélo avec ma famille. Nous faisons souvent du camping et le soir nous aimons bien jouer aux boules avec les autres campeurs.

Agnès: Je passe mes vacances à la montagne avec mes grands-parents. Il y a un grand lac près de la maison avec beaucoup de poissons. Moi et mon grand-père, nous faisons souvent de la pêche. À part ça, j'aime bien faire les boutiques en ville avec ma grand-mère.

Serge: Je vais toujours dans un centre de vacances avec ma famille. J'aime bien faire des sports un peu différents. Donc je fais du tir à l'arc. J'adore ça. C'est passionnant! Je fais aussi du ski nautique. Ce n'est pas du tout dangereux. Je trouve ça super!

A  **B**  **C**  **D**  **E**  **F**  **G**  **H**  **I** 

Exemple: **Christelle** A E **Michael** ___ ___ **Agnès** ___ ___ **Serge** ___ ___

Points	
Niveau	

B Lis et écris la bonne lettre. (Level 4)

Je passe mes vacances avec ma famille dans un centre de vacances près de La Rochelle. C'est super bien parce qu'il y a beaucoup d'activités à faire. Lundi, il y a des cours de tennis. Mardi, on organise une sortie à la plage. Je voudrais essayer le banana-riding, mais il n'y a pas ça à la plage. Alors je veux faire du ski nautique. Mercredi, il y a un concours de boules. Mes parents veulent gagner! Jeudi, il y a le tir à l'arc. Moi, je n'aime pas ça parce que c'est un peu ennuyeux. Alors, je veux faire les boutiques en ville. Vendredi, on fait un circuit en vélo et on va pique-niquer près du lac. Samedi, il y a la pêche sur lac. Mon père adore ça, mais moi, je préfère nager, donc je vais à la piscine. Dimanche, on se repose. Mes parents vont au café. Mon frère et moi, nous allons à la salle de jeux. Romain

A  **B**  **C**  **D**  **E** 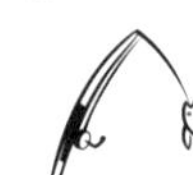 **F**  **G**  **H** 

I  **J**  **K**

Que fait Roman cette semaine?

lundi: C mardi: ___ mercredi: ___ jeudi ___ vendredi: ___ samedi: ___ dimanche: ___

Points	
Niveau	

Contrôle

Nom: ....

Lire 2

A 'a' **Read Passage A on page 128 and choose the correct words to complete the text. Write your answers on page 128. (Level 4)**

Example:	parents	(vacances)	passe-temps
1	un jour	une semaine	trois semaines
2	voyage	reste	a
3	froid	mauvais	chaud
4	pizza	gâteaux	boissons
5	amusant	difficile	ennuyeux
6	boire	manger	faire

Points	
Niveau	

B **Lis Passage A et Passage B à la page 128 et coche (✔) les six phrases correctes. (Level 5)**

Exemple: Il va en vacances avec ses parents. ☑

1 Ses parents ont une maison en Écosse. ☐
2 L'année dernière, il a passé ses vacances dans le sud de la France. ☐
3 Quelquefois, il va dans le sud de la France au printemps. ☐
4 L'année dernière, il a voyagé en avion. ☐
5 Normalement, il passe ses vacances chez ses grands-parents. ☐
6 L'année dernière, il est parti deux semaines. ☐
7 L'année dernière, il a fait beaucoup de vélo. ☐
8 En vacances, il aime aller à la plage. ☐
9 Il a beaucoup mangé au restaurant pendant ses vacances l'année dernière. ☐
10 Ses grands-parents habitent dans le sud de la France. ☐
11 Il n'aime pas faire de la pêche. ☐
12 Il aime jouer aux boules. ☐

Points	
Niveau	

5 Contrôle

Voyages et vacances

Nom: ....

Lire 2

Passage A

Boîte de réception | Messages envoyés | Brouillons

D'habitude, je vais dans le sud de la France pendant les vacances. Mes parents ont une maison au bord de la mer. On passe beaucoup de temps là-bas. On y passe (1) ________________ en août. Quelquefois, on y va aussi en avril. On (2) ________________ toujours en voiture parce que c'est moins cher.

Quand il fait (3) ________________ , je nage dans la mer. Ça, c'est génial! On aime jouer au basket sur la plage et faire des pique-niques. Quelquefois, on va en ville pour faire les magasins. Il y a une très bonne pâtisserie où on vend des (4) ________________ délicieux. On peut aussi faire du canoë, mais je n'aime pas ça. Le soir, on joue aux cartes ou quelquefois on joue aux boules. C'est très (5) ________________ , j'adore ça. Deux ou trois fois par semaine, on va au restaurant pour (6) ________________ de la soupe aux poissons. C'est la spécialité de la région.

Passage B

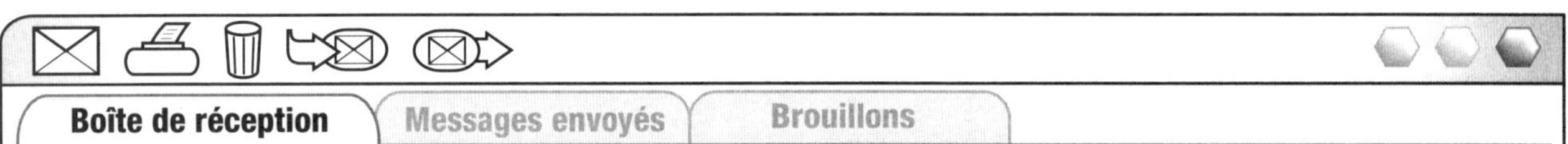

Mais l'année dernière, nous ne sommes pas allés dans le sud de la France. Nous avons décidé d'aller en Écosse parce que mes grands-parents y habitent. On a passé quinze jours là-bas, à la campagne. Normalement quand on va chez mes grands-parents, on voyage en avion parce que c'est rapide. Mais je déteste l'avion, donc on a voyagé en train. C'était moins rapide que l'avion, mais c'était très confortable.

On a fait beaucoup de promenades et de circuits à vélo. La campagne en Écosse est très belle. Mon père et mon grand-père aiment faire de la pêche, mais l'année dernière il n'y avait pas assez de poissons et c'était un peu ennuyeux. Faire de la pêche, c'est nul! J'ai bien aimé les repas du soir. Ma grand-mère a préparé des spécialités de la région. Je ne suis pas allé au restaurant une seule fois! Les vacances étaient bien, mais je préfère la plage à la campagne.

Lire 3

A **Lis Passage A à la page 130. Complète les phrases en choisissant la bonne lettre. (Level 5)**

Exemple: Marie-Yvonne est partie avec [L]

1 Elle est restée [ ]

2 Le camping était [ ]

3 Sa mère a eu [ ]

4 Son frère est resté trop longtemps [ ]

5 Marie-Yvonne a fait [ ]

5 Marie-Yvonne préfère [ ]

A très bien

B son père

C au soleil

D l'hôtel

E un accident

F de la pêche

G le camping

H à l'hôpital

I un mois au camping

J affreux

K deux semaines au camping

L sa famille

M du jet ski

Points	
Niveau	

B **Lis Passage A et Passage B à la page 130. Écris le bon prénom. (Level 6)**

Exemple: Qui est allé(e) en Angleterre l'année dernière? Maxime

1 Qui fait du camping normalement? ____________________

2 Qui n'a pas aimé ses vacances l'année dernière? ____________________

3 Qui a dû garder son frère? ____________________

4 Qui va faire du camping cette année? ____________________

5 Qui a eu du mauvais temps? ____________________

6 Qui a fait du jet-ski? ____________________

Points	
Niveau	

Contrôle

Nom: ....

Lire 3

Passage A

Normalement, nous passons nos vacances à l'hôtel, mais l'année dernière, j'ai fait du camping avec ma famille. Nous sommes partis pendant deux semaines au mois de juin. Le camping était très petit. Il n'y avait pas de restaurant, pas de piscine et pas de boutique non plus.

Il n'y avait pas d'activités sportives, même pas un court de tennis. Le premier jour, nous avons fait du vélo et ma mère est tombée. Nous avons passé l'après-midi à l'hôpital. Le deuxième jour, nous sommes allés à la plage et mon frère n'a pas mis de crème solaire et il a joué au volley sur la plage. Le soir, il était tout rouge!

Moi, je voulais faire du jet-ski, mais il y avait trop de vent et mon père a dit que c'était dangereux. Mon père, lui, il a décidé de faire une excursion en bateau – et il a vomi! Moi, j'ai choisi de faire du canoë sur le lac. L'année prochaine, je voudrais aller dans un grand hôtel. Le camping était vraiment nul!

Marie-Yvonne

Passage B

L'année dernière, nous sommes allés en Angleterre. On a passé dix jours à Londres. On a visité tous les monuments. Mon frère n'a pas aimé ça. C'est vrai qu'il a fait froid, mais mes parents ont adoré ça et moi aussi. C'était intéressant de voir une autre culture. Normalement, je préfère les vacances plus actives. J'adore faire du sport et en été, j'adore faire des sports nautiques. Cette année, on va aller dans le sud de la France. C'est bien parce qu'on va parler français! On va aller à la campagne, mais il y a un lac. On va camper. Je n'ai jamais fait du camping. Ça va être intéressant.

Maxime

L'année dernière, j'ai passé mes vacances en Espagne avec ma famille. Nous sommes allés au bord de la mer et nous avons logé dans un grand hôtel. Il y avait une grande piscine, mais il fallait surveiller les enfants de moins de 10 ans, donc j'ai passé beaucoup de temps à surveiller mon petit frère. Nous avons aussi fait beaucoup de sports nautiques et j'ai fait du jet-ski. C'était fantastique. Normalement, nous allons à la campagne et nous faisons du camping. J'adore ça. J'aime faire des promenades et du vélo, mais c'est vrai que quand il pleut ce n'est pas amusant. Je voudrais voyager et visiter beaucoup de pays. Cette année, nous allons visiter la Grèce. Ça va être génial. J'aime bien les pays chauds.

Léa

5 Contrôle

Voyages et vacances

Nom: ....

Écrire 1

A **Copie et complète les phrases pour tes vacances. (Level 3)**

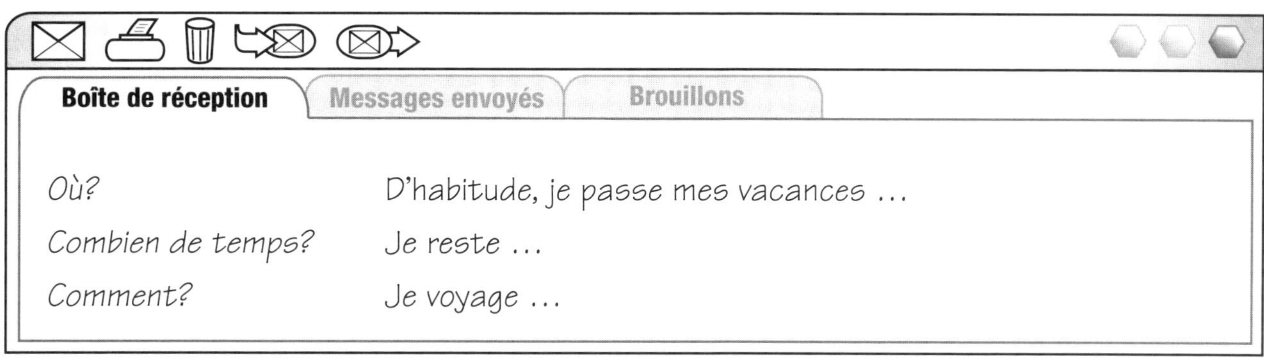

Où?	D'habitude, je passe mes vacances …
Combien de temps?	Je reste …
Comment?	Je voyage …

B **Décris ce que tu fais normalement pour les vacances (Level 4), et donne des exemples de ce que tu as fait l'année dernière (Level 5).**

Level information	Pupil support	Example
You can show achievement at Level 3, 4 or 5 depending on how you carry out the task.		
Level 3: Complete the sentences.	• Complete the sentences to describe your holiday.	*D'habitude, je passe mes vacances à la campagne en Espagne.*
Level 4: Write a short text describing your holidays. Make your writing more interesting by adding negatives, connectives, intensifiers and opinions.	• Describe your usual holidays. Say where you go, who you go with, how you get there, how long you stay and what activities you do. • Mention something you do not do.	*D'habitude, je vais en Écosse avec ma mère, son petit ami et mon frère … Je passe … Je reste …*
Level 5: As Level 4, but include a description of your last holiday. Use the perfect tense, with appropriate time expressions. Include reasons for your opinions.	• Give an account of your last holiday (where you went, how long you stayed, who you went with, how you got there, what activities you did). • Give reasons for your opinions.	*Par exemple, l'année dernière on est allés en Écosse et j'ai visité des châteaux. C'était affreux! Je préfère faire du shopping en ville.*

Contrôle

Nom: ....

Écrire 2

A Écris un email à un(e) ami(e). Tu as gagné une compétition et tu vas aller en vacances. Décris ce que tu fais d'habitude en vacances – ce que tu aimes faire, ce que tu n'aimes pas faire. Où vas-tu aller et qu'est-ce que tu vas faire avec ton argent? (Levels 4–5)

B Ton frère/Ta sœur a passé des vacances exotiques. Parle de ses expériences. Demande à ton ami(e) ses opinions/des conseils. (Level 6)

Level information	Pupil support	Example
You can show achievement at Level 4, 5 or 6 depending on how you carry out the task.		
Level 4: In your email, start with a short description of what you usually do on holiday. Say what you like and dislike. Make your writing more interesting by including negatives, connectives, intensifiers and opinions.	• Give information about your typical holiday, saying what you like and dislike about it. Mention four activities. • Say whether you/other members of your family speak a foreign language.	*D'habitude, je vais en Espagne avec ma famille; ma mère, mon père et ma sœur. En vacance, j'aime aller … mais je n'aime pas … C'est trop …*
Level 5: As Level 4, but include details of where you are going to go on holiday and what you are going to do with your winnings from the competition. Use the near future tense, with appropriate time expressions. Include reasons for your opinions.	• Describe your plans for the holiday, giving information about at least two destinations; where you are going, how, and who with. • Describe what you are going to do, linking this to your likes and dislikes. • Mention what there is in the country/city to see and to do. • Justify any opinions given.	*Au mois de juin, je vais aller en Chine avec ma famille. Nous allons visiter … J'aime visiter les monuments …*
Level 6: As Level 5, but include longer descriptions and extra detail. Extend your answers, using different tenses (present, perfect, future) where appropriate and more varied language, adapting grammatical structures.	• Include information about the experiences of a friend/brother/ sister who has had an exotic holiday in the past. • Ask your friend's opinion/advice on your plans. • When giving opinions, use more varied structures such as *assez de* and *trop de*.	*L'année dernière, ma sœur est allée au Japon. Elle a travaillé dans une école et puis elle a fait le tour du Japon … Elle pense que c'était trop … et …*

Teacher's Notes

Contrôle Module 5

Listening and reading assessment criteria
Mark scheme: 1 mark for each correct answer. Total for each task: 6 marks. For details of the sublevels see p. 167.

Écouter 1A [AT1 Level 3] 

This task tests understanding of short passages in the context of holidays. Pupils identify the topic of each exchange. There are two distractors. Play the recording twice. This task is similar to Asset Preliminary French Listening (internal), Grade 4, Task C.1.

Go to p. 167

Audioscript 22

Exemple:
- *Normalement pour les vacances, on reste en France, mais cet été on va en Espagne. Où vas-tu?*
- *Nous, on va toujours en Italie pour rendre visite à ma grand-mère.*

1 – *Quelle sorte de vacances préfères-tu?*
- *Je préfère les vacances actives.*
- *Moi, aussi.*
- *J'adore les sports nautiques, le ski nautique, le canoë.*
- *Moi, je préfère faire du vélo.*

2 – *Tu pars quand en vacances?*
- *En août.*
- *Ça va être fantastique.*
- *Oui, mais j'y vais avec mes parents! Je préfère partir avec mes amis.*
- *Pourquoi?*
- *C'est plus amusant. Parfois, c'est ennuyeux avec mes parents.*

3 – *Tu aimes faire du camping?*
- *Oui, j'adore ça. Nous faisons du camping chaque été. Nous allons toujours dans les grands campings où on trouve une piscine, un restaurant et des magasins.*
- *Personnellement, je préfère l'hôtel. C'est plus confortable.*

4 – *Où vas-tu passer tes vacances cette année?*
- *On va à la campagne.*
- *Tu aimes ça?*
- *Non, je déteste ça! C'est ennuyeux et il n'y a pas de magasins.*
- *Moi, je n'aime pas aller à la montagne. Ça aussi, c'est ennuyeux!*

5 – *Tu pars samedi?*
- *Oui, à 6h du matin!*
- *Où vas-tu?*
- *On va dans le sud de la France.*
- *Ah c'est loin, ça.*
- *Oui, je sais. Ça va prendre 5 heures.*
- *Vous y aller en voiture?*
- *Non, papa n'aime pas faire de longs voyages en voiture. On prend le train.*

6 – *Où vas-tu cette année?*
- *On va en Espagne.*
- *Vous allez à l'hôtel?*
- *Oui, on va rester trois semaines dans un grand hôtel au bord de la mer.*
- *Trois semaines! Tu as de la chance. Moi, je vais partir seulement deux semaines.*
- *Normalement on part deux semaines, mais cette année, ma mère veut rester plus longtemps.*

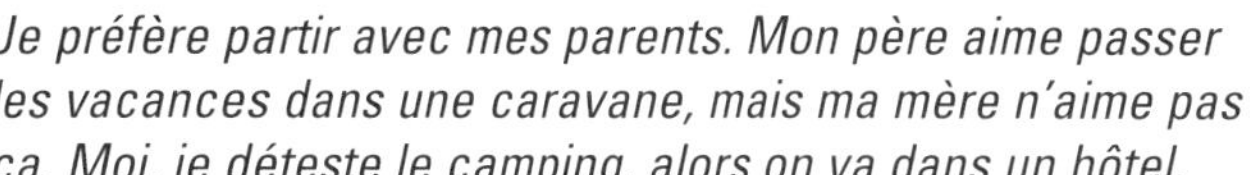

Réponses 1 F 2 C 3 D 4 I 5 A 6 E

Écouter 1B [AT1 Level 4]

This task tests understanding of a longer passage in the context of holidays. The questions are multiple choice. Play the recording twice.

Audioscript 23

Je préfère partir avec mes parents. Mon père aime passer les vacances dans une caravane, mais ma mère n'aime pas ça. Moi, je déteste le camping, alors on va dans un hôtel.

Quelquefois on va à la campagne, mais c'est un peu ennuyeux. Je préfère aller au bord de la mer, il y a plus à faire. On part toujours en voiture. Personnellement j'aime l'avion, mais c'est trop cher tout comme le train.

Cette année, on va faire beaucoup d'activités. Mon père aime faire de la pêche et cette année, il va essayer le tir à l'arc. Moi, je préfère faire du vélo. Ma mère aime jouer aux boules. Elle adore aussi faire les boutiques, mais je déteste faire ça. Je voudrais visiter d'autres pays. L'année prochaine mon père veut aller en Espagne, mais ma mère veut aller en Angleterre. Moi, je voudrais visiter l'Italie pour manger de la nourriture italienne.

Réponses 1 C 2 B 3 B 4 B 5 C 6 B

Écouter 2A [AT1 Level 4]

This task tests understanding of a longer passage in the context of holiday activities. Although it includes the near future tense, understanding of tense usage is not tested. Pupils identify what each person does, ticking the correct column. There are two distractors. Play the recording twice.

Audioscript 24

- *Alors, Henri, qu'est-ce que vous allez faire, toi et ta famille?*
- *Le matin, on va tous faire du jogging!*
- *Et après ça?*
- *Alors, mon père est un peu fatigué. Il ne veut plus faire du sport. Aujourd'hui, il va aller en ville pour acheter des souvenirs. Ma mère par contre veut bronzer, donc elle va passer la journée à la plage.*
- *Et ton frère et tes sœurs?*
- *Alors, Rachelle va prendre le train pour aller à la campagne. Il y a une belle forêt avec un lac. Kévin veut voir la Tapisserie de Bayeux parce qu'il adore l'histoire. Nathalie veut faire du sport. Elle aime nager, mais elle ne veut pas aller à la plage avec ma mère. Je crois qu'elle va louer un vélo.*
- *Et toi, Henri?*
- *Moi, je veux aller en ville pour manger des crêpes. C'est la spécialité de la région.*

Teacher's Notes

Contrôle Module 5

Réponses 1 I 2 E 3 B 4 D 5 H 6 C

Écouter 2B [AT1 Level 5]

This task tests understanding of a passage (including the ability to distinguish between past and present) in the context of holiday activities. Pupils identify the six activities done, ticking the six correct boxes. There are six distractors. Play the recording twice.

Audioscript 25

Salut! Moi, je suis Chloé. Cette année, j'ai passé mes vacances dans un centre de vacances. C'était bien parce qu'il y avait beaucoup à faire. La plage était tout près et le premier jour nous y sommes allés.

Ma sœur adore le tennis, donc le deuxième jour elle a joué au tennis. Moi, j'aime faire du ski nautique, mais il n'y en avait pas. Alors, j'ai joué aux boules sur la plage.

Normalement je déteste la pêche et je préfère faire du sport, mais le troisième jour, j'ai accompagné mon père et nous avons attrapé trois poissons. En vacances on fait toujours du vélo, mais il n'y avait pas assez de vélos. Donc moi et ma sœur, nous avons fait du tir à l'arc. C'était pas mal, mais ma sœur était nulle!

Le cinquième jour, ma mère a décidé de visiter le musée. Normalement, je vais au musée avec ma mère, mais je voulais acheter un cadeau pour mes grands-parents, donc je suis allée en ville. Le samedi soir, ma sœur et moi, nous avons décidé de jouer au golf à neuf trous, mais il y avait trop de touristes. Donc, nous sommes allées dans la salle de jeux. Le dernier jour, je voulais faire du banana-riding, mais il y avait trop de vent donc, ma famille et moi, nous sommes allés au restaurant!

Réponses A, C, F, H, I, K

Écouter 3A [AT1 Level 5]

This task tests understanding of a longer passage featuring a wider range of language and two tenses (perfect and present) in the context of holidays. Pupils tick the six correct sentences. There are six distractors. Play the recording twice.

Audioscript 26

Cette année, j'ai passé mes vacances avec ma copine à la campagne dans le nord de la France. Normalement, je passe un mois avec mes parents au bord de la mer. Mais là, j'ai passé deux semaines près de Dinard.

Ma copine, Khalida, a le même âge que moi et elle est très amusante, mais elle parle tout le temps! Nous sommes restées dans un centre de vacances où il y avait des courts de tennis et des boutiques sur place. La piscine était fermée, mais de toute façon il a fait froid et il a plu. Heureusement nous avons apporté des vêtements chauds! L'année prochaine je voudrais aller dans un pays chaud.

Dans notre chambre, il y avait un coin cuisine où j'ai préparé à manger le soir. J'adore faire ça – heureusement parce que le restaurant était très cher! Nous avons loué des vélos pour visiter la région. Il y avait beaucoup d'Anglais dans le centre et c'était bien parce que nous avons parlé avec eux et le soir nous avons joué au baby-foot ensemble. Les vacances étaient assez bien, mais il n'y avait pas assez d'activités. C'était un peu ennuyeux.

Réponses 2, 5, 6, 8, 9, 12

Écouter 3B [AT1 Level 6]

This task tests understanding of a passage (including the ability to distinguish between past, present and future) in the context of holidays. Play the recording twice.

Audioscript 27

Je préfère passer mes vacances au bord de la mer. Parfois on reste en France, parfois on va à l'étranger. Je n'aime pas aller dans le même endroit chaque année. En vacances, j'aime faire des excursions et faire un peu de sport.

L'année dernière, je suis allé en Grèce avec ma famille. Il y avait beaucoup de soleil, ce qui était bien. L'hôtel était près de la plage et était très grand. Il y avait tout – des restaurants, des boutiques, beaucoup d'activités sportives, le tennis, le golf, le basket, une piscine, tout! C'était comme un centre de vacances!

Mes parents ont bronzé et ma sœur a fait des excursions en bateau pour visiter les plages. Moi, j'ai fait de la plongée tous les jours, j'adore faire ça en vacances. J'ai vu plein de poissons exotiques. J'ai aussi essayé le ski nautique pour la première fois. C'était assez difficile … et très fatigant! Les vacances étaient incroyables et je voudrais bien y retourner.

Cette année, on va passer les vacances en Angleterre, car ma mère veut y retourner. Moi, je n'y suis jamais allé. Apparemment il y a beaucoup de monuments à visiter. C'est ce que ma mère veut faire. Moi, je veux faire les magasins et acheter beaucoup de vêtements.

Réponses 1 B 2 C 3 B 4 A 5 C 6 B

Speaking and writing assessment criteria
See the level information supplied on the Assessment sheet. For detailed Assessment criteria (including sublevels) see pages 168 and 169.

Use *Parler/Écrire 1* in the first instance if you are unsure of which level to give a particular learner.

Parler 1 [AT2 Levels 3–5]

This task tests the ability to put together a simple conversation in the context of talking about a holiday centre. Pupils who can include information on a trip to the holiday centre last year (showing use of the perfect tense in addition to the present tense) can attain Level 5.

Teacher's Notes

Contrôle Module 5

Parler 2 [AT2 Levels 4–6]

This task tests the ability to prepare and deliver a presentation about a visit to a holiday centre. Opportunities are given to work in different time frames, and to add more complex structures in order to reach higher levels.

The task gives pupils the opportunity to reach Level 6 by requiring the use of a range of tenses (past, present and future) and that they respond to simple prepared questions on the presentation. Possible questions: What did your mother do yesterday? What will your sister do tomorrow?

Lire 1A [AT3 Level 3]

This task tests understanding of short texts in the context of holiday activities. Pupils identify the two activities for each person, ticking the correct columns. There is one distractor.

Réponses **1** D, I **2** F, G **3** B, H

Lire 1B [AT3 Level 4]

This task tests understanding of a short text in the context of holiday activities. Pupils identify the activities for the days of the week, filling in the letters in the diary. There are four distractors.

Réponses
mardi I **mercredi** D **jeudi** J **vendredi** E
samedi G **dimanche** B

Lire 2A [AT3 Level 4] 'a'

This task tests understanding of a short text in the context of holidays. Pupils read Passage A (a gap-fill text) and select the missing words to complete it. The questions are multiple choice.

This task is similar to Asset Preliminary French Reading (internal), Grade 4, Task D.1. Go to p. 167

Réponses
1 trois semaines **2** voyage **3** chaud
4 gâteaux **5** amusant **6** manger

Lire 2B [AT3 Level 5]

This task tests understanding of a text (including the ability to distinguish between past and present) in the context of holidays. Pupils read Passage A and Passage B and tick the six correct sentences. There are six distractors.

Réponses 3, 6, 7, 8, 11, 12

Lire 3A [AT3 Level 5]

This task tests understanding of a text featuring a wider range of language and two tenses (perfect and present) in the context of holidays. Pupils read Passage A and complete the sentences choosing from the answers given. There are six distractors.

Réponses **1** K **2** J **3** E **4** C **5** F **6** D

Lire 3B [AT3 Level 6]

This task tests understanding of a text (including the ability to distinguish between past, present and future) in the context of holidays. Pupils read Passage A and Passage B and answer each question by writing the appropriate name.

Réponses
1 Léa **2** Marie-Yvonne **3** Léa **4** Maxime
5 Maxime **6** Léa

Écrire 1 [AT4 Levels 3–5]

Give this sheet only to pupils who are working at Levels 3–5. This task tests the ability to write a short paragraph in the context of holidays. In Section A pupils describe their usual family holiday completing the sentences supplied (Level 3). In Section B (Levels 4–5) pupils write in more detail about their typical holiday and a recent holiday: this section gives pupils the opportunity to reach Level 5 by requiring the use of the perfect tense, including appropriate time expressions.

Écrire 2 [AT4 Levels 4–6]

This task tests the ability to write a text about a holiday pupils are planning now they have won a competition, bringing in their likes/dislikes of the sort of holidays they usually have.

Pupils who feel more confident can complete both Sections A and B. Section A (Levels 4–5) gives pupils the opportunity to reach Level 5 by requiring the use of the near future tense, including appropriate time expressions. Section B (Level 6) involves a variety of time frames (past, present and future) and encourages pupils to extend their descriptions and use a wider range of structures.

Answers to Challenge, page 115
B 1D, 2B, 3E, 4F, 5C, 6A

Grammaire
Les déterminants possessifs

A Complete the chart to show the different words for *my* and *his* or *her*.

	In front of a masculine singular noun	In front of a feminine singular noun	In front of a plural noun
my			
your	ton	ta	tes
his / her			

B Complete the sentences with the correct possessive adjectives.

1 Où est ______________ baladeur? (my)
2 Il a perdu ______________ veste. (his)
3 Elle a oublié ______________ classeur. (her)
4 Donne-moi ______________ bonbons. (your)
5 Il va chez ______________ grand-mère. (his)
6 As-tu vu ______________ boucles d'oreille? (my)
7 Tu vas porter ______________ robe bleue. (your)
8 C'est ______________ CD. (your)

The table below shows how to say **our**, **your** (in the plural and formal form) and **their**. The same form is used for both masculine and feminine singular nouns.

	In front of a masculine singular noun	In front of a feminine singular noun	In front of a plural noun
our	notre jardin	notre maison	nos parents
your	votre jardin	votre maison	vos parents
their	leur jardin	leur maison	leurs parents

C Complete the sentences with the correct possessive adjectives.

Nous avons perdu
1 __________ appareil photo numérique ,
2 __________ ordinateur,
3 __________ livres,
4 __________ voiture,
5 __________ jeux de console
et **6** __________ chien!

Sortez
7 __________ cahiers,
8 __________ crayons,
9 __________ stylos,
10 __________ règles,
11 __________ gommes et
12 __________ devoirs.

Ils ont perdu
13 __________ argent,
14 __________ maison,
15 __________ voiture,
16 __________ enfants
et **17** __________ chaussures.

Learning skills

Looking up adjectives in a dictionary

When you look up the French for an **adjective** in a dictionary, it will normally give you the **masculine singular** form. Some adjectives are irregular, so a detailed dictionary will give you the feminine form, too.

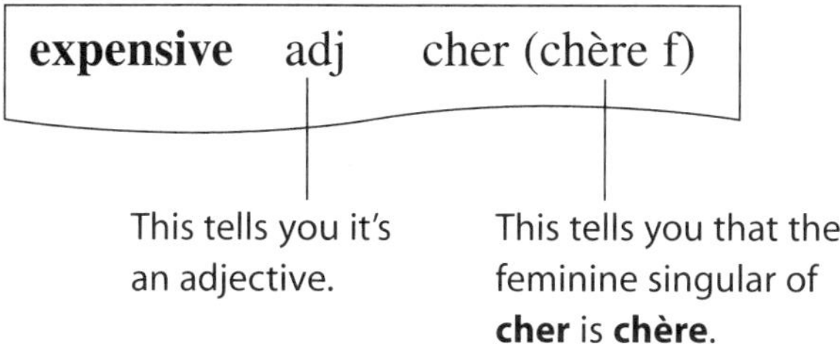

So, if you want to say 'I bought an expensive watch', you would say:
J'ai acheté une montre chère.

Most French adjectives come **after** the noun they describe. But a few important ones come **before** the noun. A detailed dictionary will tell you this.

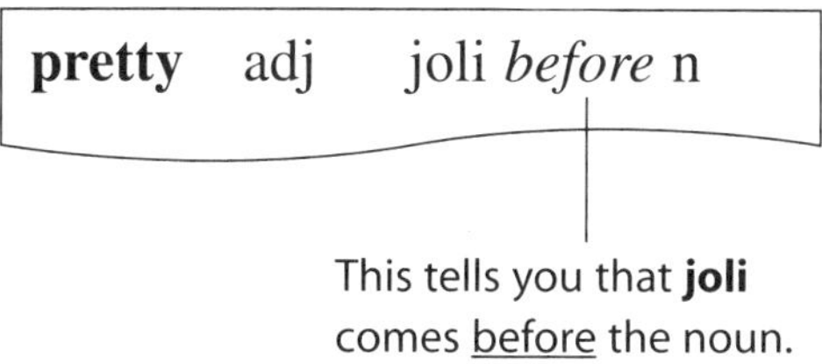

So, if you want to say 'I bought a pretty watch', you would say: **J'ai acheté une jolie montre**.

The adjective **joli** agrees with the subject, **une montre**, which is feminine, so an **-e** is added on the end.

A **Use a dictionary to work out how to say the following. Remember to:**

- **make the adjective agree with the noun (masculine or feminine)**
- **check whether the adjective is one of the few that comes before the noun.**

1 a strange camera ______________________

2 a noisy television ______________________

3 an old mobile phone ______________________

4 an old radio ______________________

5 a new keyboard ______________________

6 a new watch ______________________

7 a beautiful personal stereo ______________________

8 a beautiful car ______________________

Lesson starter

Normally, last year and this summer

Work with a partner. Use the grid below to challenge each other. One person says the letter and number of a square (B4) and the other says a sentence in the present, past or future tense. Use the following verbs: *aller, rester, jouer, visiter.*

Exemple: L'année dernière, je suis allé(e) au bord de la mer.

	A Normalement	B L'année dernière	C Cet été
1			
2			
3			
4			

Grammaire

Le présent, le passé et le futur proche

A Présent

Il **mange** beaucoup de chocolat.

B Passé

Il **a mangé** trop de chocolat.

C Futur

Il **va manger** un fruit.

A **Which tense do these words indicate? Write the numbers in the table.**

1 maintenant
2 hier
3 l'année prochaine
4 samedi dernier
5 l'année dernière
6 demain
7 en ce moment
8 dimanche prochain

Present	Past	Future

B **Underline the correct verb form to complete the sentences.**

1 Demain, **je fais/j'ai fait/je vais faire** du jet-ski.
2 Hier, **je regarde/j'ai regardé/je vais regarder** une série policière.
3 L'été prochain, **je vais/je suis allé/je vais aller** en Espagne.
4 En ce moment, **je lis/j'ai lu/je vais lire** le nouveau Harry Potter.
5 Samedi dernier, **j'achète/j'ai acheté/je vais acheter** un appareil photo numérique.

C **Complete the table with the perfect tense and the immediate future forms of the verbs.**

	Le présent	Le passé	Le futur proche
1	je regarde		
2	je travaille		
3	je finis		
4	je prends		

D **Write sentences using the verbs from task C in all three tenses.**

Exemple: Normalement, je regarde les dessins animés, mais hier, j'ai regardé une série policière et demain, je vais regarder un documentaire.

Thinking skills

Odd-one-out

A **Work in a group. Each set of verbs includes an odd-one-out, which is circled. Can you work out why it is the odd-one-out?**

1 peux	(aime)	dois	veux
2 (mange)	voudrais	vais	déteste
3 aller	rester	(travailler)	sortir
4 (faire)	visiter	finir	attendre
5 boire	lire	(prendre)	voir

B **This time, the odd-one-out is not circled. Which one is it and why? You might have different ideas from the rest of your group, so be prepared to justify your choices.**

1 préfère	déteste	veux	aime
2 vais	allons	va	voudrais
3 acheter	aller	faire	jouer
4 lu	regardé	fait	dit
5 sortir	passer	gagner	rencontrer

C **Make up more sets of odd-ones-out, using verbs, for other groups to try.**

____

____

____

____

____

Les copains **6**

Grammaire

L'infinitif

In both sentences below, there are two verbs. The second one is in the infinitive form. Remember that an infinitive in French ends in **-er**, **-ir** or **-re**.

J'**aime écouter** de la musique.
Je **voudrais acheter** un baladeur mp3.

A **Match up the French expressions with their English translations.**

1 J'aime sortir.
2 Je peux sortir.
3 Je dois sortir.
4 Je voudrais sortir.
5 Je vais sortir.

A I would like to go out.
B I must go out.
C I like going out.
D I'm going to go out.
E I can go out.

B **Write five sentences using the words in the table.**

J'aime/Je n'aime pas Je voudrais/ne voudrais pas Je dois/ne dois pas Je peux/ne peux pas Je veux/ne veux pas Je vais/ne vais pas	faire mes devoirs. dormir en classe. travailler en classe. manger en classe. écouter le professeur. devenir professeur. aller au collège. regarder la télé après 21h.

____

____

____

____

____

C **Teacher's pet. Translate these sentences into French.**

1 He likes to work in class. ______________________________
2 He must listen to the teacher. ______________________________
3 He mustn't eat in class. ______________________________
4 He cannot sleep in class. ______________________________
5 He would like to become a teacher. ______________________________

Défi

Projets, ambitions et rêves

A Look at the list of dreams and ambitions for the future. Think about them for you personally and write each letter in the appropriate part of the Venn diagrams.

A Je voudrais faire des sports extrêmes, comme le kite surf ou le parapente.
B Je voudrais rencontrer des amis dans les pays étrangers.
C Je voudrais faire du théâtre et devenir célèbre.
D Je voudrais avoir un bon emploi et gagner beaucoup d'argent.
E Je voudrais traverser le Sahara en moto.
F Je voudrais faire de la plongée sous-marine.
G Je voudrais travailler à l'étranger pour améliorer mon français.
H Je voudrais rencontrer mon héros.
I Je voudrais visiter des pays exotiques.
J Je voudrais être heureux/euse et rencontrer mon/ma partenaire de rêve.
K Je voudrais jouer au foot pour mon club préféré.
L Je voudrais acheter une belle voiture et habiter dans une grande maison.

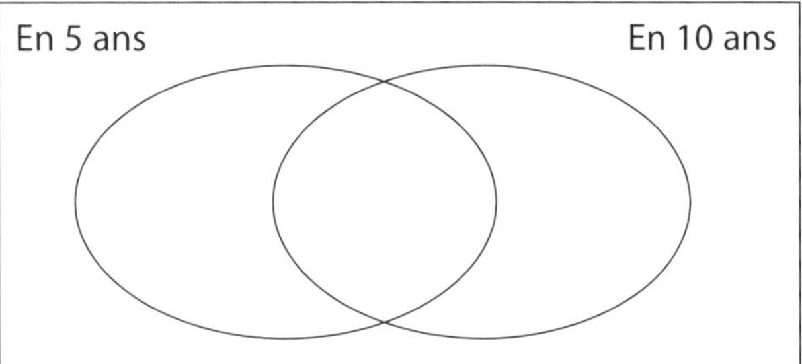

- If a sentence falls into both categories, put it in the intersecting area in the middle.
- If a sentence falls into neither category, put it in the box, but outside the circles.

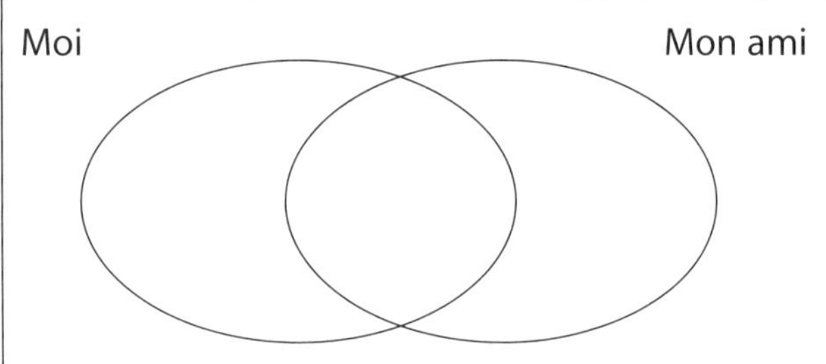

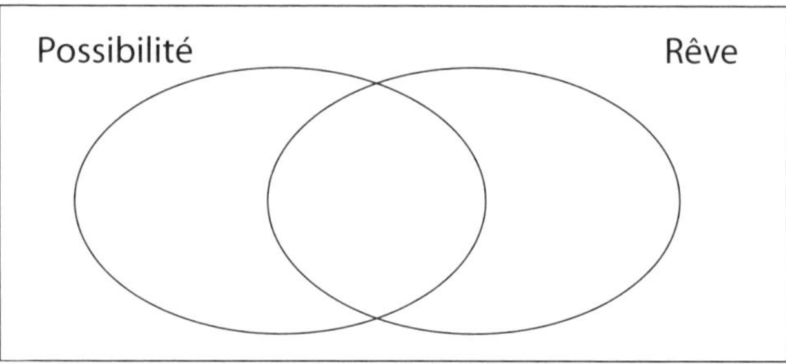

B Write three sentences about plans/ambitions/dreams of your own not covered in the list above.

____

____

____

C Quels sont tes projets pour l'avenir? Copy and complete the spider diagram: use it to structure your thoughts so you can take part in a conversation. Add more circles as required.

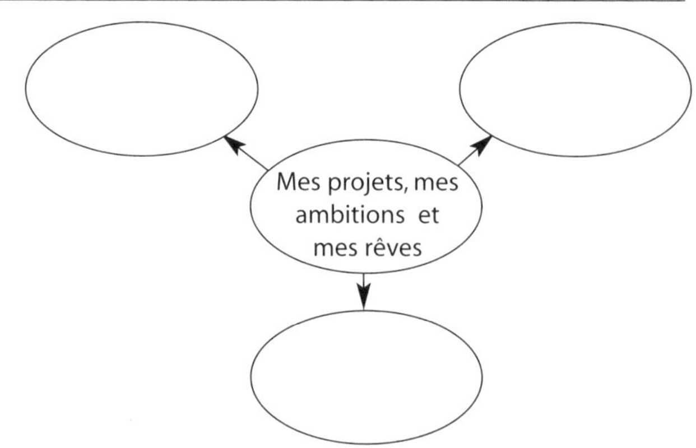

6 Défi
Projets, ambitions et rêves

Assignment 6 Challenge

Prepare a description of your thoughts and aspirations for the future. Work in groups to discuss these then critically review the group's performance. Repeat the performance in order to refine your speaking and listening skills.

Assignment 6 Support grid

Level 3	Say three things you would like to do in the future, and ask someone about his/her plans. Include a connective.	*Je voudrais faire du karting.* *Quels sont tes projets pour l'avenir?*
Level 4	Give information about your dreams and ambitions and say how they link to what you do/like doing now. Ask others about their plans. Include short descriptions and opinions. Use intensifiers, connectives and adjectives.	■ *Jan, quels sont tes rêves?* ● *Je voudrais devenir célèbre. Je joue souvent au tennis, et je voudrais être champion de tennis …*
Level 5	As Level 4, but add details of specific plans, using the near future tense. Justify opinions. Use a dictionary to say something original.	*Je voudrais faire un tour du monde. J'aime bien voyager. Par exemple, cet été, je vais aller en France …*
Level 6	As Level 5, but use a broader range of vocabulary and structures. Use the perfect tense to give examples of what you have already done. Use modals and the comparative and superlative. Ask and answer a range of related questions.	*Je voudrais faire un tour du monde. L'année dernière, ma famille et moi, nous sommes allés au Maroc. C'était fantastique. Jeannie, es-tu allée au Maroc?*

Assignment 6 Judging grid

Points per level reached as shown plus 1 point for each of the other criteria.

(L3 = **1**, L4 = **2**, L5 = **3**, L6 = **4**)		All group members worked from notes rather than a script.		
All group members participated.		All group members interacted well.		
All group members spoke clearly and confidently.		All group members contributed in assessing performance.		Total
All group members encouraged each other to participate by asking questions.				/10

Projects, ambitions et rêves: guidelines for teachers

For general guidelines on how to get the most out of the *Défi* sections, see page 14.

Use this activity instead of activities 5 and 6 on page 105 of the Pupil's Book.

1 Hand out the activity sheet and ask pupils to do exercises A–C. Activity C allows pupils to think strategically about what they are going to say in the conversation by creating a simple mind-map.

2 Pupils then conduct a discussion in groups of four. They critically evaluate their group performance, using the criteria in the judging grid. Once possible improvements have been identified, they then have the discussion again.

English Programme of Study	2.1 Key processes; speaking and listening.
Levels accessed	Levels 3–6
Key vocabulary	*Expo 2 Rouge* Pupil's Book, Module 6, pages 112–113

Vocabulaire

Opinions et passe-temps / *Opinions and interests*

Mon sport préféré, c'est ...	*My favourite sport is ...*
Mon émission préférée, c'est ...	*My favourite programme is ...*
Mes matières préférées sont ...	*My favourite subjects are ...*
Mes acteurs/ chanteurs préférés sont ...	*My favourite actors/ singers are ...*
Je n'ai pas de chanteur préféré.	*I don't have a favourite singer.*
Notre collège s'appelle ...	*Our school is called ...*
Notre cantine est moderne.	*Our canteen is modern.*
Nos profs sont rigolos.	*Our teachers are funny.*

L'argent de poche / *Pocket money*

J'achète ...	*I buy ...*
des bonbons et des chocolats	*sweets and chocolates*
des magazines	*magazines*
des cadeaux	*presents*
du maquillage	*make-up*
du matérial scolaire	*things for school*
des CD et des DVD	*CDs and DVDs*
des baskets	*trainers*
des jeux de console	*console games*
Je n'achète jamais ... de chocolat.	*I never buy ... chocolate(s).*
J'économise pour ...	*I'm saving for ...*
J'ai besoin ...	*I need ...*
J'ai besoin de baskets.	*I need some trainers.*

Les cadeaux / *Presents*

un jeu pour PC	*a computer game*
un jeu pour Gameboy	*a Gameboy game*
un jeu de société (version électronique)	*a board game (electronic version)*
un lecteur karaoké	*a karaoke machine*
une voiture radiocommandée	*a radio-controlled car*
un paquet de classeurs	*a pack of files*
Ça coûte ...	*It costs ...*
Merci pour le cadeau.	*Thank you for the present.*
Tu es vraiment généreux.	*It's really kind of you.*
C'est parfait.	*It's perfect.*

Les gadgets / *Gadgets*

le téléphone portable	*mobile phone*
le caméscope	*camcorder*
le baladeur mp3	*mp3 walkman*
le clavier électronique	*electronic keyboard*
la manette	*gamepad*
l'appareil photo numérique	*digital camera*
l'organiseur électronique	*PDA (electronic organiser)*

Les comparaisons / *Comparing things*

plus cher que	*more expensive than*
plus grand que	*bigger than*
moins grand que	*smaller than*
le meilleur cadeau	*the best present*
compliqué(e)	*complicated*
démodé(e)	*old-fashioned*
facile à utiliser	*easy to use*
difficile à utiliser	*difficult to use*
pratique	*practical*
utile	*useful*
élégant(e)	*elegant*
amusant(e)	*amusing*
cher (chère)	*expensive*
C'est génial!	*It's great!*
C'est trop cher!	*It's too expensive!*
Ce n'est pas mal.	*It's not bad.*
C'est nul!	*It's rubbish!*

Vocabulaire

Les expressions de temps	*Time phrases*
l'année dernière	*last year*
samedi dernier	*last Saturday*
normalement	*normally*
généralement	*generally*
d'habitude	*usually*
de temps en temps	*from time to time*
des fois	*sometimes*
cet été	*this summer*
l'été prochain	*next summer*
l'année prochaine	*next year*

Dans tes rêves	*In your dreams*
Je voudrais ...	*I would like to ...*
rencontrer des garçons sympas	*meet nice boys*
jouer au foot pour mon club	*play football for my club*
acheter une moto	*buy a motorbike*
faire du jet-ski	*go jet-skiing*
devenir chanteur de rock	*become a rock star*
rencontrer mon héros	*meet my hero*
célèbre	*famous*
gagner une compétition	*win a competition*
passer l'été sur la plage	*spend the summer on the beach*
visiter des pays exotiques	*visit exotic countries*
travailler sur un film	*work on a film*

Objectifs

Nom: ....

Module 5 Attainment			This module (M6) targets	
Listening			Listening	
Speaking			Speaking	
Reading			Reading	
Writing			Writing	

Before	Level 3 (Short sentences linked together, short conversations)	Mid	End
	Working with a partner, ask and answer questions on our favourite sports, television programmes and singers. **G** Use possessive pronouns.		
	Write three sentences about my class's preferences. Give information about our favourite teacher, favourite subject and favourite sport. **G** Use possessive pronouns.		
	Write three sentences about what I do with my pocket money. Say what I buy and what I am saving for.		
	Choose two gadgets and describe them. Include information on what they cost. **G** Make the adjectives agree.		

Before	Level 4 (Short texts and longer conversations, short presentations)	Mid	End
	In a short paragraph, talk about things I like/don't like, including details of my favourite actor, singer, teacher, subject and sport. Include connectives and intensifiers. **G** Include at least one negative.		
	Write a short article for the school website giving information on our school and details of our class's likes and dislikes. Describe the gym and the canteen, and mention four favourite things. Include connectives, intensifiers and opinions.		
	Working with a partner, interview each other about pocket money. Ask each other what we usually buy, what we need to buy, what we save for and what we never buy. Respond, including connectives, intensifiers and opinions. **G** Use *j'ai besoin de*.		
	Write a short paragraph giving my opinion on at least three gadgets. Mention their price and describe them, using a variety of adjectives. Include connectives and intensifiers. **G** Use comparatives and superlatives and include at least two negatives.		
	Write a formal thank you letter to a relative who has given me a birthday present. Include information about the gift and my opinion of the gift, giving reasons. Use connectives, intensifiers and opinions.		
	Give a short presentation on what I would like to do and what I would not like to do this summer. **G** Use *je voudrais* and include at least one negative.		

Objectifs

Nom: ....

Before	Level 5 (Longer texts and more detailed conversations, longer presentations)	Mid	End
	Write a text about a planned holiday. Give information about where, when, how and with whom I am going, and where I am staying. Say which activities I am going to do. Include information about where I usually go and what I usually do. Include and justify opinions. **G** Use the near future tense and the present tense. Include at least two negatives.		
	Imagine I'm going on a weekend break with my parents somewhere I don't want to go. Give a presentation about my parents' plans (where, when, how and with whom we are going), and compare these with my preferences and what I would like to do. Include and justify opinions. **G** Use the near future tense and the present tense. Use *je voudrais*. Include at least two negatives.		

Before	Level 6 (Longer texts and short talks/more detailed conversations using known language and structures in new contexts)	Mid	End
	Working with a partner, have a conversation about ideal holidays that we are both planning. Seek and give information about what my family and I like doing on holiday, and what the plans are for this holiday. Make reference to positive and negative experiences from holidays in the past. Include and justify opinions. **G** Use the perfect, present and near future tenses as appropriate. Include the comparative and superlative and at least two negatives.		
	Give a presentation on my weekend. Give information about what I usually do at the weekend, talk about last weekend as an example, and give plans for the coming weekend. Include and justify opinions. Be ready to answer simple prepared questions about the presentation. **G** Use the perfect, present and near future tenses as appropriate. Include modal verbs.		
	My teacher is wild! Write a paragraph about his/her plans and dreams for this coming year. Give details of four activities he/she is going to do, linking these to his/her likes and dislikes and past experiences. Also mention two things he/she would like to do. **G** Use the perfect, present and near future tenses as appropriate. Use *je voudrais* and the comparative and superlative and include at least two negatives.		

Personal Targets	Mid	End

Target Setting

Fill in the levels you reached in Module 5, then decide which level you are aiming for in Module 6 in each skill.

Go to the objective grid for your target level and decide which objectives you are going to focus on. You may want to include an objective from the level below or the level above, to help you make the transition from a lower to a higher level. Put a mark in the **Before** column for your chosen objectives.

To help you fill in your personal targets, you may like to refer to pages 164–166 for ideas.

Contrôle

Nom: ....

Écouter 1

A Écoute et écris la bonne lettre. (Level 3)

A 

B 

C 

D 

E 

F 

G 

H 

I 

J 

K

L 

M 

Points	
Niveau	

Exemple: Julien va passer ses vacances ... K

1 Il aime manger ... ☐

2 Il aime aller ... ☐

3 D'habitude il reste ... ☐

4 Il fait ... ☐

5 Comme sport il voudrait ☐

6 Il voudrait aussi ... ☐

B 'a' You will hear six conversations. What are they about? Match each extract you hear to the correct heading by writing a letter (A–I) in the box. (Level 4)

Example	D
1	
2	
3	
4	
5	
6	

A Jobs
B The weather
C Interests
D Sport
E TV programmes
F Going out
G Shopping
H Holidays
I Eating out

Points	
Niveau	

6 Contrôle

Les copains

Nom: ……………………………………………………………………

Écouter 2

A Écoute et écris les bonnes lettres dans la case. (Level 4)

A  
B 
C 
D 
E 
F 
G 
H 
I 
J 
K 
L 
M 
N 

Joachim aime …
Exemple: J

Points	
Niveau	

B Écoute et coche (✔) les six bonnes images. (Level 5)

Qu'est-ce qu'Amélie va faire en vacances?

A  ☐
B  ☐
C  ☐
D  ☐
E  ☐
F  ☐
G  ☐
H  ☐
I  ☐
J  ☐
K  ☐ 
L  ☐

Points	
Niveau	

Contrôle

Nom: ....

Écouter 3

A Écoute et écris les bonnes lettres dans les cases. (Level 5)

Exemple: Yannick [B]

1 Gilles [ ]

2 Michel [ ]

3 Karim [ ]

4 Thierry [ ]

5 Simon [ ]

6 Ahmed [ ]

A

B

C

D

E

F

G

H

I
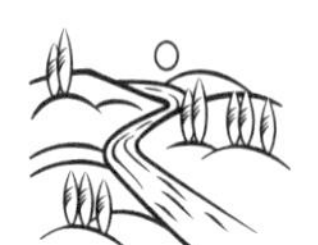

J

Points	
Niveau	

B Écoute et écris les bonnes lettres dans les cases. (Level 6)

A

B

C

D

E

F

G

H

I

J

K

L

M

Qu'est-ce que Sophie a fait/fait/va faire?

Hier (jeudi)	Aujourd'hui (vendredi)	Demain (samedi)
Exemple: L		

Points	
Niveau	

Contrôle

Nom: ....

Parler 1

Réponds aux questions de ton professeur ou de ton ami/amie. Pose des questions à ton/ta partenaire aussi. (Levels 3–5)

- Qu'est-ce que tu achètes normalement avec ton argent de poche?
- Qu'est-ce que tu achètes normalement comme cadeaux pour les anniversaires?
- Est-ce que tu économises ton argent?
- Est-ce qu'il y a des choses que tu n'achètes jamais? (Level 4)
- Qu'est-ce que tu as acheté en ville le week-end dernier? C'était comment ta visite? (Level 5)

Level information	Pupil support	Example
You can show achievement at Level 3, 4 or 5 depending on how you carry out the task.		
Level 3: Ask and answer the questions.	• In pairs, ask and respond on the following: • what you normally buy with pocket money. • what you usually buy as birthday presents for friends and family. • if you save money, and what for.	■ *Qu'est-ce que tu achètes normalement avec ton argent de poche?* ● *Normalement, j'achète des magazines ou du matériel scolaire.*
Level 4: As Level 3, but include adjectives, intensifiers, connectives and negatives in your answers.	• Ask each other if there are things you never buy with your pocket money. Respond, giving opinions. • Include details of two items you would like to buy and give your opinion of them.	■ *Est-ce qu'il y a des choses que tu n'achètes jamais?* ● *Oui. Je n'achète jamais de jeux de console. Je n'aime pas les ordinateurs.* *Je voudrais acheter …*
Level 5: As Level 4, but your conversation needs to make reference to the past as well as the present, and use appropriate time expressions. Include reasons for your opinions.	• Ask each other what you bought last weekend when you went shopping for two birthday presents, one for your best friend and one for your mother. Respond using the perfect tense (and *c'était* to give opinions) and including reasons for your choices. Describe your trip in detail.	■ *Qu'est-ce que tu as acheté en ville le week-end dernier?* ● *Je suis allé(e) en ville pour acheter des cadeaux. J'ai acheté un CD pour ma mère parce que …*

Contrôle

Nom: ....

Parler 2

Supergran! Décris Supergran et donne des détails sur ses passe-temps.

- Décris Supergran. Comment est-elle? Et sa personnalité? Qu'est-ce qu'elle porte?

- Qu'est-ce qu'elle aime/n'aime pas?

- Qu'est-ce qu'elle fait normalement le week-end? (Level 4)

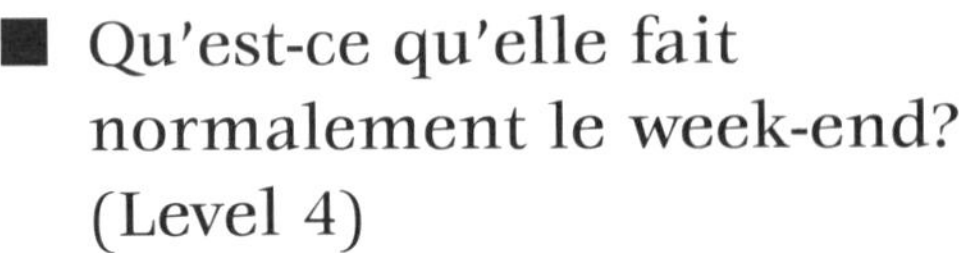

- Qu'est-ce qu'elle a fait le week-end dernier? (Level 5)

- Quels sont ses projets pour l'avenir? (Level 6)

Level information	Pupil support	Example
You can show achievement at Level 4, 5 or 6 depending on how you carry out the task.		
Level 4: Prepare and deliver a presentation. Make your writing more interesting by including negatives, connectives, intensifiers and opinions.	• Give a short description of Supergran, including information on what she's like (physically and her character) and what she wears. • Mention her likes and dislikes. • Give information on what she usually does at the weekend (four activities).	*Supergran est assez grande. Elle a les cheveux gris … et elle est très sportive et … Elle aime … mais elle déteste … Normalement le week-end, elle fait du vélo dans le parc et elle …*
Level 5: As Level 4, but add a second section including details of Supergran's antics last weekend. Use the perfect tense, with appropriate time expressions. Include reasons for your opinions.	• Give information about what she did last weekend (four activities). • Give her opinions of the activities and justify them with reasons.	*Par exemple, le week-end dernier, elle a fait beaucoup de choses! Samedi matin, elle est allée au centre de sports et elle a fait du tir à l'arc … Après ça elle …*
Level 6: As Level 5, but include longer descriptions and extra detail. Extend the presentation, using different tenses (present, perfect, near future) where appropriate and more varied language, and adapting grammatical structures. Be prepared to answer simple questions on your presentation.	• Give information about her plans for the future: what's she's going to do, where she wants to go on holiday, her hopes and dreams, etc. • Include comparatives and superlatives. • Use *depuis* to say how long she has been doing some of the things she does.	*L'année prochaine, elle va aller en France pour les vacances au bord de la mer. À l'avenir, elle veut … Elle est beaucoup plus sportive que ses enfants! Elle fait de la planche à voile depuis trente ans. Elle va … et …*

Contrôle

Nom: ....

Lire 1

A Lis et coche (✔) la bonne réponse. (Level 3)

Je m'appelle Sandihya et j'habite dans le nord de la France, à la campagne. J'ai beaucoup de passe-temps. J'aime regarder la télé, surtout les dessins animés. Je ne suis pas sportive, mais j'aime jouer aux jeux vidéo. J'adore sortir avec mes amis. À la maison, je dois ranger ma chambre. Ma mère fait le ménage et mon père fait les courses. Nous allons souvent en ville. Il n'y a pas de patinoire ou de bowling, mais on peut aller au cinéma. Ça, c'est génial. On mange souvent au fast-food. J'adore les frites, mais je n'aime pas les hamburgers. Chaque année pendant les vacances, je vais en Espagne avec ma famille. On va au bord de la mer. J'adore ça.

1 À la télé, elle aime ...

A  ☐ B  ☐ C  ☐

2 Elle aime ...

A  ☐ B  ☐ C  ☐

3 Pour aider, elle ...

A  ☐ B  ☐ C  ☐

4 Avec ses amis, elle aime ...

A  ☐ B 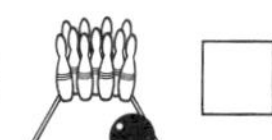 ☐ C  ☐

5 Elle aime manger ...

A  ☐ B  ☐ C  ☐

6 Elle passe ses vacances ...

A  ☐ B ☐ C  ☐

Points	
Niveau	

B Lis et écris la bonne lettre. (Level 4)

Voici une image de mes amis. Roger est petit. Il est plus petit que moi. Il a les cheveux blonds. Xavier est grand. Sa passion est la musique. Il a toujours son baladeur. Vincent est plus grand. Lui, il adore le sport. Il joue au basket et au foot. Julien est assez grand, plus grand que moi. Il est très marrant et très bavard et il a toujours son téléphone portable sur lui. Edouard est plus grand que Xavier et lui aussi a toujours son téléphone portable sur lui. Pierre est plus grand que moi, mais plus petit que Julien. Lui, il adore la musique. Avec son argent de poche, il achète beaucoup de CD. Rémy est plus petit que Roger. Il reçoit beaucoup d'argent de poche et de cadeaux. Il a tout, même un organiseur électronique, mais il est très gentil et généreux.

1 Xavier _____

2 Vincent _____

3 Julien _____

4 Edouard _____

5 Pierre _____

6 Rémy _____

Points	
Niveau	

Contrôle

Nom: ....

Lire 2

A Lis Passage A à la page 155 et complète la grille. (Level 4)

A 

B 

C 

D 

E 

F 

G 

H 

I 

J 

Miriam achète	Miriam n'achète pas
Exemple: C	

Points	
Niveau	

B Read Passage A and Passage B on page 155 and tick the six correct statements. (Level 5)

Example: Miriam gets 15 € pocket money per week. ☑

1 Last Saturday Miriam went horse riding. ☐
2 On Sunday she went cycling. ☐
3 She is saving up for a mobile phone. ☐
4 Last Saturday she watched her favourite TV programme. ☐
5 Last weekend she went shopping with her parents. ☐
6 She likes to buy music magazines. ☐
7 She watched her favourite TV programme on Saturday. ☐
8 Last Saturday the weather was bad. ☐
9 On Sunday she had a lot of school work to do. ☐
10 She never tidies her room. ☐
11 She always visits her grandad on Sunday afternoon. ☐
12 Last Sunday she went to a family celebration. ☐

Points	
Niveau	

Nom: ....

Expo 2R Reading

Lire 2

Passage A

Chaque semaine, mes parents me donnent 15 €. Ce n'est pas beaucoup! J'achète un croissant le matin au collège et avec le reste de l'argent j'achète surtout des magazines. J'adore les magazines pour jeunes filles comme Girl et Best. De temps en temps, j'achète un CD, mais ils sont assez chers. Ma mère achète le matériel scolaire pour moi. J'adore jouer aux jeux vidéo, mais ils sont très chers, donc je joue aux jeux de mon frère. Il a plus d'argent que moi! Mes parents et mes grands-parents achètent mes vêtements. Je les choisis moi-même, mais ils paient! Ma mère n'aime pas le maquillage, mais moi, j'adore ça. J'achète du maquillage assez souvent. En ce moment, j'économise pour acheter un nouveau téléphone portable.

Miriam

Passage B

Je fais de l'équitation et mes parents paient pour ça. Normalement, j'en fais le samedi matin, mais samedi dernier il y avait des orages, alors je n'en ai pas fait. D'habitude l'après-midi, je rencontre mes amis et nous allons au cinéma. Le cinéma est ma passion, mais la semaine dernière, le film n'était pas intéressant. Samedi après-midi, mes parents font des courses. Je déteste ça (c'est très ennuyeux!), mais samedi dernier, je suis allée au supermarché avec eux. C'était nul! Le samedi soir, il y a mon émission préférée à la télé, mais samedi dernier, il y avait un match de foot important et mon père et mon frère ont regardé le match. Donc je suis restée dans ma chambre et j'ai rangé mes affaires. Normalement, je ne range jamais ma chambre!

D'habitude, le dimanche matin, je regarde la télé, mais ce week-end, j'ai fait mes devoirs et j'ai révisé pour un examen. Et finalement, le dimanche après-midi je fais toujours du vélo, je suis membre d'un club. Mais c'était l'anniversaire de mon grand-père et toute la famille est allée chez mes grands-parents.

Miriam

Contrôle

Nom: ....

Lire 3

A 'a' Read Passage A on page 157 and answer the questions. (Level 5)

1 Who is Thierry going on holiday with?
- A His parents ☐
- B His friends ☐
- C His grandparents ☐

2 What do the hotel rooms have?
- A A TV ☐
- B A bath ☐
- C A balcony ☐

3 What does Thierry want to do?
- A Waterskiing ☐
- B Canoeing ☐
- C Visit the sites ☐

4 What are his parents going to give him?
- A Some money ☐
- B A new digital camera ☐
- C A new mobile ☐

5 What new clothes does he want?
- A Trainers ☐
- B Trousers ☐
- C Shorts ☐

6 What does he not eat?
- A Meat ☐
- B Cakes ☐
- C Fish ☐

Points	
Niveau	

B Lis Passage A et Passage B à la page 157 et complète les phrases en choisissant les bonnes lettres. (Level 6)

Exemple: Thierry est en vacances ... D

1 Avant de partir, il voudrait acheter ... ☐
2 Ils ont voyagé ... ☐
3 Hier, ils ont ... ☐
4 Aujourd'hui, il ... ☐
5 Demain, il va ... ☐
6 Il est anxieux parce qu'il ne veut pas ... ☐

A acheté des souvenirs.
B essayer la nourriture.
C des baskets.
D avec son école.
E rencontrer des jeunes espagnols.
F pendant la nuit.
G fait des courses.
H aller à la plage.
I visité les monuments.
J en train.
K fait de l'escalade.
L un portable.

Points	
Niveau	

Nom: ....

Lire 3

Passage A

mardi 6 juin

Dans une semaine, je vais aller en Espagne avec mon collège. Normalement, je pars en vacances avec mes parents. C'est la première fois que je vais partir avec mes amis. C'est aussi mon premier voyage en Espagne. D'habitude, je vais chez mes grands-parents dans le sud de la France.

Nous allons rester dans un grand hôtel avec piscine et salle de jeux. Toutes les chambres sont avec douche et télé-satellite, mais il n'y a pas de balcon. Je vais être avec mon meilleur ami, Rémi. Il est très rigolo et généreux. On aime les mêmes choses, mais lui, il voudrait essayer le ski nautique ou le canoë; par contre moi, je suis membre d'un club de canoë et j'en fais régulièrement, donc ce qui m'intéresse, c'est visiter le château et je crois aussi qu'il y a une très belle cathédrale.

J'économise pour acheter un nouveau portable avec un appareil photo. Je veux prendre de belles photos que je vais envoyer à ma famille. Mes parents vont me donner 200 € pour le voyage. Je voudrais aussi de nouveaux vêtements. Mes baskets sont nouvelles et très cool, mais j'ai besoin d'un pantalon noir. Ma mère voudrait m'acheter un short, quelle horreur!

J'espère que je vais aimer la nourriture. Chez moi, on mange beaucoup de viande et de pâtes. On ne mange pas de poisson parce que je suis allergique au poisson. Là où on va, c'est près de la mer et il y a beaucoup de spécialités avec du poisson! Ma mère va me donner beaucoup de biscuits et de gâteaux pour manger.

Thierry

Passage B

vendredi 15 juin

Me voilà en Espagne. Je suis en voyage avec mon collège et on passe 10 jours ici. Nous sommes partis de Paris à 18h mercredi et nous sommes arrivés à 6h jeudi matin. Nous avons voyagé en car parce que le train était trop cher.

Hier matin, nous sommes allés en ville et nous avons visité le château et la cathédrale. C'était intéressant, mais il y avait trop de soleil. Nous n'avons pas fait les magasins parce que tout le monde était fatigué, donc on est rentrés à l'hôtel et on a nagé dans la piscine.

Aujourd'hui on va à la plage. Rémi veut essayer le jet ski, mais je crois qu'il est trop jeune. Il va peut-être faire de la plongée sous-marine. Moi, je vais me reposer. Il y a un petit village avec beaucoup de boutiques pour les touristes et je vais y acheter des souvenirs pour ma famille.

On va visiter un collège demain. On va aller en classe et on va parler espagnol avec les élèves espagnols. Je ne parle pas bien l'espagnol, mais je vais essayer de le comprendre. L'après-midi, on va au centre de sport avec la classe espagnole et on va faire de l'escalade. Ça va être fantastique. Le soir, on va organiser une soirée spéciale. On va écouter de la musique, on va danser et on va manger de la paella. C'est une spécialité espagnole, mais malheureusement c'est avec du poisson. Qu'est-ce que je vais faire?!

Thierry

Contrôle

Nom: ....

Écrire 1

A Copie et adapte les phrases pour tes vacances. (Level 3)

Pour les vacances, j'aime aller en Espagne. En vacances, je porte un short et un tee-shirt. J'aime manger des œufs et du poisson. On peut nager et on peut jouer au golf.

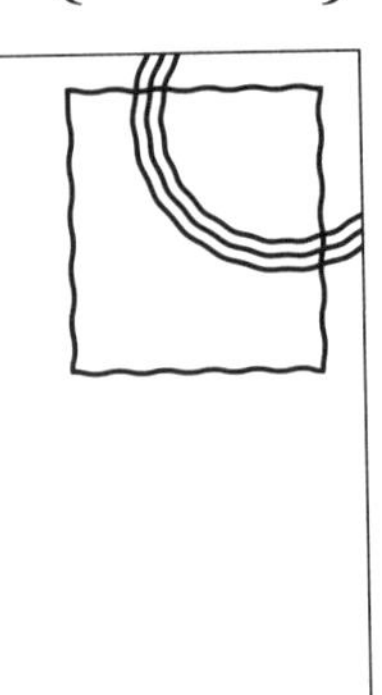

B Où vas-tu en vacances normalement? Qu'est-ce que tu fais en vacances? Qu'est-ce que tu portes? Qu'est-ce que tu manges? Qu'est-ce qu'on peut faire? (Level 4) Qu'est-ce que tu vas faire cet été? (Level 5)

 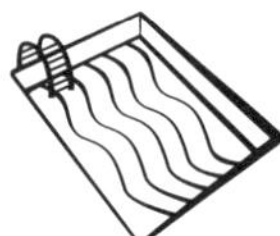   

Level information	Pupil support	Example
You can show achievement at Level 3, 4 or 5 depending on how you carry out the task.		
Level 3: Write two or three sentences, adapting the example supplied by using different details. (If you can change (e.g.) the location and include an opinion or a negative in the same sentence, you will be working towards Level 4.)	Copy the sentences adapting the information so that it describes what you do on holiday.	Copy *Pour les vacances, j'aime aller* and change *en Espagne* to your usual holiday destination.
Level 4: Write a short text about holidays. Make your writing more interesting by adding negatives, connectives, intensifiers and opinions.	• Say when and where you usually go on holiday. • Say what you usually do on holiday (give three activities). • Say what you wear on holiday. • Say what you eat and drink on holiday. • Say what you can do in the area you usually go to on holiday.	*Pour les vacances en été, je vais normalement en France. J'y vais avec ma famille. En vacances, je visite des monuments … Je mange … et je bois …*
Level 5: As Level 4, but include details of what you are going to do for your holidays this year. Use the near future tense, with appropriate time expressions. Include reasons for your opinions.	• Give information about where you are going to go this summer and what you are going to wear/eat/do there. • Give reasons for your opinions.	*Cet été, je vais aller en Italie au bord de la mer. Je vais jouer au volley et on va manger … et boire … Je vais porter …*

Contrôle

Nom: ....

Écrire 2

A Ton blog: Décris tes préférences (Level 4) et tes activités (Level 5).

- Quel est ton sport préféré?
- Quelle est ton émission préférée?
- Quelles sont tes matières préférées?
- Qui sont tes acteurs/chanteurs préférés?
- Qu'est-ce que tu aimes faire? Qu'est-ce que tu as fait la semaine dernière? (Level 5)

B Ton blog: Décris tes rêves et tes espoirs pour l'avenir. (Level 6)

Level information	Pupil support	Example
You can show achievement at Level 4, 5 or 6 depending on how you carry out the task.		
Level 4: Write a blog entry about your favourite things. Include adjectives, qualifiers, connectives and negatives.	Give information about: • your favourite sports. • your favourite programmes. • your favourite subjects at school. • your favourite actors and singers. • Include details of sports/TV programmes/subjects/actors and singers you are less keen on or don't like.	*J'aime beaucoup le sport. Mon sport préféré est le tennis. Je joue au tennis une fois par semaine. J'aime aussi le rugby …*
Level 5: As Level 4, but include details of activities you do and the activities you did last week. Use the perfect tense, with appropriate time expressions. Include reasons for your opinions.	• Give information on the activities that you do. • Include details of what you did last week, linking this to your preferences. • Justify your opinions.	*Par exemple, mardi dernier, je suis allé(e) au centre de sport avec Sam et nous avons joué au tennis. J'aime le sport parce que c'est bon pour la santé. Vendredi soir, j'ai …*
Level 6: As Level 5, but include longer descriptions and extra detail. Extend your answers, using different tenses (present, perfect, future) where appropriate and more varied language, adapting grammatical structures.	• Include information on your future plans. • Use modal verbs and other verbs followed by the infinitive to say what you can/want to/have to/prefer to do. • Use *je voudrais* to talk about your future hopes and dreams.	*Ce week-end, on va jouer au football dans le parc. Je préfère faire du vélo, mais je trouve que le football est aussi amusant …*

Teacher's Notes

Contrôle Module 6 et Fin d'année

Listening and reading assessment criteria
Mark scheme: 1 mark for each correct answer. Total for each task: 6 marks. For details of the sublevels see p. 167.

Écouter 1 [AT1 Level 3]

All modules. This task tests understanding of a short passage in the context of personal preferences/holidays. Pupils identify the picture which correctly completes each statement, writing the correct letter in the box. There are six distractors. Play the recording twice.

Audioscript 28

J'aime passer mes vacances en Italie. J'adore la cuisine italienne surtout les glaces – elles sont délicieuses. J'aime visiter les villes et les monuments. Normalement, j'y passe une semaine dans un grand hôtel près de la plage. Je fais beaucoup de promenades en vélo. Cette année je voudrais faire de la plongée sous-marine. J'espère rencontrer beaucoup de filles sympas.

Réponses 1 J 2 E 3 H 4 A 5 L 6 G

Écouter 1B [AT1 Level 4] 'a'

Modules 1–5. This task tests understanding of short passages in the context of a range of topics, including personal information. Pupils write the correct letters in the box. There are two distractors. Play the recording twice.

This task is similar to Asset Preliminary French Listening (internal), Grade 6, Task C.1.

Go to p. 167

Audioscript 29

Exemple:
- *Quels sont tes passe-temps?*
- *Au collège je joue au basket et le week-end je joue pour une équipe de foot. Je fais du judo deux fois par semaine.*

1 – *Avez-vous cette jupe en vert en 38?*
– *Attendez, je vais voir. Vous voulez l'essayer?*

2 – *Quels sont tes projets pour l'avenir?*
– *Je voudrais aller à l'université et étudier les sciences.*
– *Et plus tard?*
– *Je ne sais pas. Peut-être je serais prof dans une école.*

3 – *Je vais en boîte samedi. Tu veux venir?*
– *Non, désolé. Je dois rester à la maison et faire le ménage.*

4 – *Qu'est-ce qu'il y a ce soir?*
– *Rien d'intéressant: un jeu télévisé, qui est bête, et puis les informations.*

5 – *Alors, qu'est-ce que tu prends?*
– *Je ne sais pas. Je ne veux pas d'entrée. Qu'est-ce qu'ils ont comme plat principal?*
– *Je vais demander au serveur.*

6 – *Où habites-tu?*
– *Dans l'est de la France.*
– *Tu aimes habiter là?*
– *Oui. En été il fait très beau et en hiver il neige. C'est parfait.*

Réponses 1 G 2 A 3 F 4 E 5 I 6 B

Écouter 2A [AT1 Level 4]

Modules 1–5. This task tests understanding of a passage in the context of likes and dislikes, including holidays. Pupils identify what Joachim likes, writing down the letters of the correct pictures. There are seven distractors. Play the recording twice.

Audioscript 30

J'aime surtout écouter de la musique. Je ne regarde pas beaucoup la télé. Mon frère aime les dessins animés, mais moi, je préfère les documentaires. Je sors beaucoup avec mes amis. On ne va pas au cinéma – on préfère faire les magasins.

J'adore manger. Je ne mange pas de chips parce qu'elles sont mauvaises pour la santé, mais je mange beaucoup de gâteaux et de pâtisseries.

J'aime aussi partir en vacances. Je n'aime pas tellement aller à l'hôtel. Je trouve le camping beaucoup plus amusant. Je ne suis pas très sportif, donc en vacances je préfère me reposer et visiter la région. J'aime bien visiter les monuments – je trouve ça intéressant. Ma saison préférée est l'hiver. Mes parents adorent être au soleil, mais moi, je préfère la neige!

Réponses D, F, L, N, K, A

Écouter 2B [AT1 Level 5]

Module 6. This task tests understanding of a passage (including the ability to distinguish between the present and the future) in the context of holidays. Pupils tick the six correct pictures. There are six distractors. Play the recording twice.

Audioscript 31

Je vais partir pour trois semaines avec ma famille. Ma mère préfère la campagne, mais nous allons passer nos vacances au bord de la mer. Normalement on fait du camping, mais je déteste ça. Heureusement nous allons rester dans un hôtel.

Mon frère va faire du jet ski. Moi, j'en fais tous les week-ends, alors je vais essayer la plongée sous-marine. Ça va être génial. On peut faire de la pêche, mais je n'aime pas ça parce que c'est ennuyeux. Le soir, je vais aller au parc d'attractions avec mon frère. Mes parents n'aiment pas ça.

J'espère que je vais rencontrer des garçons au parc – cela va être marrant! Je vais aussi visiter les monuments. D'habitude je n'aime pas ça, mais il y a un très beau

Contrôle Module 6 et Fin d'année

château que je voudrais voir. En ce moment j'économise pour acheter un apparcil photo numérique. Ça coûte assez cher, mais je vais l'utiliser en vacances. Je vais prendre beaucoup de photos.

Réponses A, E, F, G, I, K

Écouter 3A [AT1 Level 5]

Module 6. This task tests understanding of a passage featuring a wider range of language and a range of verb types (the present tense and the conditional) in the context of likes/dislikes/ activities. Pupils write the correct letter. There are three distractors. Play the recording twice.

Audioscript 32

J'ai beaucoup de bons amis. Nous avons les mêmes passe-temps, mais on est très différents les uns des autres. Moi, je suis très sportif. J'adore tous les sports, mais ma passion c'est le foot. Je voudrais être joueur de foot.

Gilles aussi aime le sport. Il aime les sports un peu plus dangereux. Il est membre d'un club et le samedi il fait souvent du jet ski ou de la plongée sous-marine, mais son rêve est de travailler dans un studio et d'être acteur. Michel est moins sportif et il préfère prendre des photos. Il a un nouvel appareil photo numérique. Il économise parce qu'il voudrait acheter une moto.

Karim aime aussi le foot. Il joue pour une équipe, mais sa passion est la musique. Il est membre d'un groupe et il voudrait être chanteur plus tard. Thierry est aussi dans le groupe, mais lui il voudrait voyager et visiter beaucoup de pays exotiques.

Simon préfère rester en France. Il n'aime pas tellement la plage. Ses grands-parents ont une ferme et cet été il préfère aller là-bas. Ahmed par contre déteste la campagne. Il la trouve ennuyeuse. Il voudrait acheter une villa au bord de la mer.

Réponses **1** C **2** J **3** A **4** G **5** I **6** E

Écouter 3B [AT1 Level 6]

All modules. This task tests understanding of a passage (including the ability to distinguish between past, present and future) across a range of topics, including likes/dislikes/activities. Pupils identify which activities Sophie did yesterday, today and will do tomorrow, writing the correct letters in the appropriate box. There are two distractors. Play the recording twice.

Audioscript 33

Hier soir, je suis rentrée à 17h. Normalement, j'écoute de la musique pour me relaxer, mais j'ai promené le chien. Il s'appelle Médor et il est très rigolo. Tous les jeudis je vais à un club de basket, mais hier soir je n'y suis pas allée parce que j'avais trop de devoirs à faire. Ma mère a regardé un jeu télévisé. Personnellement je les déteste, donc je me suis couchée à 21h.

Aujourd'hui, je reste à la maison. Ce soir, il y a mon émission préférée. C'est une série policière et je la regarde tous les vendredis. Ma copine Maryse est avec moi. On aime jouer aux jeux vidéo. Normalement, on va au parc, mais il pleut!

Demain c'est samedi et c'est l'anniversaire de mon frère. D'habitude, on va au restaurant pour fêter les anniversaires, mais demain on va pique-niquer sur la plage. Ensuite, mon frère va faire du vélo avec ses amis et moi je vais prendre des photos avec mon appareil photo numérique, que mon père m'a donné pour mon anniversaire!

Réponses
hier: K, J
aujourd'hui: H, C
demain: I, E

Speaking and writing assessment criteria

See the level information supplied on the Assessment sheet. For detailed Assessment criteria (including sublevels) see pages 168 and 169.

Level information and pupil assessment support with examples are supplied on the assessment sheet. Encourage your pupils to use this to decide which level they are aiming for. Point out that they should not copy the examples given, but use them as a guide.

Use *Parler/Écrire 1* in the first instance if you are unsure of which level to give a particular learner.

Parler 1 [AT2 Levels 3–5]

Module 6. This task tests the ability to put together a simple conversation in the context of pocket money and shopping.

Pupils who can include information on a shopping trip in the past (showing use of the perfect tense in addition to the present tense) can attain Level 5.

The best way to conduct the assessment is for pupils to listen to each other's conversations while you circulate, or to listen to individual learners at the front of the class, while pupils continue with other parts of the assessments.

Parler 2 [AT2 Levels 4–6]

All modules. This task tests the ability to prepare and deliver a presentation about Supergran. The task covers a range of topic areas, and also gives pupils the opportunity to write in a variety of tenses (present to describe what Supergran usually does, perfect to give last weekend as an example, and future to talk about her plans) and to use a variety of structures, giving them the opportunity to reach Level 6.

Teacher's Notes

Contrôle Module 6 et Fin d'année

In order to reach Level 6, pupils respond to some simple questions on the presentation, from you or another pupil. For example, where Supergran lives, how old she is, etc.

The best way to conduct the assessment is to listen to individuals, either at the front of the class or as the others continue other aspects of the assessments. Pupils could record these as podcasts for marking also.

Lire 1A [AT3 Level 3]

Modules 1–5. This task tests understanding of a short text in the context of personal information. The questions are multiple choice (pictures).

Réponses **1** B **2** A **3** C **4** C **5** A **6** B

Lire 1B [AT3 Level 4]

Module 6. This task tests understanding of a short text in the context of personal information. Pupils use the text and the pictures to identify the friends, writing down the appropriate letter. There are two distractors.

Réponses **1** C **2** A **3** D **4** B **5** E **6** H

Lire 2A [AT3 Level 4]

Module 6. This task tests understanding of a text in the context of personal information/pocket money. Pupils read Passage A. They identify the items Miriam buys/doesn't buy, writing the appropriate letters in the boxes. There are three distractors.

Réponses
Miriam achète: A, G, D
Miriam n'achète pas: F, E, B

Lire 2B [AT3 Level 5]

Modules 1–5. This task tests understanding of a text passage (including the ability to distinguish between past and present) in the context of personal information/weekend activities. Pupils read Passage A and Passage B and tick the six correct statements. There are six distractors.

Réponses 3, 5, 7, 8, 9, 12

Lire 3A [AT3 Level 5] 

Modules 1–6. This task tests understanding of a text featuring a wider range of language and two tenses (present and near future) in the context of holidays. Pupils read Passage A. The questions are multiple choice.

This task is similar to Asset Preliminary French Reading (internal), Grade 5, Task A.1.

Go to p. 167

Réponses **1** B **2** A **3** C **4** A **5** B **6** C

Lire 3B [AT3 Level 6]

Modules 1–6. This task tests understanding of a text (including the ability to distinguish between past, present and near future) in the context of holidays. Pupils read Passage A and Passage B and then write the appropriate letter. There are five distractors.

Réponses **1** L **2** F **3** I **4** G **5** E **6** B

Écrire 1 [AT4 Levels 3–5]

All modules. Give this sheet only to pupils who are working at Levels 3–5. This task tests the ability to write a short paragraph in the context of holiday plans. It is divided into two sections. In Section A pupils describe what they usually do on holiday by changing the model sentences (Level 3).

In Section B (Levels 4–5) pupils write a text about their typical holiday and their plans for the coming summer: this section gives pupils opportunity to reach Level 5 by requiring the use of the near future tense, including appropriate time expressions.

Écrire 2 [AT4 Levels 4–6]

Module 6. This task tests the ability to write a text about themselves, detailing preferences and interests.

It is divided into two sections. Pupils who feel more confident can complete both Sections A and B. Section A (Levels 4–5) gives pupils the opportunity to reach Level 5 by requiring the use of the perfect tense, including appropriate time expressions. Section B (Level 6) involves a variety of time frames (past, present and future) and encourages pupils to extend their descriptions and use a wider range of structures.

Assessment rubrics

Adapte les phrases.	*Adapt the sentences.*
Ajoute de l'information sur…	*Add information on…*
Choisis (un titre pour chaque paragraphe).	*Choose (a title for each paragraph).*
Choisis (les bons mots pour compléter le texte).	*Choose (the correct words to complete the text).*
Coche (la bonne image/les bonnes images).	*Tick (the correct picture/pictures).*
Coche (la bonne case/les bonnes cases).	*Tick (the correct box/boxes).*
Coche (la bonne réponse/les bonnes réponses).	*Tick (the correct answer/answers).*
Coche (les cinq/six phrases correctes).	*Tick (the five/six correct sentences).*
Compare.	*Compare.*
Complète (les phrases/la grille).	*Complete (the sentences/the grid).*
Complète (les phrases en choisissant la bonne lettre).	*Complete (the sentences by choosing the correct letter).*
Copie.	*Copy.*
Décris.	*Describe.*
Demande.	*Ask.*
Écoute.	*Listen.*
Écris (les lettres dans le bon ordre).	*Write (the letters in the correct order).*
Écris (la bonne lettre/les bonnes lettres).	*Write (the correct letter/letters).*
Écris (le bon prénom/les bons prénoms).	*Write (the correct name/names).*
Écris (les bonnes lettres dans la case/dans la grille).	*Write (the correct letters in the box/in the grid).*
Écris (tes réponses).	*Write (your answers).*
Écris (un email).	*Write (an e-mail).*
Écris un paragraphe sur…	*Write a paragraph on …*
Fais une conversation (avec ton professeur ou ton ami/amie).	*Make up a conversation (with your teacher or your friend).*
Imagine (que) ….	*Imagine (that) …*
Invite (ton ami/amie à ta fête d'anniversaire).	*Invite (your friend to your birthday party).*
Lis.	*Read.*
Lis (la question).	*Read (the question).*
Mets (les images/lettres dans le bon ordre).	*Put (the pictures/letters in the correct order).*
Mets (les lettres dans les bonnes cases).	*Put (the letters in the correct boxes).*
Note (les détails en français).	*Note (the details in French).*
Note (les bons prix).	*Note (the correct prices).*
Parle de …	*Talk about …*
Pose des questions à ton/ta partenaire aussi.	*Ask your partner questions too.*
Prépare et fais une présentation.	*Prepare and make a presentation.*
Remplis la grille.	*Complete the grid.*
Réponds aux questions (de ton professeur ou de ton ami/amie).	*Answer (your teacher's/your friend's) questions.*
Utilise (l'exemple pour t'aider).	*Use (the example to help you).*

Personal target suggestions

The Personal Targets featured here consolidate the suggestions given in *Expo 1*, focusing on the core areas of *Listening strategies, Reading strategies, Vocabulary learning, Study skills* and *Reaching Level 5*. Suggestions on *Reaching Level 6* have been added. You can either hand out the whole list to pupils at the start of the year or copy and circulate suggestions in a different area (e.g. *Vocabulary learning*) as you begin each module.

Listening strategies

1 **Check instructions.** Before you hear the recording, look at what you are asked to do: read the rubric/instruction for the exercise, so you know what to listen out for.
2 **Review questions.** Read through all the questions before you hear the recording. You will then know the type of information you have to listen for.
3 **Guess answers in advance.** Think about the range of possible answers to the question and about the vocabulary that might come up. This will mean you are better prepared when you hear the recording.
4 **Relax.** Prepare yourself for the exercise. Stay focused but relaxed. Sometimes concentrating too hard on listening can stop you from hearing.
5 **Gist first.** You will generally hear a listening passage twice. The first time, listen to get the gist (general meaning); the second time, concentrate on the specific information you are asked to find.
6 **Note-taking.** Try different ways of noting down information. Make notes in French, make notes in English, draw symbols and images, etc. Identify the way that works best for you.
7 **Focus on key words.** It doesn't matter if you don't understand every word – focus on the ones you need to help you answer the questions and don't let yourself get distracted by language you don't need to understand.

Reading strategies

1 **Overview.** Read the whole text to get a general understanding of it (gist) first, before looking for specific details.
2 **Get ready.** Make sure that you understand exactly what you need to do. Read the rubric/instruction for the exercise, the questions and any example given carefully.
3 **Strategy 1, cognates.** Look for cognates – words that are closely related in French and English. Try to spot similarities that will help you work out what words mean.
4 **Strategy 2, context.** Use the context to work out a new word, e.g. you might not know/remember the word *dimanche*, but if you recognise *vendredi* and *samedi* in the same text, you can make an educated guess that it means 'Sunday'.
5 **References.** If you can't work out a word, do you know where to get help? In the Pupil's Book each module has a vocabulary list at the end (*Mots*) and there is a bilingual glossary at the back of the book. You will find a bilingual dictionary increasingly useful too.
6 **Strategy 3, structure of text.** The answers to an exercise are often found in order in the text. If you have found answers 1 and 3, answer 2 is probably to be found in between in the text. Look carefully there!
7 **Grammar clues.** Look for grammatical clues and read the text carefully. Is it the present tense or the perfect tense, for example? Is it *un cinéma* or *des cinémas*? Be careful and always check your answers.

Personal target suggestions

Vocabulary learning

1 **Look, say, cover, write, check**. Use this strategy to help memorise vocabulary.

2 **Post-it notes.** Write new words on Post-it notes and stick them around your bedroom, so that you keep seeing French words at different times.

3 **Word cards.** Put new words on cards with the French on one side and the English on the other, to help you test and re-test yourself when learning.

4 **Vocabulary ranking.** When you are learning a new vocabulary group, try writing out the words in a ranking order of difficulty – start with the difficult ones and spend more time learning those.

5 **Colour coding.** Write masculine words in blue and feminine words in red to help you remember gender and the correct article.

6 **Language links.** Make links in your mind when meeting new words. Are they similar to English? Is there a simple trick to remember the word? *Serpent* is similar to the English 'serpent'; *poisson* looks like 'poison' – so imagine a poisonous fish.

7 **Language patterns.** Look for patterns in the French words and use these to your advantage. Once you know the spelling of *mère*, you do not need to re-learn it in the second half of the word *grand-mère.*

Study skills

1 **Have a go!** You need to speak French to both your partner and your teacher. Don't be worried – just have a go, even if you make a mistake.

2 **Don't panic.** When your teacher explains an activity in French, use the clues: watch your teacher; look at the example; make a sensible guess.

3 **Stay organised.** Keep your French exercises/other class material together in a file or folder. Keep your vocabulary lists and grammar notes up to date and in the same place. This will make reviewing material much easier.

4 **Check and redraft.** Whenever you complete a French writing activity, read over what you have done. Focus on checking particular elements in the text, e.g. spelling and accents, adjective agreements, verb endings, etc. Then rewrite your text, making corrections as necessary.

5 **Work with others.** Working with others can make your learning more effective. Not only does it mean you can really test how your French is developing, it is also motivating to have someone else involved. Ask a friend or family member to test you on vocabulary, verb forms, etc. Work with a class partner after school to practise speaking in French.

6 **Revise regularly.** Spend some time each week looking over vocabulary and grammar you have learned so far. This will help language stick in your memory and make revising for tests much easier.

7 **Review targets.** Don't just set targets and then ignore them. Review targets regularly. Are you getting there? It will really help you improve!

Personal target suggestions

Reading Level 5

To reach Level 5, you must first be confident in using the features required for Level 4: give opinions and including connectives, intensifiers, negatives and adjectives (with the appropriate agreements).

In addition, you need to make sure that you understand and can include the following elements in your speaking and writing:

1 **Second time frame.** Talk about the past or the future as well as the present, using the appropriate tenses.

2 **Include time references.** Include appropriate time expressions to support the use of different tenses. For example, if you are talking about the past, you could use *hier soir* to make it clear you are talking about yesterday evening. You can also use time expressions to structure your thoughts, e.g. *d'abord* 'first', *et puis* 'and then', etc.

3 **Justify opinions.** Ensure that whenever you give an opinion you justify it. You can use *parce que* 'because' or *car* 'for' and then give a reason.

4 **Say something new.** Use a dictionary to find out how to alter phrases that you know in order to express exactly what you want to say. At Level 5 this would typically be a noun or an adjective.

5 **Be accurate.** Your French must be increasingly accurate, in pronunciation and fluency when speaking, and in spelling when writing.

Reading Level 6

To reach Level 6, you must first be confident in using the features required for Levels 4 and 5:

- give opinions and include connectives, intensifiers, negatives and adjectives (with the appropriate agreements).
- include time expressions to support your use of tenses, justify opinions, use a dictionary to add something new/personalise what you say and generally improve the accuracy of your French.

In addition, you need to make sure that you understand and can include the following elements in your speaking and writing:

1 **A wide range of time frames.** Refer to a variety of time frames (past, present and future), choosing the appropriate ones for the task in hand. So far you have studied: present, near future, future, perfect and imperfect tenses and some forms of the conditional.

2 **Add value.** Include more detail in your descriptions and explanations. (Make sure it is relevant and interesting!) Try to vary the grammar structures you use.

3 **Respond.** When you give a presentation, be ready to answer simple prepared questions on your topic.

4 **Customise.** Use reference materials to expand on what you know. Use a dictionary/glossary to look up a verb and change it appropriately to express the time frame you require.

Asset Languages Practice Material

Asset Languages is the assessment scheme for the DCSF Languages Ladder and is being developed as part of the National Languages Strategy by Cambridge Assessment through OCR and Cambridge ESOL.

You may decide to use this scheme to provide certification for your pupils during or at the end of Key Stage 3. For pupils of this age group, there are two possible levels of assessment:

Breakthrough (Languages Ladder Grade 3 or National Curriculum Level 3)

Preliminary (Languages Ladder Grade 6 or National Curriculum Level 6).

The scheme is extremely adaptable. You can use it to assess any or all of the four skills (listening, speaking, reading and writing): for example, pupils may take just Listening and Reading assessments (this is the most common combination). It consists of two different approaches to assessment, Teacher and External. You can combine these approaches or choose which to use, though note that only the latter leads to an external qualification.

Expo 1–3 Nouvelle Éditions provide a series of practice tasks for Asset assessments in the receptive skills of Listening and Reading. Each Listening and Reading *Contrôle* section contains an Asset-type task, highlighted with a special symbol 'a'. In the teacher's notes, references are given to the equivalent sample tasks on the Asset website. There is a range of Teacher and External task types, giving your pupils the practice they will need if you decide to adopt the Asset assessment scheme. If you don't, you will nevertheless benefit from the variety that these new task types add to the *Contrôles*.

As Asset tasks in the productive skills of Speaking and Reading are much more flexible and open to customised response, we have not provided Asset-type tasks for these. Our carefully-graded speaking and writing *Contrôles* contain the necessary practice for the Asset assessment scheme.

For more information about the scheme, please visit the Asset Languages website.

Assessment criteria [listening and reading]

	6 marks	4–5 marks	3 marks	0–3 marks
Level 3	3a	3b	3c	working towards Level 3
Level 4	4a	4b	4c	working towards Level 4
Level 5	5a	5b	5c	working towards Level 5
Level 6	6a	6b	6c	working towards Level 6

Assessment criteria (speaking)

Each level is divided into three sublevels: *Effective communication, Generally effective communication* and *Some effective communication.* These sublevels detail performance requirements within the level only and do not relate to other levels. So, although a student performing at 5c has achieved only *Some effective communication*, he/she is still performing at a higher level than a 4a student, who has achieved *Effective communication* within level 4.

Level 3

Short phrases/whole sentences as part of an exchange

3a Effective communication: clear pronunciation and intonation; accurate French. (3–4 exchanges, fairly fluent conversation; ability to substitute vocabulary items)

3b Generally effective communication: a few mistakes in pronunciation, intonation and accuracy. (2–3 exchanges)

3c Some effective communication: mistakes in pronunciation, intonation and accuracy, which sometimes impair communication. (2–3 exchanges)

Level 4

Structured conversation: more detailed answers including adjectives, qualifiers, connectives and negatives

4a Effective communication: a few mistakes in pronunciation, intonation or grammar. A range of verbs, connectives, qualifiers, opinion phrases and negatives used. Generally accurate in using grammatical knowledge to substitute words and phrases.

4b Generally effective communication: mistakes in pronunciation, intonation or grammar, which occasionally impair communication. Different verbs, connectives, qualifiers, opinion phrases and negatives used. Fairly accurate in using grammatical knowledge to substitute words and phrases.

4c Some effective communication: mistakes in pronunciation, intonation or grammar, which often impair communication. Limited range of verbs used and a connective, a qualifier, opinion phrase or negative occasionally included. Some attempt to substitute words/phrases: generally inaccurate when attempted.

Level 5

Short conversation or talk including present tense with either the perfect or near future

5a Effective communication: a few mistakes in pronunciation, intonation or grammar. Correct use of the present tense with either the perfect or near future of a wide range of verbs. A wide variety of time expressions, connectives, qualifiers, opinion phrases and negatives included.

5b Generally effective communication: some mistakes in pronunciation, intonation or grammar, but these do not impair communication. Generally correct use of the present tense with either the perfect or near future of a range of verbs. Some time expressions, connectives, qualifiers, opinion phrases and negatives included.

5c Some effective communication: mistakes in pronunciation, intonation or grammar, which sometimes impair communication. Fairly correct use of the present tense with some use of either perfect or near future of a limited range of verbs. A limited number of time expressions, connectives, qualifiers, opinion phrases and negatives included.

Level 6

Short prepared conversation or talk including range of tenses, with responses to simple prepared questions

6a Effective communication: good pronunciation and intonation; a few mistakes in grammar. Occasionally hesitant but confident delivery. Appropriate use of a range of tenses (present/perfect/imperfect/(near) future) of a wide range of verbs. Inclusion of more detailed/extended responses, including opinions. A variety of structures and the use of grammar in new contexts.

6b Generally effective communication: generally good pronunciation and intonation; some mistakes in grammar. Generally appropriate use of a range of tenses (present/perfect/imperfect/(near) future) of some verbs. Some inclusion of more detailed/extended responses, including opinions. Different structures used and some use of grammar in new contexts.

6c Some effective communication: fairly good pronunciation and intonation; some mistakes in grammar. Some use of a range of tenses (present/perfect/imperfect/(near) future) of a limited number of verbs. Occasional inclusion of more detailed/extended responses, including opinions. Limited use of different structures/grammar in new contexts.

Assessment criteria (writing)

Each level is divided into three sublevels: *Effective communication, Generally effective communication* and *Some effective communication.* These sublevels detail performance requirements within the level only and do not relate to other levels. So, although a student performing at 5c has achieved only *Some effective communication*, he/she is still performing at a higher level than a 4a student, who has achieved *Effective communication* within level 4.

Level 3

Short phrases written from memory; short paragraphs (two or three sentences) written with support

3a Effective communication: only a few mistakes in spelling, accents or grammar.

3b Generally effective communication: some mistakes in spelling, accents or grammar, which do not impair communication.

3c Some effective communication: mistakes in spelling, accents or grammar, which sometimes impair communication.

Level 4

Short texts written from memory

4a Effective communication: a few mistakes in spelling, use of accents or grammar. A range of verbs, connectives, qualifiers, opinion phrases and negatives used. Often accurate in using grammatical knowledge to substitute words and phrases.

4b Generally effective communication: some mistakes in spelling, use of accents or grammar, which occasionally impair communication. Different verbs and connectives, qualifiers, opinion phrases and negatives used. Sometimes accurate in using grammatical knowledge to substitute words and phrases.

4c Some effective communication: mistakes in spelling, use of accents or grammar, which sometimes impair communication. A limited range of verbs used and occasionally a connective, a qualifier, an opinion phrase or a negative included. Little attempt to substitute words/phrases: generally inaccurate when attempted.

Level 5

Short texts featuring the present tense with either the perfect or near future

5a Effective communication: few mistakes in spelling, use of accents or grammar. Correct use of the present tense with either the perfect or near future of a wide range of verbs. A variety of time expressions, connectives, qualifiers, opinion phrases and negatives included.

5b Generally effective communication: some mistakes in spelling, use of accents or grammar, which do not impair communication. Often correct use of the present tense with either the perfect or near future of a range of verbs. Some time expressions, connectives, qualifiers, opinion phrases and negatives included.

5c Some effective communication: mistakes in spelling, use of accents or grammar, which sometimes impair communication. Some use of the present tense with either the perfect or the near future of a limited range of verbs. A limited number of time expressions, connectives, qualifiers, opinion phrases and negatives included.

Level 6

Longer texts giving and seeking information and opinions

6a Effective communication: few mistakes in grammar. Appropriate use of tenses of a wide range of verbs to talk about the past, present and future. Able to use a variety of structures, produce descriptive language and adapt grammar to new contexts.

6b Generally effective communication: occasional mistakes in grammar. Often appropriate use of tenses of a wide range of verbs to talk about the past, present and future. Different structures used and some use of descriptive language and grammar in new contexts.

6c Some effective communication: some mistakes in grammar. Some appropriate use of tenses of a wide range of verbs to talk about the past, present and future. Some use of different structures and of descriptive language and grammar in new contexts.

Assessment Grid
Bilan fin d'année

	Listening	Speaking	Reading	Writing
		Salut!		
Module 1 Famille et domicile				
Module 2 Temps libre				
Module 3 Les sorties				
Module 4 Manger et boire				
Module 5 Voyages et vacances PARIS				
Module 6 Les copains